Modern Pastoralism and Conservation

MODERN PASTORALISM AND CONSERVATION
Old Problems, New Challenges

edited by

Troy Sternberg and Dawn Chatty

The White Horse Press

Cover photo © Marc Foggin

British Library Cataloguing in Publication Data
A catalogue record for this book is available from the British Library

ISBN   978-1-874267-74-4

CONTENTS

LIST OF ILLUSTRATIONS AND TABLES

List of Illustrations and Tables

Chapter 9

AUTHOR BIOGRAPHIES

Dawn Chatty

Dawn Chatty is University Professor in Anthropology and Forced Migration and Deputy Director of the Refugee Studies Centre, Queen Elizabeth house, University of Oxford, UK. Her research interests include coping strategies and resilience of refugee youth, nomadic pastoralism and conservation, gender and development, health, illness and culture. Her most recent books include: *Dispossession and Displacement in the Modern Middle East* (Cambridge University Press, 2010); *Dispossession and Forced Migration in the Middle East and North Africa* (ed. with Bill Finlayson, Oxford University Press, 2010); *Deterritorialized Youth: Sahrawi and Afghan Refugees at the Margins of the Middle East* (ed. Berghahn Books, 2010); *Nomadic Societies in the Middle East and North Africa: Facing the 21ˢᵗ Century* (Brill, 2006); *Children of Palestine: Experiencing Forced Migration in the Middle East* (ed. with Gillian Lewando-Hundt, Berghahn Books, 2005); and *Conservation and Mobile Peoples: Displacement, Forced Settlement and Sustainable Development* (ed. with Marcus Colchester, Berghahn Press 2002). Email: dawn.chatty@qeh.ox.ac.uk

Marc Foggin

J. Marc Foggin is a Canadian biologist with over 15 years of experience in community-based conservation and sustainable development in China, with geographic focus on the Tibetan plateau region. His prior work includes conservation initiatives for endangered Asian wildlife species, grassland ecology and management, support for development of local governance, environmental education, and community development. He also has worked in Mongolia and Pakistan. With degrees from McGill University (1993) and Arizona State University (2000), he is the founding Director of the international non-profit organisation, Plateau Perspectives (URL: http://www.plateauperspectives. org). Email: foggin@plateau perspectives.org

Anatoly M. Khazanov

Anatoly M. Khazanov is Ernest Gellner Professor of Anthropology (Emeritus) at the University of Wisconsin-Madison. He is Fellow of the British Academy, Corresponding Member of the UNESCO International Institute for the Study of Nomadic Civilizations and Honorary Member of the Central Eurasian Society. He has published and edited 19 books and volumes and is the author of over 200 articles and other scholarly publications. Among his monographs is *Nomads and the Outside World* (2ⁿᵈ edition, The University of Wisconsin Press, 1994) also translated and published in South Korea, Kazakhstan and Russia. For many years he has been doing extensive field work, mainly in Central Asia and Russia. His current research interests include the origins of pastoralism and pastoral nomadism, historical anthropology of the nomads of the Eurasian steppes, pastoral nomadism in the contemporary world and other related issues. Email: khazanov@wisc.edu

Saverio Krätli

Saverio Krätli is Editor of *Nomadic Peoples*. He works as an independent researcher and scientific advisor, specialising in the interface between pastoral producers, science, and development. His main fieldwork experience has been amongst the WoDaaBe (central Niger), Turkana (Kenya) and Karamojong (Uganda). Email: saverio.kratli@gmail.com

Angela Kronenburg García

Angela Kronenburg García studied cultural anthropology at the University of Leiden in the Netherlands and is currently a Ph.D. candidate at Wageningen University. Her MA thesis was on the relationships between the Naimina Enkiyio forest and Loita Maasai ritual practices in south Kenya. She describes how and why the forest is used as a site for rituals and ceremonies, and shows how emerging conflicts over the forest are mediated through ritual. Her Ph.D. research builds on the MA thesis and explores the Naimina Enkiyio forest conflicts further. Resource conflicts are now linked to political struggles and changing property relations over land. Angela is currently in the final phase of her Ph.D. and about to complete her dissertation. Email: angela.kronenburg@wur.nl

Stephen Moiko

Stephen S. Moiko has studied Anthropology at the University of Nairobi, Kenya and at McGill University, Canada for his doctorate. His research interests have revolved around the changing dynamics of land use in rangeland environments, particularly in sub-Saharan Africa. Within this field, he is especially interested in issues of land tenure and property rights systems, pastoral systems and livelihoods, conservation and sustainable use of resources, rural development, common property regimes (CPRs), resource governance institutions and, more recently, food security. Email: stephen.moiko@mail.mcgill.ca

Salem Mezhoud

Salem Mezhoud is an applied anthropologist and a consultant specialising in human rights and post-conflict reconstruction. After studying at London University (SOAS) and the university of Paris, he taught at the Sorbonne for three years and then worked as a journalist (BBC World Service and other media) specialising in Africa and world affairs. For the past 25 years he has worked for a number of human rights organisations and UN agencies (OHCHR, OCHA, UNICEF) in Northern and West Africa as well as South East Asia, focusing on refugees and internally displaced persons, child rights and indigenous and minority rights. He has worked extensively in the Sahel and was in charge of the UN Humanitarian Coordination Unit for OLS Sudan. Lately he has worked on stabilisation and transitional justice in post-conflict countries. He has held visiting scholarships and research fellowships at the Woodrow Wilson International Center for Scholars, Columbia University, King's College, London. Email: salemervey@aol.com

Clare Oxby

Clare Oxby is Senior Lecturer at the Institute of Social Anthropology, University of Bern, Switzerland. She spent a formative year living with Tuareg nomadic camel herders in Niger in preparation for her Ph.D. at the School of Oriental and African Studies, University of London. Her work has spanned the aid / development and university worlds. For several years she was the pastoralist and livestock projects adviser at the Overseas Development Institute, London. She then worked for various aid and development agencies especially the UN Food and Agriculture Organization, in West, Central and East Africa, Madagascar, Indonesia and Sri Lanka. The work focused on the needs of nomadic livestock-keepers and shifting cultivators and on the integration of livestock-keeping within agricultural systems. She has taught Social Anthropology at the universities of Sussex, Perugia and Oxford. She is currently researching social change in Niger's pastoral zone including international migratory networks based there. Email: clare.oxby@btinternet.com

Troy Sternberg

Troy's research focuses on how natural hazards interact with societies and the environment in the Gobi Desert, Asia. Research focuses on hazard identification, social exposure and resilience and evolving climate and hazard impact on human systems. He investigates how drought, *dzud* (extreme winter) and climate influence human opportunity and security in the Gobi Desert region of northern China and southern Mongolia. Troy is a British Academy Post Doctoral Fellow and Leverhulme Grant recipient in the School of Geography, University of Oxford. He recently co-edited the volume *Changing Deserts: Integrating People and Their Environment* (2012). Email: troy.sternberg@geog.ox.ac.uk

Emily T. Yeh

Emily T. Yeh is an Associate Professor of Geography at the University of Colorado, Boulder, specialising in nature–society relations, and environment and development in Tibetan areas of China. Over the past fifteen years, she has conducted field research on conflicts over access to natural resources, environmental history, emerging environmentalisms and the political economy and cultural politics of development and land use change in Tibet. She has also worked on the cultural politics of identity in the Tibetan diaspora and on interdisciplinary projects investigating the vulnerability of herders to climate change and the determinants of grassland degradation on the Tibetan plateau. Her work has appeared in journals such as *Society and Space, Environment and Planning*

A, *Environmental History, Conservation and Society, The China Quarterly* and *Annals of the Association of American Geographers*. Email: emily.yeh@colorado.edu

Gongbu Zhaxi

Gongbu Zhaxi is a senior lecturer in Natural Resource Management at the Agriculture College of Tibet University. He is also General Manager at Plateau Perspectives and a close colleague of Marc Foggin. With a Masters degree from University of Hawaii (2005), he is now carrying out his doctoral research in Xian, China, focused on Quinoa plant breeding in the Tibetan plateau region. Email: gongbu@plateauperspectives.org

FOREWORD

The Commission on Nomadic Peoples (CNP) is an integral part of the International Union of Anthropological and Ethnological Union Sciences (IUAES). The IUAES is a global society that consists of university, institutional and national organisations specialising in anthropology and ethnology. The Commission on Nomadic Peoples was founded in the 1970s to focus on nomadic peoples. The Commission draws together researchers, practitioners, government and non-government officials and crosses language and cultural divides. In 2009 the Commission on Nomadic Peoples took part in the 16th IUAES Congress in Kunming, China. This book is a collection of papers presented at the Congress.

The CNP organised three academic panels that brought together researchers and specialists interested in nomadic pastoralism across the world. Over four days of talks the key issues and critical concerns facing pastoralism were presented and discussed by scholars and students. Led by Dawn Chatty, Chair of the Commission on Nomadic Peoples, and honouring Anatoly Khazanov's lifetime achievements, the sessions encapsulated the evolution, strengths and challenges of pastoralism in the 21st century. Two perspectives were stressed; the first highlighted pastoralism in an international context, drawing on research in Africa, the Middle East, South America and parts of Asia. The second focus was on pastoralism in the host nation, China, and identified both the impact of rapid development on nomadic practices and livelihoods and the country's growing integration into the global pastoral research community. The session provided the opportunity to compare findings, identify patterns and methodologies and expand academic networks for future engagement and expanded cooperation.

Modern Pastoralism and Conservation: Old Problems, New Challenges is a direct outcome of the CNP sessions at the IUAES Congress. Its purpose is to present a broad compilation of recent pastoral research covering different regions and approaches that were addressed at the Congress. The objective nature of pastoralism as an area of study and the common political ecology approach of many of the papers give the book its coherent perspective. The papers presented address key points raised at the conference. These include the nature and viability of pastoralism, its practice in different parts of the world and the challenges it faces from policy, population, the environment and socio-economic development. Issues of transformation and sustainability run throughout the chapters. The changing nature of pastoralism makes knowledge of today's pastoral world essential; the papers were selected to provide a broad context of pastoralism and enhance understanding of this unique livelihood and lifestyle.

The volume commences with a paper by the Commission's 2009 Lifetime Achievement recipient, Anatoly Khazanov. Prof. Khazanov received his Ph.D. from Moscow State University in 1966 where he worked on the archaeology of nomadic cultures. At the USSR Academy of Sciences his focus shifted to social anthropology and the examination of nomadic pastoralism and the development of complex societies. His extensive body of work is capped by the classic book *Nomads and the Outside World* (1984). Since 1990 he has been at the University of Wisconsin-Madison where he continues to work and contribute to international pastoral research and debate. His chapter analysing nomadic pastoralism begins the volume; it is a fitting synthesis of the state of pastoralism today. The chapter, and book, benefit from Khazanov's long study and considered assessment on the topic. *Modern Pastoralism and Conservation: Old Problems, New Challenges* highlights the integration of mobile pastoralism into the globalised world, identifies the difficulties of transition and modernisation and notes the inevitable decline of traditional pastoralism, themes that are evident in the following chapters.

Framed by Khazanov's essay on the state of pastoralism in the world, the book follows nomadic peoples and their lives from West to East Africa, the Arabian Peninsula and the Inner Asian regions of western China and Mongolia. Saverio Krätli examines the complexities of cattle breeding amongst the WoDaaBe herders of Niger. The matriarchal lineage of the cattle population maintains diversity and economic functionality; the systems stresses cattle reliability and performance over peak productivity and livestock numbers. The paper argues that among the WoDaaBe cattle raising and mobility are part of a multifaceted understanding of herding that transforms natural unpredictability into a key resource. In the following chapter Salem Mezhoud and Clare Oxby disentangle the 'forced displacement' of herders from concepts of pastoral migration. Using examples from the Sahel, particularly Mali and Niger, and South Sudan the authors stress the vulnerability of herders to institutional displacement and government neglect while lacking access to international mechanisms and potential claims and redress under human rights law.

Stephen Moiko, an active herder, addresses the rapid transformation of Kenya's Maasai pastoral community. His chapter highlights policies of land individuation vs. communal resource management. The Maasai are at a crossroads that contrasts the security of land tenure with the flexibility to adapt to fluctuating resources that customary communal tenure offers. His case study of the Olkiramatian Group Ranch stresses 'property rights systems attuned to ecological conditions, indigenous knowledge and institutional structures'. Also in Kenya, Angela Kronenburg García investigates land appropriation strategies in Loita Masaailand. This encompasses processes of land demarcation, individualised appropriation of previously collective pasture, social approaches to possession and conditions of diminishing land availability. Appropriation strategies, grounding claims and living in the 'grey zone' between access and property are now key features of Loita Maasai life and law.

Dawn Chatty, Chair of the Commission on Nomadic Peoples, writes on the Harasiis mobile pastoralists of Central Oman. Efforts towards biodiversity conservation, such as through nature reserves, can be at odds with local pastoralists whose wellbeing depends on access to vegetation over vast areas. Difficulties faced by an Oryx

Foreword

Sanctuary in the Jiddat-il Harasiis exemplify how sustainable conservation depends on the goodwill of indigenous populations. In arid lands the drive for bio-conservation requires consideration of the rights and interests of mobile pastoral communities, such as the Harasiis, to develop sustainably.

Shifting to Asia, Troy Sternberg considers the factors that shape pastoralism in Mongolia. This stresses the local environment, long tradition and history, including 70 years as a Soviet satellite state and the pressure of rapid adjustment to a market economy since 1990. Herding transformation reflects the declining (formerly positive) role of the state, collapsing infrastructure and a cultural shift toward modern lifestyles. A changing climate, access to water and market conditions will encourage or constrain future pastoralism on the steppe.

Two final chapters reflect on pastoralism in the Chinese context. Chinese herding is dominated by strong government control of policy and livelihood patterns that often contrast with the divergent interests of the pastoral minority communities. Emily Yeh examines China's environmental governance and ecological modernisation through large-scale ecological construction projects. Such projects in western China have become a form of reterritorialisation, with different citizens having different societal value dependent on a group's alignment with state interests. Thus environmental 'greening' becomes a means of state power over marginal groups, such as the pastoral community, across the region. Foggin and Zhaxi's evaluation of ecological migration on the Tibetan plateau presents migration as way to meet conservation and human development goals. To assess the planned relocation of pastoralists the authors draw on Canada's experience resettling indigenous populations. The paper questions the efficacy of ecological migration and theorises that a more socially stable and sustainable approach would include community engagement and the ability to maintain pastoral livelihoods.

This book, made up of a selection of the academic presentations at the CNP sessions at the 2009 IUAES Congress, develops a global perspective on the wide-ranging approaches and challenges in the pastoral world. The volume includes original papers and articles previously published in peer-reviewed journals. Together the chapters provide a snapshot of nomadic pastoralism in 2009. The editors thank Prof Jijiao Zhang and Dr Fachun Du of the Institute of Anthropology and Ethnology, Chinese Academy of Social Sciences for their assistance and support for the Chinese edition of the book and their work organising the 2009 IUAES Congress. The Commission on Nomadic Peoples looks forward to new research and pastoral scholarship at the next IUAES conference in Manchester, England in 2013.

Dawn Chatty and Troy Sternberg

Oxford, 2012

CONTEMPORARY PASTORALISM: OLD PROBLEMS, NEW CHALLENGES[1]

Anatoly M. Khazanov

University of Wisconsin, Madison

I will start with terminology because it is sometimes confusing and misleading, and results in the wrong conclusions. One should discriminate between the pure pastoral nomadism, which, as some scholars claim, is coming to its end (Humphrey and Sneath 1999), other forms of traditional, subsistence-oriented mobile pastoralism and pastoralist mobility in general that is characteristic of many various forms of stock-breeding as long as they utilise natural pastures (Khazanov 1994, 15 ff.).

While commercialised and somewhat industrialised ranch-stock breeding is practiced in the USA, Canada, Australia, New Zealand, Argentina and a few other countries, there are still many millions of people in the world for whom mobile pastoralism remains the main economic activity. They are living mainly in Africa, in the extended Middle East, in Central and Inner Asia, in South Asia and in the Far North. In Africa, the pastoralist population is estimated at 268 million, over a quarter of the total population (African Union 2010). In some countries, such as Niger, Djibouti or Somalia, mobile pastoralists still constitute the majority of population; in many others they constitute a significant minority. Thus, in Mongolia, a country with a population of 2.5 million people, about 400,000 thousand are pastoralists, while half the population directly or indirectly depends on pastoralism (Fernandez-Gimenez 1999, 4). The remarkable resilience of mobile pastoralism, despite numerous gloomy predictions to the contrary, is indeed not accidental.

Climate and environment are not subject even to our post-industrial civilisation. It is worth keeping in mind that pastoralism was originally developed as an alternative to cultivation in the regions where the latter was impossible, or economically less feasible (Khazanov 1994, 85 ff.). In many of these areas the situation remains basically the same. In Mongolia, pastures constitute 74.8 per cent of the total area, arable lands

---

1. This is a revised and augmented version of a paper originally published in Mongolia. See Anatoly M. Khazanov. Pastoralists in the 'Age of Globalisation': Challenges of the 21st Century, in Jörg Janzen and Batboldyn Enkhtuvshin (eds.) *Dialog between Cultures and Civilizations. Present State and Perspectives of Nomadism in a Globalizing World.* Proceedings of the International Conference, Ulaanbaatar, August 9–14 2004. Ulaanbaatar 2008, pp. xiii–xxviii.

only 0.8 per cent; in Kazakhstan, the ratio is 68.8 and 12.9 per cent; in Turkmenistan, 61.6 and 3 per cent; in Kyrgyzstan, 42.9 and 7.2 per cent. In Sudan, only one third of the land is potentially arable. In sub-Saharan Africa in general, the arid zone accounts for 37 per cent, and the semi-arid zone for another 18 per cent of its land area (Jahnke 1982). Thus, mobile stock-breeding may retain some advantages in comparison with other forms of economic activity and remain a rational and sustainable system for utilising natural resources in the arid and semi-arid zones. Moreover, new ecological thinking holds that in many dry zones pastoralism is more environmentally benign than cultivation.

Still, one must admit that, at present, traditional, subsistence-oriented pastoralism is experiencing many difficulties and has to adjust to the new realities. Our times are often called the 'age of globalisation', but globalisation is just a new stage in the ongoing modernisation process. To avoid any misunderstanding I would like to make one clarification. When I write about modernisation I do not imply simplistic views which hold that the developing countries should copy the Western models and repeat the Western stages of development. I perceive modernisation as economic growth based on technological innovations, with corresponding changes of socio-political and cultural institutions. I would also add that, as world practice has demonstrated time and again, successful and long-term modernisation, especially in our age of the transnationalisation of information, production and finance, is inseparably linked to the market economy. All other ways of modernisation eventually lead to a dead end.

However, it is difficult for traditional economies not only to compete with, but even to adapt to the modern economies. Therefore, it is difficult, in principle, to maintain traditional mobile pastoralism within the contemporary, increasingly globalised economic climate. It is evident that traditional pastoralism should somehow be modernised. The unsolved problem, however, is how to do this in the least painful way for pastoralists themselves.

Considering the great variety of ecological, socio-political, and economic conditions of pastoralists in different countries and in different parts of the world, it is not surprising there are no general recipes applicable to every situation. Still, it is worth noting that two major and radical approaches to modernisation of traditional pastoralists that have been suggested and experimented with, have in many cases proved to be inadequate.

The first solution was the communist one. It was based on nationalisation and/or collectivisation of the stock and pastureland, not infrequently accompanied by forced sedentarisation of the pastoralists. In its extreme form – collectivisation plus sedentarisation – this model was first applied in the Soviet Union, in the late 1920s and early 1930s. Later, some other countries adopted the whole model, or more often, either its collectivisation or sedentarisation parts: Iran, in the 1930s; Mongolia, in the 1950s; China, in the 1960s; Somalia, in the 1970s; Eritrea, in the 1990s. Generally, this method was a failure.

Contemporary Pastoralism

It is true that in the Soviet Union the pastoralist process of production was eventually somewhat modernised, but this was done in an inefficient and misguided way. Livestock breeding had lost its traditional character, but was never organised on rational economic principles. In the Soviet Union and Mongolia, in the late communist period, the prime goal was to increase numbers of stock by any means. This should not be surprising indeed, since even in Mongolia urban dwellers suffered chronic shortages of milk and meat products (Fernandez-Gimenez 1999, 19).

However, an increase in stock numbers was achieved by large subsidies and disregard for the production cost, and especially for the rapidly deteriorating environment. Vast areas of fertile pastures in Kazakhstan and Turkmenistan have been turned into sand deserts; other pastures are rapidly degrading. In Kyrgyzstan, overgrazing resulted in degradation of 1.7 million hectares of pastureland (according to some data, even 3.5 million hectares), while another 30 per cent of pastures lost productivity (Dzoldoshev 1997, 168; Kliashtornyi 1999, 61). In Uzbekistan, more than 30 per cent of pastures in the desert and semi-desert zones are in various stages of degradation (Aripov 1997, 139). In China, nearly 90 per cent of usable grassland is considered 'degraded' because of species change and productivity loss (Li and Huntsinger 2011). In its Xinjiang province, salinisation and desiccation affected about 4.7 million hectares (Benson and Svanberg 1998, 141), while the average productivity of rangeland has fallen by 30 per cent since the 1960s (Banks 1999, 298).

Besides this, all pastoralist activities were put under the day-to-day control and supervision of appointed managerial staff, which denied any initiative on the part of pastoralists themselves. The lack of personal responsibility and stimuli made the work of herders dull and uninspiring, while narrow specialisation within appointed groups brought about the loss of the whole complex of pastoralist skills.

It is true, however, that the post-communist period was also marked everywhere by many negative developments in the pastoralist sector. In the 1990s, one of the most striking characteristics of the situation in the region was that in its main stock-raising countries, Kazakhstan and Kyrgyzstan, as well as in the Russian North, pastoralist specialisation had become unprofitable to the majority of households and farms due to the high input prices, undeveloped market channels and low prices for animal production. Other conspicuous characteristics had been a serious decrease in stock numbers, which was somewhat stabilised only in the last few years, and a decrease in pastoralist mobility. These negative developments were mainly the result of the state's premature retreat from its former role as a provider of subsidies, credits and input-supply systems, which was accompanied by widespread corruption and embezzlement (Khazanov *et al.* 1997; Khazanov *et al.* 1999; Khazanov and Shapiro 2005; Kerven 2003).

In the early 1990s, some scholars from Central Asia and other countries predicted the revival of traditional forms of mobile pastoralism in the region. So far, nothing like this has happened. Communal forms of land tenure and pasture utilisation destroyed in the Soviet period have not been restored and the role of kinship-based ties in the organisation of pastoralist production remains insignificant. At the same time, the transition to market-oriented forms of pastoralism and animal husbandry is also blocked for many pastoralists. In some post-communist countries, there is the danger of re-peasantisation and even pauperisation of the majority of those who remain in the pastoralist sector. Instead of becoming small-scale but efficient market-oriented produc- ers, these people may be locked into the role of subsistence farmers with no capital.

Another solution advocated mainly by some experts from Western countries is transformation of traditional pastoralists into commercial stock producers (Ingold 1978, 121), or even into capitalist ranch-owners. However, these recommendations did not take into account the environmental and social conditions in many Third World coun- tries. The ranch system that emerged in the United States and in some other countries during the second half of the nineteenth and first half of the twentieth centuries was by no means a result of the development of traditional pastoralist economies. Rather, it was created and introduced anew.

From the outset, the ranch system was aimed at production of livestock exclu- sively for sale and was operating within profit-oriented market economies. There was no introductory period. In the western United States, commercial ranching rapidly replaced subsistence-based herding with communal grazing lands after the USA took over the Mexican territories. On the Plains and in the Prairies an opportunity for expanding ranching emerged after the extirpation of bison. Ranchers might, and still may, enjoy their peculiar subculture, social status, lifestyle and quality of life, which for them were more than money, but they could not survive without being market oriented and producing for profit. In the beginning, the rapid growth of the East Coast and European beef markets guaranteed cattlemen high prices and profits, especially after the introduction of refrigerator cars, in 1869, and refrigerated ships, in 1875. Livestock owners were businessmen, not infrequently absentee cattle barons, who possessed the capital, technological know-how and means to develop the intensive system of fenced ranching with irrigated pastures, machinery, motorised transport, tame-seed forage plants, selective breeding and artificial insemination, shelters for animals in the winter and so on (Dale 1960; Atherton 1961; Bennett 1985; Barsh 1990; Jordan 1993; Starrs 1998; Huntsinger and Starrs 2006). Still, it is remarkable that in the United States and Canada most rangelands belong not to individual ranchers but to various government agencies and the ranchers have to lease them or to get grazing permits. Today even in the USA many family-owned ranches are monospecialised. They are relying on cattle alone and are facing growing difficulties connected to their limited profitability. It is hard for them to compete with the agro-industrial enterprises, which are using rela- tively cheap grain and agricultural by-products to feed cattle. Besides, contemporary ranchers are sedentary people, and often their cattle are for the most part stationary.

In the short run, it would be unrealistic to expect similar developments in many Third World countries, where the relative costs of labour versus capital are unlikely to be consistent with large-scale, capital intensive operations. This is why many scholars are now advocating much more gradual transformation of traditional pastoralism. In fact, one may already single out three stages in its attempted development. In the beginning, most attention was paid to the technological improvements in stock-breeding within the framework of traditional pastoralist social organisation and land tenure. In other words, livestock development took priority over pastoralists' development.

However, the real world is often quite a different place from the one assumed by those development experts who supposed that appropriate technological inputs would automatically yield desirable economic and social outputs. As Gorse and Steeds (1987, 10) noted:

> Planners have often misunderstood the logic of traditional production systems, and have thereby overestimated the ease with which improvements could be introduced and underestimated the negative consequences of intended improvements.

Many early developmental projects in Africa failed or resulted in unforeseen repercussions because administrators and planners ignored the peculiarities of the social organisation and land tenure of pastoralists. Thus, attempts at intensifying traditional pastoralism by applying modern technologies not infrequently gave rise to overstocking, overgrazing, degradation of vegetation, soil and water, and even to desertification (see for example Reining 1978; Goldschmidt 1981, 104 ff.; Handule and Gay 1987; Bernus 1990, 166–7).

Later, in the 1970s and in the early 1980s, an understanding came that it would be very difficult to introduce effective innovations without general changes in social systems. The World Bank, the FAO, the European Union, USAID and other donors, apparently influenced by the 'tragedy of commons' theory (Hardin 1968, 1243–8; Hardin and Baden 1977; cf. Hardin 1988) began to promote individualised land tenure, assuming that it would be more efficient and productive than the communal (Fratkin 1997). This theory, which is still very influential in China (Banks 1999, 300; Taylor 2006), holds that if a resource belongs to everybody, nobody is interested in its preservation; therefore, situations where stock is privately owned but pastures are common property inevitably result in overgrazing. In fact, this theory is wrong because it has failed to take into account a plethora of ethnographic data on pastoralists and does not distinguish between open access to pastures and their communal tenure, sometimes with further regulations (McCay and Acheson 1987; Berkes *et al.* 1989; Paine 1994, 187–8).

No wonder that the new trend in development policy has brought, at best, ambiguous results. The traditional pastoralists usually lack both the experience and the necessary capital to start market-oriented ranch enterprises. It is not surprising that the development of capital-intensive livestock production, and sometimes speculative investments, usually led to a concentration of benefits in only a few hands (Waters-Bayer and Bayer 1992, 4).

Commodification of livestock and labour resulted in the emergence of absentee herd owners and hired herders. Thus, in Turkey, Iran, Kenya, Tanzania, Botswana, some West African countries and several others, it is not pastoralists but sedentary businessmen with managerial experience and people with good connections in the governments who have established commercial enterprises (see for example Bates 1980, 125 ff. on Turkey; Beck 1980 and Bradbury 1980 on Iran; Pelican 2002 on Cameroon; Little 1985; Galaty 1992; Ellwood 1995, 9 on Kenya; Arhem 1985 on Tanzania; Hinderink and Sterkenburg 1987 on Botswana; Maliki 1986 on Niger; Salih 1990a on Sudan; and Waters-Bayer 1988 on Nigeria). Even the advocates of ranch schemes admit that concentration of large tracts of land in the hands of a few individuals creates a new set of social and political problems (see for example Awogbade 1987, 25–6).

This inevitably leads to an increasing number of displaced and unemployed persons who, in the currently prevailing conditions in many developing countries, are often denied viable possibilities for adjustment and alternative employment. At the same time, at present, pastoralist systems in Africa, as well as in some other parts of the world, are no longer capable of reabsorbing these people without help from outside sources which are at best insufficient and often inefficient, and at worst are non-existent.

Only recently are some scholars and experts coming to the conclusion that modernisation of traditional pastoralists cannot be carried out in isolation from the broader political and developmental issues. There are two main obstacles that hinder successful modernisation of traditional pastoralists. The first is connected with their growing political weakness and subjugated positions in many post-colonial states. Not infrequently, these states remain alien to the pastoralists. The latter cannot escape them, as they were sometimes capable of doing in the past, but they do not benefit from the state either. When they run away from the state, as the pastoralists of Madagascar have literally tried to do in the quite recent past (Kaufmann 1998), the state runs after them; and the state is much stronger.

The second obstacle consists in double marginalisation of the pastoralists. They are becoming increasingly marginalised within national systems of Third World countries, which, in turn, are marginalised within regional and global economic systems. These countries are often euphemistically called the 'developing' ones; however, in fact, many of them, especially in Africa and in some parts of the Middle East, are not developing but stagnating. In all, the pastoralists have to adjust to external forces of great magnitude, which are beyond their control.

In some respects, the colonial period was easier for pastoralists than what followed. It is true that they lost their political independence, that the colonial power confiscated some of their lands, regulated their migratory routes, and forced them to pay taxes. However, some exceptions notwithstanding, in general, those powers were often satisfied with the maintenance of order and did not intentionally try to undermine the traditional way of life and social organisation of the pastoralists.

In the post-colonial period, many national governments and ruling elites demonstrate much stronger anti-pastoralist bias (Azarya 1996, 69 ff.; Manger 2001, 29; Claudot-Hawad 2006, 655 ff.; Keenan 2006, 918 ff.). They consider the pastoralists as not sufficiently productive and, at the same time, as a disruptive and unruly element that has to be pacified and domesticated. In 1973, when the Sahel was affected by a severe drought and many pastoralists lost their stock, Ebrahim Konate, at that time the

Secretary of the Permanent African Interstate Committee for Drought Control, expressed his satisfaction with the situation with remarkably cynical frankness. He stated: 'We have to discipline these people, and to control their grazing and their movements. Their liberty is too expensive for us. Their disaster is our opportunity.' (Marnham 1979, 9)

Terms for nomads, like 'Yörük' in Turkey, or 'Kuchi' in Afghanistan, have become derogatory labels. (Actually, nowadays, only about 200 families of the Sarikacili Yörük practise seasonal migrations – Aysa Hilal Tuztas, personal communication). In Kenya and Uganda, negative images of pastoralists as backward and unproductive people, locked into a way of life that belongs to the past, are a commonplace in the mainstream political and popular discourses (Krätli 2006, 124–7). In Saudi Arabia the Bedouin stand not only for ancestors but also for 'backward people', 'primitive', or even 'savage' (Fabietti 2006, 573). The governments of some Central Asian countries are glorifying their 'nomadic heritage' but are doing very little, if anything at all, to assist their pastoralists in practice. No wonder that in many countries, pastoralists are currently facing more threats to their way of life than ever before in their long history.

Population growth, mining, industrial development and urbanisation result in the encroachment of sedentary populations into territories occupied by the pastoralists. This is often encouraged by the national governments. Not only in Central Asia, but in such countries as Nigeria, Mali, Cameroon, Ethiopia, Sudan, Kenya, Algeria, Syria, Israel, Turkey, Iran, India and some others, many pasturelands were appropriated by the state, or were simply seized by agriculturalists to be put under the plough (Lewis 1987; Galaty and Johnson 1990; Galaty and Bonte 1991; Koehler-Rollefson 1992; Smith 1992; Ma 1993, 173; Sheehy 1993, 17–30; Abu-Rabi'a 1994, 15; Galaty *et al.* 1994; Medzini 1998; Benson and Svanberg, 1998, 141; Claudot-Hawad 2006, 672).

In Nigeria, in 1957, 67 per cent of the land was utilised as pastures; by 1986, the area of pastureland had decreased to 39 per cent (Gefu and Gelles 1990, 39, 40). Even in Mongolia, according to some estimates, between 1957 and 1994, the total grazing area was reduced from 140 to 125 million hectares for urbanisation purposes, tilling, extension of roads and steppe tracks, etc. (Szynkiewicz 1998, 208). In the Scandinavian and Russian Arctic, many pasturelands utilised by reindeer were lost to hydroelectric development, extractive industries and other projects (Morris 1990; Vakhtin 1992; Paine 1994; Krupnik 1998). Not infrequently, herding lands are also lost to game parks and urban areas (Anderson and Grove 1987; Kaufmann 1998, 136–7; Chatty 2001; Lenhart and Casimir 2001, 10 ff.; Rao 2002; Chatty and Colchester 2002). In addition, pastoralists face increasing dislocation brought about by droughts, famines, banditry, military conflicts and civil wars.

Many national governments and governmental agencies force the pastoralists to sedentarise. Actually, the allegedly permanent battle between the desert (or the steppe for that matter) and the sown is an oversimplification of a great variety of real situations and is profoundly ahistorical. Nevertheless, already in 1979, the Fifteenth International African Seminar held at Ahmadu Bello University made a remarkable statement:

Anatoly M. Khazanov

> The conference notes that the nomadic aspect of the life of pastoralists is no longer
> tenable in the face of ever greater pressure on land, and that it is not in the interests of
> the pastoralists themselves to continue to lead a nomadic or semi-nomadic way of life.
> (Adamu and Kirk-Greene 1986, xvii; see also Khogali 1981; Salih 1990, 64 ff.)

In principle, sedentarisation and urbanisation of at least some mobile pastoralists is inevitable and even desirable under contemporary conditions, if it channels the surplus labour in the pastoralist sector into other occupational activities. It may even facilitate an increase in economic efficiency of those who remain involved in mobile pastoralism. However, at present, sedentarisation of pastoralists faces many difficulties, such as shortage of land suitable for cultivation and demographic pressure. It is very difficult to turn to cultivation when arable land is already occupied by other people, who are numerically and politically stronger. As a result, the pastoralists often have to sedentarise in marginal areas, where cultivation is risky and unpredictable to the extent that the sedentary themselves consider such lands of little use for cultivation.

Thus, at present, sedentarisation can hardly be considered a general solution for the majority of pastoralists. As Salzman (1980, vii) aptly remarked:

> Sedentarisation, viewed as an inevitable and necessary step in furthering progress and
> advancing civilization, and pressed upon nomadic peoples by external forces, can have
> detrimental consequences not only for the nomadic peoples themselves but for the large
> societies of which they are part.

Likewise, for a growing number of pastoralists who are moving into the cities and become urbanised, the problem of employment is quite acute in many countries.

In the past, traditional pastoralist economies were never deliberately profit-oriented or consistently aimed at meeting market demands, although they almost always had a barter exchange or even a market component. Nowadays, the pastoralists, whether they like it or not, are increasingly becoming involved in state, regional or international systems based on a monetary economy, with a corresponding shift from use-value to exchange-value and commoditisation of livestock and its products. At the same time, their engagement with the market is proceeding in unfavourable conditions of state intervention and expanding world markets.

Products of animal husbandry from the developed countries are dominant on the world markets and it is very difficult for pastoralist produce in developing countries to compete with them. Moreover, export produce from the developed countries has seized a significant share of the markets in some developing countries, while the pastoralists there face many difficulties in selling their own produce. If one visited supermarkets in the major cities of Kazakhstan in the 1990s, one would find a great variety of meat, sausage, cheese and even butter produced in Australia, New Zealand, the countries of the European Union, almost everywhere except Kazakhstan. The local produce was sold mainly in bazaars. The situation has changed for the better only in the last few years. Many milk products and other foodstuffs in Mongolia are imported from other countries. In the second half of the 1980s and in the early 1990s, European

Community dumping of low-grade industrial beef, pork and offal on coastal West African markets depressed demand for Sahelian fresh beef and small ruminant meat (Holtzman and Kulibaba 1996, 90–2). Most milk products available in Cameroon are imported from European countries or regionally produced on the basis of imported products (Pelican 2002).

This situation has an almost ironic side. While many international agencies, like the World Bank, argue that in Third World countries agriculture, including pastoralism, should be self-sustaining, in all developed countries it enjoys direct or indirect subsidies and other support from governments and/or consumers. Thus, subsidies to farmers in the OECD countries exceed the GDP of Africa (Krätli 2006, 134). However, one should take into account that in developed countries only a small percentage of the population is involved in agriculture, while in developing countries the agriculturalists constitute more than half the population.

In some countries, price control and other policies exercised by national governments are unfavourable to pastoralists even with regard to the local markets. In China, since the 1980s, comparative price advantages have moved in favour of crop production relative to animal husbandry (Williams 1997, 346). In 1998 in Mongolia, meat cost less than a third of its 1990 value in terms of flour (Sneath 2002, 172). Meat prices in Africa in general are artificially low (John Galaty, personal communication). In Kenya, arbitrary quarantine regulations deny access to livestock markets to many pastoralists, while others receive preferential treatment.

Besides, subsidies by themselves far from always change the situation for the better and really assist development. I can refer to the example of some Arab countries, especially the oil-producing ones. They support the Bedouin in the form of money payments, land allocations, job offers in the military, police, administration and so on. As a result of this policy, many people have moved into other sectors of national economies and societies. One might expect that this would facilitate modernisation of pastoralism and intensification of its production. Nothing like this has happened, however. It seems that in this case subsidies and subventions serve not as incentives for development but rather as compensation for a lack of development. There are but a few ranch and commercial stock-breeding enterprises in those countries, which are unable to satisfy their needs. Nowadays, countries like Saudi Arabia, Kuwait, Oman, Libya and even Jordan, have to rely upon imported meat and even dairy foodstuff (see for example Marx 2006, 85 on the Middle East in general; Katakura 1977; Cole 1981; Fabietti 1982; Lancaster and Lancaster 1986; Kostiner 1990, 244 ff.; Cole 2006 on Saudi Arabia; Scholz 1981; Jansen 1986 on Oman; Behnke 1980 on Libya; Abu Jaber and Gharaibeh 1981; Hiatt 1984 on Jordan). At the same time, a policy of sedentarisation pursued in some Arab countries has not been very successful either. It has resulted in deterioration of fragile ecosystems of the steppe regions (Bocco 2006; Fabietti 2006).

One may complain about unfair competition and limited export opportunities for the developing countries as much as one wants; but this is how things are in practice at the moment. To provide but one of many possible examples I can refer to the

Mongolian case. Cashmere is the only product of animal husbandry that the country successfully exports. It is the second largest producer of cashmere in the world (21 per cent of the world market). The increased breeding and raising of goats has had a negative impact on the environment. At the same time, the export tax put on raw cashmere by the Mongolian government does not work well because of widespread smuggling. A recent crash in cashmere prices on the world market has negatively affected both government revenues and immediate producers' incomes.

Moreover, while the developed countries build various barriers, like rigorous quality constraints, which prevent the import of animal products from the developing countries, the governments of the latter, not infrequently, encourage imports and control producer and consumer prices to keep them at a lower level for the growing urban population.

So far, I have mentioned various schemes suggested and implemented by planners, experts on development and government officials. But what about social scientists, especially anthropologists? In many cases we have been sitting on the fence complaining about the decay of traditional pastoralism but unable to offer a viable and practical alternative (see, for example, Raikes 1981, 250; cf. Sandford 1996, 179).

It should not be surprising, then, that attempts at dialogue between anthropologists and developers and governmental officials have not been very fruitful so far. When administrators and planners began to advance and implement schemes aimed at transformation of traditional pastoralists into commercial livestock producers, this brought them into direct conflict with the majority in the anthropological community. Thus, we pointed out time and again that our opponents did not realise that production is not only an economic activity; it is also a socially and culturally constructed activity. Perhaps this attitude was the best expressed by Baxter (1987, i): 'Almost all, indeed maybe all, the development interventions to date had not helped the impoverished pastoralists at all, nor had they added a cent to the wealth of any nation.' This opinion is echoed by Scoones (1996, 3):

> The last 30 years have seen the unremitting failure of livestock development projects across Africa. Millions of dollars have been spent with few obvious returns and not a little damage. Most commentators agree that the experience has been a disaster, so much so that many donors and other international agencies have effectively abandoned the dry zone in their development efforts.

In the past I too was very critical of many development projects suggested by various international organisations and implemented by national governments in Third World countries (see, for example, Khazanov 1998, 12 ff.). I am still critical of many of those projects. However, now I am coming to the conclusion that my general attitude to the principal goal of advocated development, which I shared with many other anthropologists, was, to some extent, unfair and unrealistic. Explicitly or implicitly, we, the anthropologists, resent most development projects because they undermine those types of social organisation, culture, values, etc. that are connected with traditional pastoralism. Essentially, our criticism has a certain anti-modernist touch, although we rarely admit this.

However, practical experience is teaching us that traditional forms of social organisation and of associated social behaviour are often becoming counterproductive and inappropriate in the age of globalisation. It is true that so far mobile pastoralism in the developing countries has survived despite all kinds of development schemes, rather than because of them. Many development projects were ill-devised. Attempts at transforming mobile pastoralism from above, initiated, designed and implemented by the state through purely administrative measures in most cases have not brought the desired results. International and national aid was sometimes directed at the wrong goals, misused and then prematurely withdrawn. For example, in the 1990s, assistance to African pastoralists by international agencies was much less than in the 1960s and 1970s. Soviet aid amounted to more than a third of annual GDP in Mongolia. Its withdrawal was one of the main reasons for the economic crisis in the country in the early 1990s.

The same can be said about national assistance to and investment in the pastoralist sector of economies in the rare cases when this takes place. Thus, in China, only a small portion of agricultural development resources goes into improving livestock production (Williams 1997, 346–7). In Mongolia, the level of investment in pastoralism is low and was declining steadily in the 1990s. The percentage of all bank loans granted to borrowers outside the capital, Ulaanbaatar, has fallen each year throughout the 1990s, from 46 per cent in 1993, to 11 per cent in 1998 (Sneath 2002, 173).

In any case, excessive paternalism, even if benevolent, will not help. The problem is not only what to do with the mobile pastoralists, but also what the pastoralists have to do themselves in order to cope with challenges of globalisation. It goes without saying, however, that the pastoralists must become full-fledged citizens of modernising states and have a voice in decision-making. They should not only be listened to; they should be directly involved in the planning and implementation of development programmes. At the same time, learning from previous mistakes, national governments and international agencies should do more by providing the pastoralists with various kinds of input: education, water service, veterinary care, transportation facilities, stock insurance, information, market infrastructure, credits, etc. Some protectionist measures should not be excluded either.

Only the future will tell whether these recommendations, and many similar ones, remain wishful thinking. Still, the general trend of transformation of mobile pastoralism in the twenty-first century seems to me quite clear and unavoidable. Let us face the truth. In many countries, mobile pastoralism in its current forms is no longer a viable economic option. In East Africa, in the Middle East, in Central Asia and in the Russian North the inability of many pastoralists to subsist primarily by means of livestock has become a common theme.

Modernisation, which is highly beneficial in general, at the same time, was, is and will remain a merciless selection process. It is uneven and differential. It has its winners, its losers and those whose rewards are delayed. Those who fail to cope with it either perish, or, at best, are relegated to the margins of the developed world. They will be denied access to proper education, advanced medical services, the telecommunications revolution, a chance of improving their living standards and many other benefits of modernity because directly or indirectly these benefits are intrinsically connected with the market-oriented economy. Without modernisation the mobile pastoralists face the risk of being further marginalised and alienated, or of becoming 'museum exhibits' or even 'zoo groups', an exotic attraction for urban romantics and tourists. Contrary to Krupnik (2000, 54), I am by no means sure that 'flagging public spirit and herders' pride can be boosted via outreach and exhibit programmers, publication of elders' narratives, historical photographs, catalogues and classical ethnographies addressed primarily to local audiences.' There is nothing wrong with this and other similar suggestions. Besides, they help to keep anthropologists occupied. But it would be very naïve to expect them to really change the situation for better.

In order to continue being pastoralists, people should benefit from their capability of being pastoralists. It is indeed high time for anthropological attention to shift from a concern for a 'way of life' to a concern for the people who have to live it under dire circumstances. Episodic revivals of more or less traditional pastoralism, in one country or another, are more connected to temporary factors than to dominant trends in contemporary development. Thus, in Somalia this revival was connected with the disintegration of the state. In Mongolia, in the early 1990s, it was connected with the collapse of the communist command economy, which resulted in high unemployment rates. Modernisation is an irresistible force and there is no viable alternative to it. This is what the anti-globalists do not want to comprehend.

In all probability, spatial mobility will remain an important characteristic of stock breeding in many arid environments. The complete transformation of mobile pastoralists into sedentary cultivators or town-dwellers would mean that vast desert and semi-desert territories unsuitable for cultivation would cease to be used for food production and would be left to lie as waste land. Besides, it is worth remembering that crop cultivation is more environmentally degrading than pasturing. Apparently, the general trend in pastoralists' development will be connected with the growing commercialisation and monetarisation of production, introduction of modern livestock technology and other innovations. Probably, one will witness the better definition of leasing and ownership rights and, in some countries, even the introduction of individual land tenure. One may only hope that the appropriate land tenure arrangements will be flexible enough to adjust to environments, especially non-equilibrium ones, which are characterised by high climatic variability. There is also a danger of substituting short-term maximisation of production for long-term optimisation.

Modernisation brings not only technological and economic changes, but social and cultural changes as well. Some pastoralists will benefit from these developments, but I am afraid that many will find themselves at the losing end. These changes may increase further the tensions within pastoralist groups, already evident in many countries. They may result in the erosion of many traditional social institutions, bonds, statuses, values, loyalties and authenticities, as well as in growing economic inequality.

Actually, these processes are already quite conspicuous in Africa (see, for example, Bovin and Manger 1990) and other parts of the world. They may have other disruptive consequences, since the mere destruction of the traditional forms of social organisation will hardly bring a vital new system; on the contrary, this may result in social disorganisation and dislocation. In any case, more people will have to leave pastoralism and move into other sectors of economy. In the worst scenario more pastoralists may become destitutes, whose physical survival will depend on the international relief organisations.

Still, the situation with contemporary mobile pastoralism is not absolutely grim. It seems that some individual governments and international organisations are beginning to comprehend its importance and benefits for national and regional economies, while the pastoralists themselves are adjusting to the changing conditions, just as they were always doing in the past. Thus, in Kazakhstan, in the last few years, domestic demand for meat, milk and dairy produce is mainly satisfied, and in 2010 the government set an ambitious goal: to increase production for export. Remarkably, 85 per cent of market production is produced by small-size private farms, which proves their viability given proper conditions.

In September 2010, a new document, 'A Policy Framework for Pastoralism in Africa', was adopted by the African Union. It still contains some dubious statements. Thus, it claims that the worsening situation of pastoralists is the result of their inability to adapt to a changing world under the combined effects of natural and human factors. Nevertheless, the document admits the need to abandon the biased perception of pastoralism as an archaic livestock production system and of pastoralists as suffering the self-inflicted choice of an obsolete traditional lifestyle. The document also states that, given the cross-border character of pastoralism, a pan-African policy on pastoralism is long overdue. This policy should integrate the pastoralists in the mainstream market economy and national policy process. The document contains another important recommendation, namely that the collective land rights of pastoralists need to be protected against infringement by claims to private property and alternative forms of land use (African Union 2010). However, this document is not binding, and it remains to be seen whether, and to what extent, its recommendations are implemented in practice.

It is impossible to predict in detail exactly what forms the integration of mobile pastoralism in the developing countries into the globalised market will take. Apparently, there will be various forms, including transitional ones, which may be quite different from each other in terms of land tenure, degree of specialisation, and many other parameters. In all, this process will continue to be very painful, and will bring a lot of resentment. Perhaps it is possible to somewhat alleviate its negative collateral effects, but hardly to avoid them completely. However, hopefully mobile pastoralism will eventually become more competitive and more productive along the lines of market-oriented economic production. In any case, like it or not, the decay of traditional pastoralism seems to me inevitable.

18

Anatoly M. Khazanov

BIBLIOGRAPHY

Abu Jaber, K.S. and Gharaibeh, F.A. 1981. 'Bedouin Settlement: Organizational, Legal, and Administrative Structure in Jordan', in D. Aronson, J.D. Galaty, and P.C. Salzman (eds.) *The Future of Pastoral Peoples*. Ottawa, International Development Research Centre: 294–300.

Abu-Rabi'a, A. 1994. *The Negev Bedouin and Livestock Rearing: Social, Economic and Political Aspects*. Oxford, Berg Publishers.

Adamu, M. and Kirk-Greene, A.H.M. (eds.) 1986. *Pastoralists of the West African Savanna*. Manchester, Manchester University Press.

African Union 2010. Department of Rural Economy and Agriculture. *Pastoral Policy Framework in Africa: Securing, Protecting and Improving the Lives, Livelihoods and Rights of Pastoralist Communities*. Addis Ababa.

Anderson, D. and Grove, R. (eds.) 1987. *Conservation in Africa: People, Policies and Practice*. Cambridge, Cambridge University Press.

Arhem, K. 1985. *Pastoral Man in the Garden of Eden: The Maasai of the Ngorongoro Conservation Area*. Uppsala, Uppsala Research Reports on Cultural Anthropology.

Aripov, U. 1997. 'Karakulevodstvo i aridnoe kormoproizvodstvo v Uzbekistane: sostoianie i problemy razvitiia', in A. Khazanov, V. Naumkin, and K. Shapiro (eds.) *Pastoralism in Central Asia*. Moscow, University of Wisconsin-Madison and Russian Center for Strategic Research and International Studies: 134–141.

Atherton, L. 1961. *The Cattle Kings*. Bloomington, University of Indiana Press.

Awogbade, M.D. 1987. 'Grazing Reserves in Nigeria', *Nomadic Peoples* (NS) **23**: 19–30.

Azarya, V. 1996. *Nomads and the State in Africa: The Political Roots of Marginality*. Leiden, African Studies Centre.

Banks, T. 1999. 'State, Community and Common Property in Xinjiang: Synergy or Strife?' *Development Policy Review* **17**: 293–313.

Barsh, R.L. 1990. 'The Substitution of Cattle for Bison on the Great Plains', in P.A. Olson (ed.) *The Struggle for the Land: Indigenous Insight and Industrial Empire in the Semiarid World*. Lincoln and London, University of Nebraska Press: 103–126.

Bates, D.G. 1980. 'Yörük Settlement in Southeast Turkey', in P.C. Salzman (ed.) *When Nomads Settle: Processes of Sedentarization as Adaptation and Response*. New York, Praeger: 124–139.

Baxter, P.T.W. 1987. 'Introduction', in P.T.W. Baxter (ed.) *Property, Poverty and People: Changing Rights in Property and Problems of Pastoral Development*. Manchester, University of Manchester: i–vii.

Beck, L. 1980. 'Herd Owners and Hired Shepherds: The Qashqa'i of Iran', *Ethnology* **19**, 3: 327–352.

Behnke, R. 1980. *The Herders of Cyrenaica: Ecology, Economy and Kinship among the Bedouin of Eastern Libya*. Urbana, University of Illinois Press.

Bennett, J.W. 1985. 'Range Culture and Society in the North American West', *Folklore Annual*: 88-104.

Benson, L. and Svanberg, I. 1998. *China's Last Nomads. The History and Culture of China's Kazakhs.* Armonk, New York, M.E. Sharpe.

Berkes, F., Feeny, D., McCay, B.J., and Acheson, J.M. 1989. 'The Benefits of the Commons', *Nature* **340**: 91-93.

Bernus, E. 1990. 'Dates, Dromedaries, and Drought: Diversification in Tuareg Pastoral Systems', in J.G. Galaty and D.L. Johnson (eds.) *The World of Pastoralism: Herding Systems in Comparative Perspective.* New York, Guilford Press.

Bocco, R. 2006. 'The Settlement of Pastoral Nomads in the Arab Middle East: International Organizations and Trends in Development Policies 1950–1990', in D. Chatty (ed.) *Nomadic Societies in the Middle East and North Africa. Entering the 21st Century.* Leiden-Boston, Brill: 302–330.

Bovin, M. and Manger, L. (eds.) 1990. *Adaptive Strategies in African Arid Lands.* Uppsala, The Nordic Africa Institute.

Bradburd, D.A. 1980. 'Never Give a Shepherd an Even Break: Class and Labor among the Komachi', *American Ethnologist* **7**, 4: 603–620.

Chatty, D. 2001. 'Pastoral Tribes in the Middle East and Wildlife Conservation Schemes: The Endangered Species?' *Nomadic Peoples* (NS) **5**: 104–122.

Chatty, D. and Colchester, M. (eds.) 2002. *Conservation and Mobile Indigenous Peoples.* Oxford, Berghahn.

Claudot-Hawad, H. 2006. 'A Nomadic Fight against Immobility: the Tuareg in the Modern State', in D. Chatty (ed.) *Nomadic Societies in the Middle East and North Africa. Entering the 21st Century.* Leiden and Boston, Brill: 654–681.

Cole, D. 1981. 'Bedouin and Social Change in Saudi Arabia', *Journal of Asian and African Studies* **16**, 1–2: 128–149.

Cole, D. 2006. 'New Homes, New Occupations, New Pastoralism: Al Murrah Bedouin 1968-2003' in D. Chatty (ed.) *Nomadic Societies in the Middle East and North Africa. Entering the 21st Century.* Leiden and Boston, Brill: 370–372.

Dale, E.E. 1960. *The Range Cattle Industry: Ranching on the Great Plains from 1865 to 1925.* Norman, University of Oklahoma Press.

Dzoldoshev, K. 1997. 'Sostoianie pastbishch i problemy proizvodstva i zagotovki v Kyrgyzstane', in A. Khazanov, V. Naumkin, and K. Shapiro (eds.) *Pastoralism in Central Asia.* Moscow, University of Wisconsin-Madison and Russian Center for Strategic Research and International Studies: 168–177.

Ellwood, W. 1995. 'Nomads at the Crossroads', *New Internationalist* **266** (April): 7–10.

Fabietti, U. 1982. 'Sedentarization as a Means of Detribalization: Some Policies of the Saudi Arabian Government towards the Nomads', in T. Niblock (ed.) *State, Society and Economy in Saudi Arabia.* London, Croom Helm.

Fabietti, U. 2006. 'Facing Change in Arabia: The Bedouin Community and the Notion of Development', in D. Chatty (ed.) *Nomadic Societes in the Middle East and North Africa. Entering the 21st century.* Leiden and Boston, Brill: 573–598.

Fernandez-Gimenez, M.E. 1999. 'Reconsidering the Role of Absentee Herd Owners: A View from Mongolia', *Human Ecology* **27**, 1: 1–27.

Fratkin, E. 1997. 'Pastoralism: Governance and Development Issues', *Annual Review of Anthropology* **26**: 235–261.

Galaty, J. 1992. '"The Land is Yours": Social and Economic Factors in the Privatization, Subdivision and Sale of Maasai Ranches', *Nomadic Peoples* **30**: 26–40.

Galaty, J. and Bonte, P. (eds.) 1991. *Herders, Warriors, and Traders: Pastoralism in Africa*. Boulder, Westview Press.

Galaty, J.G. and Johnson, D.L. (eds.) 1990. *The World of Pastoralism: Herding Systems in Comparative Perspective*. New York, Guilford Press.

Galaty, J.G., Hjort af Ornas, A., Lane, Ch., and Ndagala, D. (eds.) 1994. The Pastoral Land Crisis: Tenure and Dispossession in East Africa. *Nomadic Peoples* **34/35** (special issue).

Gefu, J.O. and Gelles, J.L. 1990. 'Pastoralists, Ranchers and the State in Nigeria and North America: A Comparative Analysis', *Nomadic Peoples* **25–27**: 34–50.

Goldschmidt, W. 1981. 'The Failure of Pastoral Economic Development Programs in Africa', in J.G. Galaty, D. Aronson, and P.C. Salzman (eds.) *The Future of Pastoral Peoples*. Ottawa, International Developmental Research Centre: 101–118.

Gorse, J.E. and Steeds, D.R. 1987. *Desertification in the Sahelian and Sudanian Zones of West Africa*. Washington, DC, World Bank.

Handule, A. and Gay, C.W. 1987. 'Development and Transitional Pastoralism in Somalia', *Nomadic Peoples* **24**: 36–43.

Hardin, G. 1968. 'The Tragedy of the Commons', *Science* **162**: 1243–1248.

Hardin, G. 1988. 'Commons Failing', *New Scientist* **22** (October).

Hardin, G. and Baden, J. 1977. *Managing the Commons*. San Francisco, W.H. Freeman.

Hiatt, J. M. 1984. 'State Formation and the Encapsulation of Nomads: Local Change and Continuity among Recently Sedentarized Bedouin in Jordan', *Nomadic Peoples* **15**: 1–11.

Hinderink, J. and Sterkenburg, J.J. 1987. *Agricultural Commercialization and Government Policy in Africa*. London and New York, KPI.

Holtzman, J.S. and Kulibaba, N.P. 1996. 'Livestock Marketing in Pastoral Africa: Policies to Increase Competitiveness, Efficiency and Flexibility', in I. Scoones (ed.) *Living with Uncertainty. New Directions in Pastoral Development in Africa*. London, Intermediate Technology Publications: 79–94.

Humphrey, C. and Sneath, D. 1999. *The End of Nomadism? Society, the State and the Environment in Inner Asia*. Durham and Cambridge, Duke University Press/White Horse Press.

Huntsinger, L. and Starrs, P. 2006. 'Grazing in Arid North America: A Biogeographical Approach', *Sècheresse* **17**, 1–2: 219–234.

Ingold, T. 1978. 'The Rationalization of Reindeer Management among Finnish Lapps', *Development and Change* **1**: 103–122.

Jahnke, H. 1982. *Livestock Production Systems and Livestock Development in Tropical Africa*. Kiel, Kieler Wissenschaftverlag Vauk.

Jansen, J. 1986. *Nomads in the Sultanate of Oman: Tradition and Development in Dhofar*. Boulder, Westview Press.

Jordan, T.G. 1993. *North American Cattle-Ranching Frontiers: Origins, Diffusion and Differentiation*. Albuquerque, N.M, University of New Mexico.

21

Contemporary Pastoralism

Katakura, M. 1977. *Bedouin Village: A Study of a Saudi Arabian People in Transition*. Tokyo, University of Tokyo Press.

Kaufmann, J.C. 1998. 'The Cactus Was Our Kin: Pastoralism in the Spiny Desert of Southern Madagascar', in J. Ginat and A.M. Khazanov (eds.) *Changing Nomads in a Changing World*. Brighton, Sussex Academic Press: 124–142.

Keenan, J.H. 2006. 'Sedentarization and Changing Patterns of Social Organization amongst the Tuareg of Algeria', in D. Chatty (ed.) *Nomadic Societies in the Middle East and North Africa. Entering the 21st Century*. Leiden and Boston, Brill: 916–939.

Kerven, C. (ed.) 2003. *Prospects for Pastoralism in Kazakhstan and Turkmenistan. From State Farms to Private Flocks*. London and New York, Routledge Curzon.

Kerven, C. 2003. 'Agrarian Reform and Privatization in the Wider Asian Region', in C. Kerven (ed.) *Prospects for Pastoralism in Kazakhstan and Uzbekistan. From State Farms to Private Flocks*. London and New York, Routledge Curzon.

Khazanov, A.M. 1994. *Nomads and the Outside World*. 2nd edn. Madison, The University of Wisconsin Press.

Khazanov, A.M. 1998. 'Pastoralists in the Contemporary World: The Problem of Survival', in J. Ginat and A.M. Khazanov (eds.) *Changing Nomads in a Changing World*. Brighton, Sussex Academic Press: 7–23.

Khazanov, A., Naumkin, V., and Shapiro, K. (eds.) 1997. *Pastoralism in Central Asia*. Moscow, University of Wisconsin-Madison and Russian Center for Strategic Research and International Studies.

Khazanov, A., Naumkin, V., Shapiro K., and Tomas, D. (eds.) 1999. *The Kazakhstan Livestock Sector in Transition to a Free Economy*. Moscow, University of Wisconsin–Madison and Russian Center for Strategic Research and International Studies.

Khazanov, A. and Shapiro, K. 2005. 'Contemporary Pastoralism in Central Asia', in R. Amitai and M. Biran (eds.) *Mongols, Turks and Others: Eurasian Nomads and the Sedentary World*. Leiden, Brill: 503–534.

Khogali, M.M. 1981. 'Sedentarization of the Nomads: Sudan', in D. Aronson, J.G. Galaty, P.C. Salzman, and A. Chouinard (eds.) *The Future of Pastoral Peoples*. Ottawa, International Development Research Centre: 302–313.

Kliashtornyi, S. 1999. 'Sel'skokhoziaistvennaia revoliutsiia' v Kyrgyzstane i predpolagaemye tendentsii dal'neishego razvitiia', in A. Khazanov, V. Naumkin, K. Shapiro, and D. Thomas (eds.) *The Kazakhstan Livestock Sector in Transition to a Market Economy*. Moscow, University of Wisconsin-Madison and Russian Center for Strategic Research and International Studies: 60–70.

Koehler-Rollefson, L. 'The Raika Dromedary Breeders in Rajasthan: A Pastoral System in Crisis', *Nomadic Peoples* **30**: 74–83.

Kostiner, J. 1990. 'Transforming Dualities: Tribe and State Formation in Saudi Arabia', in P.S. Khoury and J. Kostiner (eds.) *Tribes and State Formation in the Middle East*. Berkeley: University of California Press: 226–251.

Krätli, S. 2006. 'Cultural Roots of Poverty? Education and Pastoral Livelihood in Turkana and Karamoja', in Caroline Dyer (ed.) *The Education of Nomadic Peoples. Current Issues, Future Prospects*. New York and Oxford, Berghahn Books: 120–140.

Anatoly M. Khazanov

Krupnik, I. 1998. 'Understanding Reindeer Pastoralism in Modern Siberia: Ecological Continuity versus State Engineering', in J. Ginat and A.M. Khazanov (eds). *Changing Nomads in a Changing World.* Brighton, Sussex Academic Press: 223–242.

Krupnik, I. 2000. 'Reindeer Pastoralism in Modern Siberia: Research and Survival During the Time of Crash', *Polar Research* **19**, 1: 49–56.

Lancaster, W. and Lancaster, F. 1986. 'The Concept of Territory among the Rwala Bedouin', *Nomadic Peoples* **20**: 41–48.

Lenhart, L. and Casimir, M.J. 2001. 'Environment, Property Resources and the State: An Introduction', *Nomadic Peoples* (NS) **5**, 3: 6–20.

Lewis, N.N. 1987. *Nomads and Settlers in Syria and Jordan 1800–1980.* Cambridge, Cambridge University Press.

Li, W. and Huntsinger, L. 2011. 'China's Grassland Contract Policy and its Impacts on Herder Ability to Benefit Inner Mongolia: Tragic Feedbacks', *Ecology and Society* **16**, 2. <http://www.ecologyandsociety.org/vol16/iss2/art1/>.

Little, P. 1985. 'Absentee Herd Owners and Part-Time Pastoralists: The Political Economy of Resource Use in Northern Kenya', *Human Ecology* **13**, 2: 131–151.

Ma, R. 1993. 'Migrant and Ethnic Integration in the Process of Socio-Economic Change in Inner Mongolia: A Village Study', *Nomadic Peoples* **33**: 173–191.

McCay, B.M. and Acheson, J.M. (eds.) 1987. *The Question of the Commons: The Culture and Ecology of Communal Resources.* Tucson, University of Arizona Press.

Maliki, B. 1986. 'The Changing Structures of Livestock Ownership among Pastoralists in Niger', *Bulletin of the Institute for Development Anthropology* **4**, 1: 3–5.

Manger, L. 2001. 'Pastoralist-State Relationships among the Hadendowa Beja of Eastern Sudan', *Nomadic Peoples* (NS) **5**, 2: 21–48.

Marnham, P. 1979. *Nomads of the Sahel.* London, Minority Rights Group Report, 33.

Marx, E. 2006. The Political Economy of Middle Eastern and North African Pastoral 'Nomads', in D. Chatty (ed.) *Nomadic Societies in the Middle East and North Africa. Entering the 21ˢᵗ Century.* Leiden and Boston, Brill: 78–97.

Medzini, A. 1998. 'Bedouin Settlement Policy in Israel 1964–1996', in J. Ginat and A.M. Khazanov (eds.) *Changing Nomads in a Changing World.* Brighton, Sussex Academic Press: 58–67.

Morris, C.P. 1990. 'Hydroelectric Development and the Human Rights of Indigenous People', in P.A. Olson (ed.) *The Struggle for Land: Indigenous Insight and Industrial Empire in the Semiarid World.* Lincoln and London, University of Nebraska Press: 193–209.

Paine, R. 1994. *Herds of the Tundra: A Portrait of Saami Reindeer Pastoralism.* Washington and London, Smithsonian Institution Press 1994.

Pelican, M. 2002. 'From Cultural Property to Market Goods: Changes in Economic Strategies and Herd Management Rationales of Agro-Pastoral Fulbe in North West Cameroon'. A paper submitted to the workshop 'Collective and Multiple Forms of Property in Animals' held at the Max Planck Institute for Social Anthropology, Halle/Saale.

Raikes, P.L. 1981. *Livestock Development and Policy in East Africa.* Uppsala, The Scandinavian Institute of African Studies.

Rao, A. 2002. 'Pastoral Nomads, the State and a National Park: the Case of Dachigam, Kashmir', *Nomadic Peoples* (NS) **6**, 2: 72–98.

Reining, P. (ed.) 1978. *Handbook on Desertification Indicators*. Washington, DC, American Association for the Advancement of Science.

Salih, M. 1990. 'Agro-Pastoralists Response to Agricultural Policies: The Predicament of the Baggara, Western Sudan', in M. Bovin and L. Manger (eds.) *Adaptive Strategies in African Arid Lands*. Uppsala, Scandinavian Institute of African Studies: 59–75.

Salih, M. 1990a. 'Government Policy and Options in Pastoral Development in the Sudan', *Nomadic Peoples* **25–27**: 65–78.

Salzman, P.C. 1980. 'Preface', in P.S. Salzman (ed.) *When Nomads Settle: Processes of Sedentarization as Adaptation and Response*. New York, Praeger: vii–viii.

Sandford, S. 1996. 'Improving the Efficiency of Opportunism: New Directions for Pastoral Development', in I. Scoones (ed.) *Living with Uncertainty. New Directions in Pastoral Development in Africa*. London, Intermediate Technology Publications: 174–182.

Scholz, F. (ed.) 1981. *Beduinen im Zeichen des Erdöls: Studien zur Entwicklung im Beduinischen Lebensraum Südost-Arabiens*. Wiesbaden, Dr. Ludwig Reichert Verlag.

Scoones., I. 1996. 'New Directions in Pastoral Development in Africa', in I. Scoones (ed.) *Living with Uncertainty. New Directions in Pastoral Development in Africa*. London, Intermediate Technology Publications: 1–6.

Sheehy, D.P. 1993. 'Grazing Management Strategies as a Factor Influencing Ecological Stability of Mongolian Grasslands', *Nomadic Peoples* **33**: 17–30.

Smith, A.B. 1992. *Pastoralism in Africa: Origins and Development Ecology*. London and Athens, Christopher Hurst and Ohio University Press.

Sneath, D. 2002. 'Producer Groups and the Decollectivization of the Mongolian Pastoral Economy', in J. Heyer, F. Stewart, and R. Thorp (eds.) *Group Behaviour and Development. Is the Market Destroying Cooperation?* Oxford, Oxford University Press: 161–184.

Starrs, P.F. 1998. *Let the Cowboy Ride: Cattle Ranching in the American West. Creating the North American Landscape*. Baltimore, John Hopkins University Press.

Starrs, P.F. and Huntsinger, L. 1998. 'The Cowboy and Buckaroo in American Ranch Hand Styles', *Rangelands* **20**, 5: 36–40.

Szynkiewicz, S. 1998. 'Contemporary Mongol Concepts on Being a Pastoralist: Institutional Continuity, Change and Substitutes', in J. Ginat and A.M. Khazanov (eds.) *Changing Pastoralists in a Changing World*. Brighton: Sussex Academic Press: 202–222.

Taylor, J.L. 2006. 'Negotiating the Grassland: the Policy of Pasture Enclosures and Contested Resource Use in Inner Mongolia', *Human Organization* **65**, 4: 374–386.

Vakhtin, N. 1992. *Native Peoples of the Russian Far North*. London, Minority Rights Group.

Waters-Bayer, A. 1988. *Dairying by Settled Fulani Agropastoralists in Central Nigeria*. Kiel: Wissenschaftsverlag Vauk.

Waters-Bayer, A. and Bayer, W. 1992. 'The Role of Livestock in the Rural Economy', *Nomadic Peoples* **31**: 3–18.

Williams, M. 1997. 'The Desert Discourse of Modern China', *Modern China* **23**, 3: 328–355.

~ 2 ~

CATTLE BREEDING, COMPLEXITY AND MOBILITY IN A STRUCTURALLY UNPREDICTABLE ENVIRONMENT: THE WODAABE HERDERS OF NIGER[1]

Saverio Krätli

IUAES Commission on Nomadic Peoples

INTRODUCTION

In a Sahelian ecosystem, with temperatures up to and above 50 °C at the peak of a nine-month-long dry season, where it is difficult to feed even sheep and goats, the WoDaaBe herders produce the largest cattle breed in West Africa. The rare colonial

---

1.   This paper was originally published in *Nomadic Peoples* **12**, 1 (2008) and is published here with only minor changes. Since 2008, when this article was first written, some aspects of its findings have been further developed (Krätli and Schareika 2010) and some have found their way into a process of reflection on pastoral mobility in West and East Africa by a large base of stakeholders, promoted by the Howard G. Buffet Foundation (HGBF). This resulted in the publication of *Modern and Mobile*, a booklet offering an overview on the current understanding of pastoral mobility, specifically directed to policy makers (IIED and SOS Sahel 2009). Recent pan-African and regional policies now acknowledge pastoralism as the most important and sustainable economic activity in the rangelands, making a substantial contribution to both national and regional economies. The consultative draft of the 'COMESA Policy Framework for Food Security in Pastoralist Areas' states: 'Pastoralists have developed a diverse range of strategies, institutions and networks *to exploit the unpredictability of arid environments to their economic advantage. Livestock mobility and the carefully controlled breeding of animals to feed selectively on the best quality pastures highly dispersed in time and space are two of the more critical strategies that allow them to create economic value rather than mere survival in difficult environments.*' (COMESA 2009, 4, italics added) The African Union Pastoral policy framework, adopted in January 2011, 'recognizes the need to incorporate and support existing or emerging policies at national and regional levels which to varying degrees all aim to ... *maximize efficient livestock production by enabling pastoral mobility*' (AU 2010, 23 and 29, and Principle 4.1.7, italics added). The AU-IBAR background paper to the EAC Heads of State Retreat on Climate Change and Food Security (December 2010), finds that: 'In the East African region, the expansion of arid lands due to climate change provides *unmatched comparative advantage to pastoral systems* ... hotter conditions coupled with shifting rainfall patterns could make up to one million square kilometers of marginal African farmland no longer able to support even subsistence-level farming. However, this land ... could still support livestock ... *more resistant to climate change impacts than crops because of its mobility*' (AU-IBAR 2010, 8, italics added).

veterinarians who looked closely at these animals, did not conceal their astonishment at such an achievement, recording that the WoDaaBe '[thanks to their mobility] win every year, in spite of unforgiving Nature, this challenge of breeding animals whose feeding requirements (given their size) are out of proportion with the capacity of the pastures' (Mornet and Koné 1941, 179). Today, despite the major droughts of the 1970s and 1980s, and decades of unfavourable rural development policies, the WoDaaBe are still very much in business. Their Bororo zebu[2] has not only a significant presence on the internal beef market in Niger, but remains the most appreciated cattle on the export market (Djariri *et al.* 2003).

The well of Idinghiri is almost exactly 100 kilometres north of Tchin Tabaraden, Niger. Jiima's camp is another five kilometres away. In mid-June 2008, at ten o'clock, the sky is bright, with a temperature of 47 °C. The family herd, mainly of Bororo zebus, is 'out' for the morning graze, a few hundred metres in the opposite direction to the well. Jiima's elder son, Medji, is with them. He walks slowly, the herding stick across his shoulders, now and again saying smooth 'cattle-words' in a low voice. The mahogany cattle, with long, lyre-shaped horns, are scattered in groups of two or three. A few seem to forage more on their own. There are six young calves, mostly keeping close to their mothers, as yet unweaned but sometimes trying a bit of grass. The last rainy season, nine months ago, was a good one. Jiima's camp has been here for a bit more than a week, but the bush around, and as far as one can see, is covered with grasses 20–30 centimetres tall. Most of it is *geenal dimal* (*Schonefeldia gracilis*) and *saaBeewal* (*Echinochloa colona*). The cattle also feed on tree leaves and bushes. The young leaves and branches of the *Bamammbi (Calotropis procera)* are very popular, particularly during the break at the well, after watering. Some cattle are well rehearsed in bending the long vertical branches of this shrub with their head in order to reach its most tender part. They bite off the top half a metre of the branch and chew it skilfully on one side of the mouth like a cigar, without letting it drop on the ground. Despite it being the end of the dry season, pasture is excellent and the animals are in relatively good shape. With a herd about 30 head strong (Jiima sold six in the last ten months), the family has milk twice a day and in the evening we struggle to finish it. In Idinghiri, Jiima is way out of his habitual dry-season territory. He is from the WoDaaBe Gojanko'en but Idinghiri is mainly used by WoDaaBe Bii Korony'en. After the death of his father, when Jiima was a young child, his mother married within the Bii Korony'en group. Jiima's wife is from the same Bii Korony'en family on her mother's side. In 1996, Jiima gave her maternal uncle a heifer under *habbana.e* contract.[3] In part, that is how this

---

2. The WoDaaBe refer to their own breed of cattle as *na'i boDeeji* (lit. 'red cows'). In the scientific literature, this zebu breed is mainly referred to as Red Bororo, M'Bororo or Red Fulani (cf. Joshi *et al.* 1957; Bourn *et al.* 1992; Mason 1996). For short, in this paper I simply use the term Bororo, referring specifically to the *na'i boDeeji* of Niger. The historical analysis of the sources reveals fundamental flaws in the scientific characterisation of this breed (Krätli 2008b).

3. In the *habbana.e* contract, a heifer is 'attached' to the herd of a friend or close relative until she calves twice (which could take between three and ten years). The cow is then returned to its original owner (ideally pregnant with a third calf), whilst the calves are kept (as a gift).

26

Saverio Krätli

year he was able to take his herd to spend the dry season in the bush of Idinghiri. The abundance of good grass means that the herders are not in a hurry to move. Jiima will stay near the well until secure information about the rain will confirm the availability of new grass. From that moment on, he will take his family and his cattle away from the security of the well, relying on surface water whilst tracking untouched pasture of the best quality.

This paper explores the WoDaaBe mobile production strategy from the perspective of their breeding system. Based on my Ph.D. research (Krätli 2007), the paper looks at how the successful implementation of this strategy requires very particular cattle populations and how the breeders secure their selection and continuity. Finally, the paper draws implications for the understanding of pastoral mobility.

BACKGROUND

The WoDaaBe differentiate mobility according to function rather than degree. Working in Eastern Niger, Schareika *et al.* (2000) recorded four kinds of movement: migration in response to an otherwise uncontrollable crisis (*perol*); migration between two or more zones of different ecological settings at the beginning and end of the fresh-pasture period, in order to keep their herds 'at the front of the season' (*baartol*); movement between pasturelands within the same ecological settings, in order to keep their herds

Figure 1. Bororo cows at the cattle market of Tchin Tabaraden.

on the kind of pasture that is known to be most beneficial to them (*goonsol*); and adjustment movements in order to secure the constant availability of such a pasture even around the camp (*sottol*). As we will see, this view of mobility is rooted in a profound understanding of the relationship between pasture and herd production, differentiating by its beneficial effects: from the most manifest, such as putting on weight rapidly and keeping in good health, to more intangible ones, such as the effect of particular combinations of plants on the animals' appetite or on the taste of the milk (Figure 1).

This complex scenario is only partially represented in the current debate on pastoral mobility, even within the so-called 'mobility paradigm' (Niamir-Fuller 1999), where mobility is often described in terms of a more or less intense response to spatial and temporal variations of fodder supply (due to erratic precipitation). In contrast to the understanding held by the WoDaaBe, the conceptualisations of mobility operational in the policy-related literature on pastoral development focus on gradients of intensity rather than diversity of function; on supply rather than quality; and on reactivity rather than proactivity, with mobility seen as a coping strategy (minimising damage) rather than a production strategy (enhancing performance) (de Haan *et al.* 2001; Rass 2006; ALive 2006).

Yet range ecology has long been aware of pasture quality dynamics linked to plant development, soil diversity and erratic precipitations. Following six years of unconventional research,[4] including the unprecedented field observations of transhumant zebus by Diallo (1978) and Traoré (1978), Breman and De Wit (1983)[5] drew attention to the relationship between animals' feeding selectivity and the transient nutritional value of fodder plants. Cattle cannot compensate for poor pasture by trading quantity for quality. On the contrary, a poor diet triggers a drop in intake capacity. Thus the possibility of feeding selectively can have dramatic effects on production:

> In order to survive in the dry season, and for good production in the rainy season, the animals have to graze selectively … Diallo … showed that almost throughout the year the protein content in the herbage consumed by zebu was 2 to 5 percent higher than the average content of the grazed rangelands (Breman and De Wit 1983, 1343).

This attention to pasture quality was built into the early conceptualisation of opportunistic tracking by the 'new range ecology':

> The producer's strategy within non-equilibrium systems is to move livestock sequentially across a series of environments … exploiting optimal periods in each area they use … Herd management must aim at responding to alternate periods of high and low productivity, with an emphasis on exploiting environmental heterogeneity rather

---

4. When Henk Breman started work in Mali in 1976, he was a young biologist, with a sensitivity to the local perspective but no formal background in range ecology, a position that, in his own view, led him to invest energies in a line of research that would not normally have received the attention of a trained range ecologist at the time (Henk Breman, personal communication, 2008).

5. I am grateful to Carol Kerven for drawing my attention to this work and the recent studies of pastoral systems looking at plant phenology.

Saverio Krätli

than attempting to manipulate the environment to maximize stability and uniformity (Behnke *et al.* 1993, 14–15).

More recently, new interest is gathering around this dimension, documented in work on pastoral systems in Kazakhstan, where plant 'phenology' is found to be the driving force for livestock mobility (Alimaev 2003; see also Kerven *et al.* 2006; Alimaev and Behnke 2007).

Although variations in pasture quality have always been in the spotlight of the 'new range ecology' as part of the ecological dynamics, the dimension of transient quality within the life of fodder plants and its relation with feeding selectivity in livestock – known to be pivotal to producers' strategies – has remained a marginal concern. A recent overview of the debate around the adequacy of equilibrium or non-equilibrium models to represent the ecology of the drylands still appears perfectly comfortable with quantitative notions of 'livestock numbers' and 'grazing pressure' and with a representation of pastoral mobility as a coping strategy against variability (Vetter 2005).

Qualitative difference with regard to livestock has received even more limited attention. By and large, non-equilibrium perspectives looking at livestock systems have focused on population dynamics of grassland and animals, either in relation to management issues (Oba *et al.* 2000; Homewood *et al.* 2001; Anderies et al. 2002; Uphoff *et al.* 2006; on Niger, Hiernaux 2000; Schlecht *et al.* 2000) or as a consequence of environmental adaptation (i.e. different survival rates) between breeds (Bayer and Waters-Bayer 1995; also Bayer 1989). Some of the studies in this direction have looked at the links between local breeds and herd-management practices in relation to range ecology, touching upon herders' manipulation of animals' diet (Bayer 1990; 1986), but without venturing into the analysis of such links in the context of the breeding systems.

Non-equilibrium thinking in range ecology has led some authors to propose a model of pastoralists' economic strategy alternative to the standard 'risk-aversion' framework and based on 'high-reliability systems' theory (Roe *et al.* 1998). These scholars contend that livestock systems in harsh environments are often better understood as developed to harness and exploit unpredictable variability as a key resource, rather than trying to minimise and externalise it as in risk-aversion models – hence the affinity with high-reliability systems such as nuclear power stations or air traffic control. Overall, the direct or indirect ecological perspective of the works looking at animal production within the non-equilibrium model meant that the actual breeding systems, and particularly their dynamics of animal–human interactions, have largely remained out of the picture.[6]

Outside ecology, but equally relevant for animal production and breed development, challenges to the equilibrium paradigm have also been made within biology. In particular, these challenges concern the conceptualisation of the organism–environment interaction and the nature of inheritances. Key works in this direction draw attention

---

6. An exception is the breeding in organic farming, and the 'family breeding' method practised by some farmers in the Netherlands (cf. Baars *et al.* 2003). I am grateful to Brigitte Kaufmann for drawing this work to my attention).

to the overwhelming empirical evidence for fundamental circularity of cause and effect in organism–environment interaction: organisms engage in the positive alteration of the selective pressures acting upon them (Lewontin 1983; Salthe 1993; Van de Vijer *et al.* 1998; Salthe 2000; Oyama 1985; Griffiths and Gray 1994; Oyama *et al.* 2001; Griffiths and Gray 2005).[7] Most of these works challenge the gene/environment dichotomy, rejecting its assumption of pre-existing and independent configurations on either side – whether instructions that shape the organism from within or niches/environmental 'problems' that shape populations from without (Oyama *et al.* 2001; Odling-Smee *et al.* 2003).

Today, new developments from many branches of biology (including genetics itself) challenge the gene-centred version of evolutionary theory, the model that provides the overarching framework to the current scientific understanding of animal breeds and breeding. A reconsideration of the concept of inheritance in this light demands to extend it beyond the DNA elements, to include the transmission of ecological and cognitive elements, that is, of 'any resource that is reliably present in successive generations, and is part of the explanation of why each generation resembles the last' (Griffiths and Gray 2001, 196).

Such a notion of 'extended inheritance', finally, comes to terms with the critical mass of empirical data difficult to accommodate within the present model. As nicely summarised in a recent overview of the issue, such a growing body of data indicates that 'there is more to heredity than genes; some hereditary variations are non-random in origin; some acquired information is inherited; [and that] evolutionary change can result from instructions as well as selection' (Jablonka and Lamb 2005, 1). The concept of 'extended inheritance' (also 'multiple heredity systems') strikes one as particularly useful in the face of high environmental variability, for its capacity to address information transfer not only at the scale of the generational cycle but also within the lifetime of individuals.

The integration of complex dynamics in the models of ecology and evolutionary change opens up new and exciting dimensions in our understanding of animal breeding and production in structurally unpredictable environments, as the analysis of the WoDaaBe cattle-breeding system will show. Unpredictable distribution of precipitation in time and location makes the Sahelian rangeland an unforgiving place for herding, where even small management mistakes can easily escalate with disastrous consequences. On the other hand, it is precisely the spatial and temporal diversity in the vegetative cycle of the bush (caused by random precipitation and further enhanced by the diversity of soils and plants) that can be turned into an advantage and a powerful resource. Producers under these conditions can treat environmental variability as a

---

7. In scientific work from outside the Western tradition, challenges to the linear model of organism–environment interaction have a longer history. As early as 1941 Japanese primatologist Kinji Imanishi regarded the circular influence of organism and environment as the crucial question of biological enquiry and criticised the orthodox theory of evolution for 'considering living things apart from their way of living' (Imanishi 2002, 74; a good discussion of the work of Imanishi in relation to these issues is in de Waal 2002).

Saverio Krätli

problem and develop strategies geared towards minimising their exposure to it (high-input and risk-aversion systems). On the other hand, as already suggested in the quote above from Behnke *et al.* (1993), they can actively seek such exposure and specialise in the exploitation of variability (high-reliability systems, in the model by Roe *et al.* 1998). The breeding/production system run by the WoDaaBe – described below – is a striking example of this latter form of specialisation.

METHODOLOGY

The research integrated, within a development studies perspective, different sets of knowledge cutting across social anthropology, applied animal behaviour, and range management, as well as the herders' expertise. Fieldwork was carried out amongst several groups of WoDaaBe herders in central Niger, from August to December 2002; November 2003 to July 2004; and November 2004 to March 2005 (Figure 2).

Data generation used standard methods from social anthropology and a set of tools developed in the course of the research from a range of participatory techniques. The resulting 'Herd Analysis Exercise' (HAE) embedded multiple cross-checking

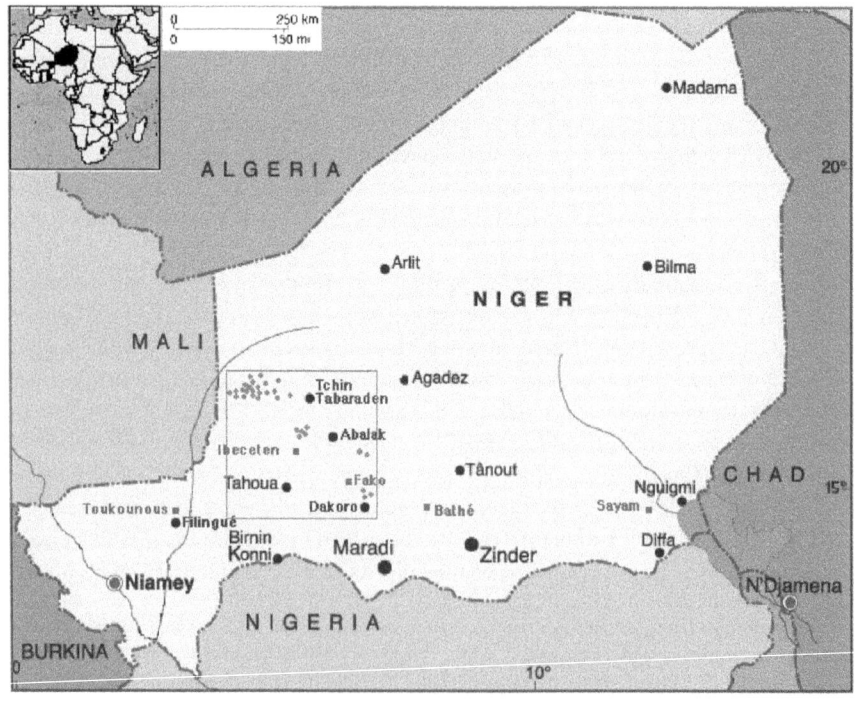

Figure 2. The fieldwork area (indicated with dots).

devices and was specifically designed for handling memorised cattle genealogies. The HAE is a seven-stage process:

1. The herder's family tree.
2. The breakdown of the herd into its different lineages.
3. The analysis of the origin/ownership of each lineage.
4. An overview of particular features of each lineage.
5. A time line.
6. The collection of detailed genealogical history of each lineage going as far back as the herder can remember.
7. And finally, the analysis of all the lineages that have entered and exited the herd during the period under consideration.

The genealogical data used in this paper refer mainly to two herds of respectively 28 and 66 head (over 20 years, about 260 head in total) belonging to kin households within the Ute'en baleeBe sub-group of the Gojanko'en clan. These data were analysed against four sets of HAE data from other clans, a broader body of semi-structured interviews and the literature on the WoDaaBe. There were differences in management 'style' between households, mainly due to different types of resource access, availability of labour and animals (and family habits). Overall, the herders I met agreed on the fundamental tenets of the breeding system described below, although some, by general recognition, applied them more strictly than others.[8]

Systematic herd analysis found that the herders in the sample could remember with remarkable precision the genealogy of virtually every animal born into their herd over the last 20 years (that is, after the 1984 drought), including pinpointing its year of birth (with the help of a timeline and in relation to the age of the dam).[9] This genealogical knowledge also included the name of the bull that sired the animal in question, the name of the bull's owner, and often the season of the fertilisation and the households in the neighbouring camps. The herders remembered the cow's age at the time of her first calf, and the age of bulls when they were used as sires for the first time, or when they had been castrated. The age of an animal at the time of its sale or death, the reason or cause, and even the name of the market, were also remembered; so were many details concerning the actual origin of each animal. In the case of heifers used in 'loan contracts' (*haBBanaaji*, sing. *haBBana.e*), the herders usually knew at what age

---

8.   The WoDaaBe use the term '*garsoo*' to describe a herder who shows particular dedication to the job, has above-standard competence and breeds exceptionally good cattle. The two data-sets providing the empirical evidence for this paper come from such dedicated herders.

9.   With an approximation of about ten months with regard to the western calendar, due to the different way of quantifying age (i.e. counting the rainy seasons).

the animal had been given out, at what age and after how many calvings it had been returned, whether the calves were male or female and what had happened to them.[10] Most stages of the HAE were partially overlapping, providing effective ground for triangulation as the work developed (for example with questions repeated at different stages of the analysis, or when bulls from one genealogical set also appeared as sires in another set). Slow-paced analysis of an entire herd by the same team, and the inclusion of dates and ages, enabled us to spot and investigate incongruities as they emerged.

Database analysis of this information provided detailed cross-sections of the herds at any given year within the period under consideration, including the age, ancestors and exact kin relationships of each animal in the herd. Series of cross-sections provided dynamic reconstructions of animals' reproductive histories, mortality and marketing patterns. Finally, combining these data with human genealogies and life histories enabled the reconstruction of circulation patterns of sires (through borrowing for a fertilisation) and dams (through loan contracts) across herds, and therefore to identify the actual network of breeders. The breeding practices emerging from this work were then analysed in the context of the WoDaaBe's strategies of production and in the light of scientific knowledge on the links between ruminants' behaviour and their productive/reproductive performance under extensive conditions.

PRODUCTION STRATEGY

The WoDaaBe are full-time herders. They specialise in cattle breeding and produce for the beef market.[11] They operate with very low external inputs[12] in one of the harshest and more unpredictable environments on the planet, usually far away from basic services and with a relatively weak political command over pasture and water access.

Comprehensive studies of their production system in Niger agree in identifying cattle reproduction as the herders' main strategic concern (Bonfiglioli *et al.* 1984,

---

10. The two households in this sample proved particularly reliable during the HAE. In other cases, the data were not as coherent and precise. However, all herders interviewed clearly believed that having a sound knowledge of the herds' genealogy was part and parcel of a herder's competence.

11. Marketing of Bororo females for breeding purposes is extremely low, although WoDaaBe herders (more often from within the same extended family) do occasionally buy or exchange cattle with one another. Outside these circles, productive females are only marketed out of very pressing need. Bororo bulls are more accessible on trading channels (although reproduction bulls (*kalhali*) are normally castrated before being marketed). Some Touareg herders use Bororo bulls to cross-breed their Azawak zebus, particularly the Kel Egheris (Gourma Rharous) in Mali (Ibrahim ag Youssouf, personal communication). Amongst the other Gourma-Rharous groups, the Kel Serere, Kel Gossi, Kel Ulli, Ifulanen and Igawodaren have also been known to keep herds of Bororo (Mike Winter, personal communication).

12. Veterinary services are difficult and expensive to access. Drugs and vaccinations can be bought at local markets but their efficacy, from the perspective of the herder, is erratic. Feed supplement is used at the end of the dry season, particularly for calves and milking cows. The cost, however, is often so high that herding households find it more convenient to simply give the most needy animals some of their own millet.

282; Schareika 2003, 4).[13] Actual yearly production strategies can be affected by several factors, most importantly herd size, availability of labour and competence, the extension of the household's social network and, at times, insecurity. However, as long as the combination of these factors allows, the strategy preferred by the WoDaaBe is to keep a high rate of reproduction within the herd by focusing on the quality of animal nutrition. With some differences in 'style' between households, the herders concentrate on two overarching rules: keeping the herd for as long as possible where it can feed on fodder plants in their most nutritional stage of development; and making sure that their animals can take as much advantage as possible from such a strategy. Different soils and plant species, together with the erratic Sahelian rainfall, mean that even within a relatively small territory the pasture does not develop everywhere at the same time. Grass might be past its best in certain locations whilst in others there is still nothing but sand. The herders exploit these differences, moving carefully in order to always keep their livestock on prime pasture, in a stage of development when its nutrients have not yet been consumed for growing (Schareika *et al.* 2000).

In the conditions under which the WoDaaBe operate, this strategy leads to a highly diversified animal diet and particularly complex patterns of mobility. During my fieldwork, when Tuareg and WoDaaBe used the same dry-season water-point, the pasture within roughly 0–10 kilometre radius from the well was mainly used by the former – although one could find WoDaaBe in the belt within a 5–10 kilometre radius at the beginning of the season. Only the WoDaaBe, however, exploited the hard-to-reach belt of grazing land within 10–30 kilometre radius, where they could find much better pasture, both in terms of quality, quantity and variety (the quality and intensity of grazing between journeys compensates, in the view of the WoDaaBe, for the greater time needed to travel to the well). Not all cattle, even amongst the other local breeds in Niger, can sustain the rapid marches and painstaking watering regime that this strategy involves, never mind flourish by taking full advantage of the nutritional opportunities that it offers. So what is so special about the herds of the WoDaaBe?

HERD FORMATION AND CATTLE-LINEAGE SYSTEM

Herds are *developed* from heifers allocated to a newborn boy by close relatives (typically the father, the paternal grandfather and uncles) and left to reproduce within the family herd until the offspring can sustain a new herding household (usually 25–30 years later). As amongst other pastoral groups in West and East Africa, this system of pre-inheritance (*sukka.e*) provides each new generation with the necessary means of production, but also sets up the conditions by which each new generation of herders literally grow up together with their own herds. By the time a new herd developed in this way is ready for independent production, the herder has spent at least twenty years working daily with the animals, observing them on the range for thousands of

---

13. Building on these studies, my work adds to the analysis of the dimension of the breeding system.

hours and seeing the lineages, and the sub-lines within them, prospering or struggling over a variety of conditions.

The WoDaaBe name all newborn calves (males and females) after their mothers,[14] thus structuring their herds along matrilineal lineages.[15] New lineages are started from 'matriarchs' bought at the market, when the name of the animal is unknown or when the animal is not a Bororo. WoDaaBe usually rename these animals in their own language (Fulfulde). Cattle names are primarily markers that enable the herders to monitor cattle lineages across human generations. On the other hand, the flexibility and adaptability of their use suggests that the naming system is also a working tool in the breeder's hands. By clustering cattle along maternal lines, the naming system has a direct influence on the way herders perceive individual animals in relation to one another and the way they conceptualise temporal dynamics of performance within the herd.

Cattle lineages are transmitted across the generations of a WoDaaBe family through the system of pre-inheritance. With each human generation, a more or less different 'team' of matriarchs from various lineages is gradually put together to develop into a new herd. My findings show that this process takes place according to a sophisticated system of selection, with production at the core of the herders' concern. Lineages also circulate within the network of breeders through the institution of *haBBana.e*. In these loan contracts a heifer is moved into another herd for a period of several years before returning to the owner. Although loan contracts are often used to support friends and relatives with unviable herds, they also take place independently of the economic need of the receiver (it is common for receivers to also be givers at the same time).

CONTROLLING CATTLE REPRODUCTION

Despite the absence of material constraints (not even night enclosure), cattle reproduction in the sample herds was strictly controlled. The Bororo zebu have periods of oestrus as brief as a few hours. Intensive management secured timely detection and thus preparation for planned dam–sire matching for virtually every fertilisation[16] (a cow expected to enter oestrus soon is kept at the camp during the night grazing).

Only about four per cent of the bulls born into the herds over 20 years had been regularly used for reproduction (the others being castrated or, more often, sold out of necessity before they reached reproductive age). The herds rarely had more than one or two reproduction bulls (at times none). In the case of these 'special bulls' (*kalhali*, sing. *kalhaldi*), careful matching of well-known lines is the rule: the father of a *kalhaldi* is always a *kalhaldi* and the mother is always from a lineage that has produced *kalhali*.

---

14. Similar matrilineal cattle-naming systems are also found amongst other groups of pastoralists (cf. Andom and Omerw 2003; Galaty 1989; Bernus 1981).

15. I use the term 'lineage' in its conventional meaning within anthropology, referring to a descent-group from a known common ancestor. I follow Bonfiglioli (1988) in maintaining the WoDaaBe's analogy between cattle and human genealogies.

16. Over the 20-year period captured by the HAE, accidental fertilisations were below 3 per cent.

Cattle Breeding, Complexity and Mobility

With the exception of the *kalhali*, attention to avoid inbreeding, promote diversity and secure good-quality bulls seemed to be key to decision making concerning dam–sire matching. Sires were borrowed from outside the herd in about 90 per cent of births, even when a 'pedigree' sire was actually present in the herd. Dams were matched to a different sire at almost every fertilisation. Inbreeding was rare and the risk of breed degradation normally avoided.[17] This was made possible by organising the breeding population along matrilineal lineages and by maintaining a detailed memory of animals' genealogies within the network of breeders (including the patrilineal genealogies of selected sires). Lineage names are more than genealogical earmarks. By clustering cattle along maternal lines, the naming system has a direct influence on the way the herders perceive individual animals in relation to one another and the way they conceptualise temporal dynamics of performance within the herd (for example, a herder's expectations of the productivity of a young animal are affected by the overall performance of its maternal line). Both these processes are key variables in herders' decision making about selection.

Although herders showed stronger attachment to particular lineages, usually due to links with the family history, this did not translate into maximising their size within the herd. On the contrary, herds typically included several lineages, with diversity between them being deliberately sought after and preserved. The analysis of animals' reproductive history showed a significant degree of heterogeneity, with each lineage within the herd presenting a specific pattern of reproductive performance (age at first calf, male/female calf mortality, male/female ratio in births). Moreover, analysis of cattle marketing over the 20-year period in the sample indicated a well-defined strategy, with poorly performing animals being selected out according to a combination of both their level of performance and the degree of economic pressure. Also heifers in poorly productive sub-lines, within the respective lineages, were more likely to be marketed before reaching reproductive age. Such a strategic marketing targeted individuals and sub-lines struggling to reproduce[18] under the operating conditions of the WoDaaBe production strategy. Whilst 'harvest' marketing (young males, and large old cows) peaks in the early cold dry season (October/November), when the animals are at their best, 'culling' marketing peaks at the beginning of the rainy season, when maximum strain on the animals' feeding capacity gives contrast to differences in performance.

Both selective mating and the marketing strategy, although sensitive to individual animals' fertility and milk yield, were concerned with production history rather than peak production. The breeding system was geared towards the maintenance (within the herd or, at least, the immediate network of breeders) of cattle lineages with a *long record* of performance: the 'original lineages' (*na'i iririiji*). These *na'i iririiji* are always Bororo. The expression 'original lineages' (in French, *vaches d'origine*) is the usual translation

---

17.   Inbreeding was limited to 'cousins', while the animals belonging to the same lineage were not normally allowed to mate.

18.   With the exception of the 'bull-cow' (*nagge ngaarye*, cf. Bonfiglioli 1981) welcomed for its stabilising role as a go-between.

but should not be associated with notions of pedigree or purebred. The concept of *na'i iririiji* (sing. *nagge iririiye*) does not define descendants from animals of inherent and superior qualities. On the contrary, as we will see, the concept applies only backwards, with hindsight: it is the current presence in the herd after several human generations that denotes the quality of a certain lineage, not its ancestors. That one often finds original lineages with names that the WoDaaBe only give to Azawak cattle – therefore betraying a distant Azawak matriarch – supports this view. Certain lineages flourish in the family herd for fifty or even a hundred years (cf. Bonfiglioli 1988), whilst others disappear after one year or two, eliminated by death or, more often, selected out by the herders' strategic marketing. The genealogical data remain mute with regard to the ultimate objectives of this selection. However, empirical evidence on what the WoDaaBe breed their cattle for, is necessarily embedded in the productive herds: which functions have to be performed by the animals for the production strategy to be successful, and what does it take for cattle to perform such functions well and reliably? A lot of human work, competence and long-term commitment goes into engineering both herd and environment in ways that will shortly become more evident.

SECURING A RELIABLY PRODUCTIVE HERD

In the course of the year, the animals feed on combinations of plants from more than forty varieties. Most of these plants can be especially beneficial or, conversely, can cause serious problems to the animals according to the season (Bonfiglioli 1981).[19] Feeding on poorly nutritious dried-out grasses during the hot dry season can abate the appetite just when the animals would need to eat most. The WoDaaBe prevent this problem through management, 'supplementing' their cattle's diet by promoting shrub and tree browsing as well as grazing of grasses. When availability allows for choice, only the most nutritious parts of the plants are eaten.

The Bororo's browsing habits on the range have been well recorded (Boutrais 1995; Schareika 2003). With the nutritional value of the bush being subject to extreme seasonal variations, the animal nutrition programme followed by the herders is to minimise weight loss during the long dry season and maximise recovery during the period of available fresh vegetation. Their primary objective is to prepare the animals for reproduction and withstanding the next dry season. At the beginning of the rainy season, the most difficult moment in the year, management input increases sharply (Bonfiglioli et al. 1984) and every effort is made in order to enable the herd to feed on the new grass as soon as possible. Every day of advantage, at this stage, can have a significant impact on the success of the animals' reproductive cycle and their condition at the beginning of the following dry season.

---

19. Some of these dangers can be very insidious. *Cenchrus biflorus*, for example, is dangerous if eaten during the dry season because the hollow stalk often contains sand (Ibrahim ag Youssouf, personal communication).

Cattle Breeding, Complexity and Mobility

The success of the WoDaaBe production strategy rests on the capacity of their herds to perform complex functions as required. Their harsh operating environment offers no resting point. The performing herd must be capable of successfully engaging with challenge all year round, year after year. First of all, the animals must be capable of physically reaching the grazing patches chosen by their herders and at the desired time. An exceptional capacity for mobility is therefore critical. For this reason, maintenance of mobility is embedded in the system to the point of being implicit, as part of the definition of cattle as such (it is often said by the WoDaaBe that the, less mobile, Azawak zebus 'are not real cattle' because 'they can't walk').

Once on prime pasture, not all the vegetable mass available will be equally nutritious.[20] The animals must be capable of selectively ingesting the most nutritious bites and digesting them efficiently (as per their herders' strategy). In order to do so, they must know which plants to feed on and which ones to avoid and must be able to ingest them or, more often, to ingest the 'right' parts of the plant. A WoDaaBe's herd of Bororo will make use of the available pasture in a very different way from other local cattle breeds (for example, the Azawak).[21] Eating efficiently and selectively from a wide range of bush plants – including not only grass species but, according to the season, shrubs and trees, and even wild melons and water lilies – requires competence in negotiating many different terrains, plant shapes and defence systems. In many cases competence must be season-specific. Interviews with Peul agro-pastoralists from Eguidi (south of Maradi, Niger), support the view that the productivity of Bororo herds rests substantially on extra-genetic factors. Whilst all the Peul herders from Eguidi take their cattle on transhumance to the north (near Abalak) for the rainy season, some of them return in October and some in January. One of the key reasons for this difference, they said, is because the herds of those who return in October 'are not accustomed to graze on the northern pasture during the dry season'. Although all the herds in question are of Bororo cattle from the same village and managed in very similar ways on the same range, sometimes by people from the same extended family, some do well whilst others have to return south earlier because on the northern pasture 'they lose weight' (Krätli 2008a).

At the beginning of the rainy season, when even small nutritional gains are crucial to the success of the entire year, eating the new short grass on sandy soil (whilst avoiding the potentially fatal ingestion of sand) requires a specific foraging technique. Cattle must use the front teeth, more like goats do, instead of their usual twining and pulling with the tongue. The herders are aware of this difference, and have a name (*noppina*)

---

20. An analysis of the quality of grass in the diet of the African buffalo found that 'seemingly equal swards often consist of different clones, which would suggest that different patches of even the same food species at the same time can be different from the herbivore's point of view' (Prins 1996, 259).

21. According to both WoDaaBe and Touareg herders, as well as staff of the Niger livestock service, while the Azawak graze all the grass from a patch, the Bororo only browse through the best bites. A French veterinarian writing about the browsing habit of Bororo herds in Cameroon, noticed that 'foraging is so selective that at the end of the season the animals are in the grass up to their bellies' (Brouwers 1963, quoted in Boutrais 1995, 281).

for this alternative foraging technique (also Bonfiglioli 1981; Schareika 2003). They favour it morphologically, by preferring sires with a slender head and a small muzzle, and cognitively by integrating in their herd management system, elements that enable and promote the social transmission of knowledge amongst their animals (as we are going to see). To summarise, therefore, for the WoDaaBe cattle nutrition programme to work, their herds must be capable of reaching, choosing, ingesting and efficiently processing the highly nutritious diet their herders lead them to.

Studies on Ruminant Feeding Behaviour

From empirical studies of ruminants' feeding behaviour, we know that none of the complex functions listed above can be taken for granted (Provenza and Balph 1987; Launchbaugh *et al.* 1999a; Ganskopp and Cruz 1999).[22] Cattle are creatures of habit, and their first inclination would be to stick to feed and grounds that are familiar to them (Hodder and Low 1978; O'Reagain and Schwartz 1995; Burritt and Provenza 1997; Howery *et al.* 1998; cf. also Provenza and Launchbaugh 1999; Emmick and Provenza 2004). We also know that the morphological and physiological bases of diet preferences can be breed specific (Bailey 1999; Howery *et al.* 1996). On the other hand, these scholars underline the 'intertwined nature of learned and innate behaviours' (Launchbaugh *et al.* 1999b, 28). Even features such as digestive and detoxification abilities (the enzyme system) have been found to be affected by experiential learning (Distel and Provenza 1991; Robbins *et al.* 1991; Distel *et al.* 1994). Feeding competence amongst ruminants is acquired in two ways: from previous post-ingestive experience of trial and error (a long, potentially dangerous, and therefore understandably 'conservative' process); and/ or through the example of influential herd members who possess it already, typically the dam. Learning is recognised as being sensitive to social dynamics (for example, can be socially transmitted; is affected by social relationships) and historical continuity (for example, can be cumulative and trans-generational, and is affected by previous learning events: learning event *n* affects the environment of learning event *n'*) (Provenza and Balph 1987; Provenza and Cincotta 1993; Launchbaugh et al. 1999b). The understanding of feeding behaviour as mediated by cognitive variables and circularity of cause and effect (recursive causation) accounts at least partly for the heterogeneous distribution of this skill across a breeding population.

The social dimension of feeding does not only account for the spread of dietary competence in a more rapid and safer way than through individuals' trial and error. Social influence can also have a negative impact on feeding performance. Antagonism

---

22. Distinguishing between this perspective, based on empirical observation, and optimal foraging theory, Provenza and Cincotta (1993, 78) underline that: 'Functional models (for example, optimal foraging theory) [...] do not [...] explain empirical observations such as why: 1. individuals within species select different kinds and amounts of forages (Provenza and Balph 1988; 1990); 2. wild and domesticated herbivores over-ingest plants that contain toxins (Provenza et al. 1992); 3. herbivores do not necessarily select foods of the richest nutritional quality (for example, most energy-rich foods) when given a choice (Grovum 1988)'.

between foraging animals can disrupt the best-designed nutrition programme and cause unsustainable loss of energy (Dumont and Boissy 1999; Macdonald and Mosley 2006). Direct competition in feeding or even the mere proximity of dominant individuals (whether or not in the presence of fodder scarcity), affects the intake of lower-ranking animals (Bennett et al. 1985; Bennett and Holmes 1987). Similarly, the overall foraging performance can be disturbed by particular features of the feeding site (for example a difficult terrain or the overwhelming presence of disliked vegetation or parasites) and particularly by high environmental temperature (Williamson and Payne 1978; Kadzere *et al.* 2002). Even in these circumstances, acquired information can be crucial. Cattle experience in mastering thermoregulatory strategies and foraging has been found to add a considerable advantage to morphological abilities (Morand-Fehr and Doreau 2001; Brewer 2005). For example, good timing of feeding and resting, exploiting shade and negotiating difficult terrain significantly enhance the thermoregulatory advantage provided by morphological traits such as a thick and movable hide of high vascularity and an agile and narrow body high from the ground. Finally, animals performing well in all the aspects of feeding discussed above, can still be severely affected by stress associated with human handling and management practices (Seabrook 1972; Rushen *et al.* 1997; Waiblinger *et al.* 2002; cf. also for a general overview Waiblinger *et al.* 2006).

WoDaaBe Manipulation of Cattle Feeding Habits

The cattle-breeding system based on maternal lineages and the WoDaaBe herd management strategies (described below) are designed to favour the social transmission of knowledge within the breeding population. In this respect, even the *haBBana.e* contract can be seen as a way (on the part of the giver) of accessing the feeding competence developed within a different herd operating under relatively different conditions. The herders are careful to abate antagonistic behaviours and the production of stress that could undermine knowledge sharing and overall herd performance. Antagonistic bulls (and cows), for example, are quickly removed from the herd. Socially triggered differential nutrition within the herd is minimised by artificially enhancing the herd's internal cohesion (through nurturing social bonds and hierarchical stability).

Such a sophisticated management system involves an intense degree of human manipulation of the cattle–environment interaction, with closely controlled animals led to perform complex sets of functions. According to applied animal behaviour science, this would be a recipe for high levels of stress in the animals. Yet, daily and nightly routines of human-driven tasks are performed by these cattle in virtually complete absence of coercion. The cattle bred by the WoDaaBe know nothing of enclosures, follow their herder of their own accord (rather than requiring to be herded from the rear[23]) and it is common, in the bush, to see entire herds controlled by one or two young children

---

23.   Driving a herd from the front, as opposed to from the rear, is a complex and skilled practice, common in full-fledged pastoral systems, but usually ignored amongst less specialised cattle-keepers. In Eritrea, Tigrinya speaking pastoralists in the lowlands also drive their herds from the front, whilst farmers keeping cattle in the highlands, herd their animals from the rear (Andom and Omerw 2003).

waving only a twig. Indeed, although sophisticated and intensive, the WoDaaBe herd management is so smooth and light-handed that it appears, from the outside, as if the Bororo zebus bred by the WoDaaBe were actually committed to 'co-operating' with their herders. Behind such an impression there is, in fact, a characteristic 'attitude' of these animals, the development and maintenance of which is a key aspect of the WoDaaBe breeding/production system

HERD MANAGEMENT

The WoDaaBe are fine observers of their animals' behaviour. Their language, Fulfulde, has a rich vocabulary describing behavioural patterns in livestock. A herder's praising of his own herd typically includes references to behavioural features. At the core of the herders' ethological competence are an educated attention to what their animals eat and an understanding of the links between individual feeding preferences and production, particularly with regard to the qualities and quantity of milk and to the animal's health and reproductive process. Herd management exposes the animals to a wide and functionally selected range of experiences (for example, the encounter with a great variety of fodder plants, foraging conditions and herding 'styles' through intense herd mobility and through the circulation of females resulting from loan contracts across the breeding network). It also promotes a stable and non-conflictual social environment within the herd, and facilitates the transmission of knowledge along both vertical and horizontal social relationships.

The system is modelled on cattle behavioural and social-organisation patterns that have also been observed by scientists studying wild populations of cattle and other ruminants. Practices as structural as limiting the herd (*sefre*) to about 50 individuals, and their organisation through the matrilineal naming system, reproduce the social organisation of feral cattle (Lazo 1994, 1995). On the other hand, studies of cattle in 'excessively large' groups under domestication show a sharp increase in aggressive interactions, as 'individual animals appear to have difficulty in memorizing the social status of all peers' (Bouissou *et al.* 2001, 130).[24] The integration of cattle-specific behavioural patterns (for example, herd size and matriarchal social structure, herding from the front, grooming) pervades the WoDaaBe herd management system down to its smallest aspects.[25] During the watering process, for example, in order to allow

---

In northern Nigeria, the herds of pastoral Fulani have been recorded to follow their herders even swimming across broad rivers (de St Croix 1972).

24.   Splitting of large herds, a phenomenon that behavioural ecologists call 'fusion–fission pattern', is known across several ruminant species. Competition within the herd has been found to be less severe in small herds (Prins 1996).

25.   With reference to pioneering work in applied ethology amongst FulBe pastoralists (Hinrichsen 1979; Lott and Hart 1979), Waiblinger *et al.* remark that the reliance on 'species-specific' patterns is what 'may provide the basis for the success of Fulani herdsman in the control of cattle' (2006, 191). On the advantages of integrating imitations of species-specific behavioural patterns in the management system, cf. Grandin (1987); Seabrook and Bartle (1992); Seabrook (1994).

every animal to drink, exuberant individuals are disciplined by beating them with a stick on the horns (and only on the horns) in a way that simulates horn clashing in antagonistic behaviour between conspecifics.

The integration of species-specific behaviour is consistent with an approach to herd management characterised by the systematic use of habituation practices and a preference for gentle handling over coercion. In the WoDaaBe myth of domestication, the cows are initially attracted by the campfire of a child-herder, then gradually follow him away from their hiding place, of their own accord (cf. Stenning 1959; Dupire 1962; Loftsdóttir 2000).[26]

This persuasive management style is key to constructing the social organisation of the herds of the WoDaaBe and their characteristic, functional patterns of animal–human interaction. Calves are allowed to spend several hours per day with their dams, both around the camp in the evening and during the morning grazing. The proximity of the feeding site to the camp, enables even the very young calves to accompany their dams on the range for a part of the day. In this way they are also gradually socialised into the group of adults. On the other hand, the calves stay together in the afternoon. Social bonds are even fostered during the night, as the young calves grow accustomed to one another tethered to the calf-rope, side by side in order of age, usually in the same relative position. Bonds with the herders are cultivated with equal attention. Ethological studies have pointed out that following calf–dam separation in weaning, calves experience a compensating drive to socialise, which can be exploited for habituating them to interacting with humans (Boivin *et al.* 1992). Under WoDaaBe management, the group of calves remain separated from their dams for a few hours per day well before weaning starts, when the herd leaves for the afternoon grazing. During these early periods of separation from their mothers, calves wander around the camp, and are exposed to intense positive interaction with children (who play with them and groom them) and women (who groom them, light the cattle fire and, as weaning begins, give them supplementary feed and extra care) (Figure 3).

The Bororo's singular selective attachment to humans (referred to as being *geeti*) is perhaps the behavioural feature most appreciated by the herders. The Bororo are exceptionally vigilant and nervous animals, yet obedient and docile with their herders. By integrating human-triggered stress-relief mechanisms into the management system (for example, social bonds with members of the herding household, the cattle fire at the camp, grooming), the WoDaaBe exploit their animals' propensity to stress as an asset to ensure their dependence on human handling. Bororo are bred to *need* the presence of the herder in order to relax. The WoDaaBe's persuasive management turns on its head the issue of management-related stress. As in the case of environmental variability, also in this respect the animal breeding/production system operated by the WoDaaBe exploits what is considered a problem, as a source of unpredictability, in Western animal science.

---

26. Still today, in every WoDaaBe camp a 'cattle fire' is lit every evening. The animals like to rest incredibly close to it. The smoke protects them from parasites.

Saverio Krätli

Figure 3. Bororo cow eating from a bush.

CATTLE BREEDING IN A STRUCTURALLY UNPREDICTABLE ENVIRONMENT

All the institutional arrangements of the WoDaaBe cattle-breeding system work together to secure the reliable exploitation of unpredictability. They do so by embedding redundancy and variability into the system (albeit within the margins of functionality). Three are particularly important.

First, by organising their cattle into matrilineal lineages (operating selection within but not between lineages), the WoDaaBe both nurture and structure animal variability within their herds and, by extension, within their cattle-breeding population at the various scales of the breeding network (extended family, clan, clusters of clans, etc.).[27] Rather than seeking a homogenous population maximised in respect of a specific productive trait (like milk or beef, as in standard breed selection), they introduce redundancy. Although very clearly defined morphologically, the Bororo breed is a segmented population, with a variable number of similarly (but not uniformly) performing sub-groups. Culling poorly performing lines through marketing contributes to keeping each lineage within the boundaries of reliable functionality relative to the household's production strategy. In a way similar to the use of redundancy in high-reliability systems or of portfolio diversity in economics, structuring animal variability into dynamic patterns of lineage-based diversity scales down the randomness of the operating conditions and increases the overall reliability of herd performance.

---

27. In the language of high-reliability-system analysis: 'managing performance fluctuations within controlled upper and lower limits and margins (bandwidths) as opposed to strategies for invariant performance' (Roe and Schulman 2008, 13).

Second, the breeders exploit the capacity for both genetic and extra-genetic inheritance in their cattle-breeding population. In other words, they use their animals' capacities *as living things*. In particular, breeders use the cattle's capacity to actively engage with their environment (including not only the range but also the other animals in the herd and the humans in the herding household); their capacity for responsive change during their lifetime; and their capacity for transmitting such resources along kin and social networks.

Third, the breeders rely on lineage duration (rather than peak productivity) as the primary criterion for selection.[28] Reproduction bulls (*kalhali*), either in the herd or borrowed from within the breeding network, are always from original lineages (both parents). Although original lineages are not maximised at the cost of the others, they are sought after and particularly sheltered from non-strategic marketing (for example the unwilling marketing of productive survivors after a drought). There is lineage duration when a lineage gives a consistently functional performance within the production strategy over an extended period of time including events of severe stress.

Besides these key elements – structuring animal variability, exploiting extra-genetic inheritance, and relying on lineage duration as the primary criterion for selection – keeping the system running is a matter of ensuring that sets of functionalities enabling the herd to take the maximum advantage of the WoDaaBe programme of animal nutrition, are effectively disseminated throughout the breeding network. This process is neither improvised nor erratic. Circulation of semen and cattle uses institutionalised channels (for example, sire borrowing and loan contracts of productive cows), closely integrated with the WoDaaBe social organisation. A household's mobility also plays an important role in accelerating the breeding process. Analysis of herds including both original and recent lineages, shows that original lineages are the ones most intensively circulated. Circulation is more intense within the extended family, particularly amongst cousins. As original lineages are only revealed through history, the system welcomes high levels of lineage diversity and encourages the continuous development of new lineages (for example, through the acquisition of females from outside the WoDaaBe breeding networks). In favourable conditions, this results in a variety of distinct although largely overlapping functional groups of original lineages (i.e. successful configurations of functionalities relative to the production strategy). As long as a viable number of original lineages are operating at any one point in time, lineages can disappear or be introduced without significant disturbance to the system as a whole. Original lineages themselves, if accidentally lost from a family herd, can usually be regenerated by acquiring another productive member of the lineage from the breeding population at the next scale of the network of breeders.

Through inheritance and loan contracts, lineages are typically exposed to a variety of herding 'styles' (within the overall production strategy characteristic of the WoDaaBe). As a consequence, the reliability of original lineages is tested across both time and space. By being centred on the original lineages, the WoDaaBe breeding/

---

28. For a quantitative discussion of this point, see Krätli (2007).

production system achieves reliability at each scale of the breeding network. Behind the WoDaaBe's commitment to their characteristic breeding/production system lies this confirming 'test' of duration. Half-a-century-old lineages in the breeding population are a mirror of families' economic history and constitute robust evidence of both the performance and the resilience of the breeding network in the face of uncertainty. Following the major droughts in the 1970s and 1980s, the pattern of livestock property in Niger has changed substantially. Amongst the producers with entitlements similar to those enjoyed by the WoDaaBe, but relying on different strategies, almost all have lost their assets and their economic autonomy.[29] On the other hand, despite the often-unsympathetic policies, the majority of WoDaaBe households, even if impoverished, are still in business.

PASTORAL MOBILITY: A SECOND LOOK

For most of the time, herders do not move *away from* scarcity of pasture, but rather move *to* places where they expect to have sustainable access to the best pasture available in relation to their herd's foraging habits. In other words, a large proportion of their mobility is about quality not quantity. Such a quality is highly transient. During the rainy season, the most nutritional stage of grass lasts for no more than a couple of weeks. A household on the move, arriving in an area with plenty of grass beyond this stage would normally carry on. During the dry season they would take the herd a few more kilometres away from the well rather than set up camp on pasture that is plentiful but unsatisfactory (Figure 4). Seeking to enable the animals to feed on a diversified diet, as we have seen, adds a further dimension to this notion of mobility for quality. Finally, mobility is embedded in herd management practices and in the social organisation of the groups of producers. We have seen several examples of this: circulation of sires; mobility of knowledge through the circulation of female animals within and across networks of breeders; mobility as instituted generators of variability in the patterns of social networks/resource access (inter-clan marriages open up new opportunities for herd mobility). How much and how well these less visible forms of mobility are effective depends, to a large degree, on the physical mobility of people and animals. The relative circulation of the households in the network of breeders greatly increases the pool of sires available to each one of them, speeds up the generation and access to animal knowledge and multiplies the opportunities for boosting social capital through friendship and marriage.

At the present low levels of external inputs, the mobility of WoDaaBe herding households is key to achieving standards of productivity, from the bush, higher than those that could be achieved if the supply of pasture was stable in time and space. I contend

---

29. Several sources indicate that during the major droughts, the WoDaaBe in Niger, although suffering severe losses, were hit significantly less than other pastoral groups with similar or even higher resource entitlements. Cf. Habou and Danguioua (1991) on the drought of 1984; Bernus (1977) and Mesnil (1978) on that of 1969–73; and SZE – Pécaud (1933) on that of 1931.

Cattle Breeding, Complexity and Mobility

Figure 4. Bororo resting after watering.

that the complex practice of mobility deeply embedded in the WoDaaBe production strategy and breeding system can be seen as key to a form of sustainable 'intensification' of production in non-equilibrium environments. Intensive production is associated, in agricultural sciences, with the use of high inputs of resources (other than labour). External inputs are used to isolate the animals from the natural environment, so that their 'productive potential' might fully manifest itself. The very notion of productive potential, as a value of productivity in ideal absence of disturbances, rests on the possibility of separating animals and environment. In less than ideal conditions, natural adaptation is supposed to fill the gaps left open by insufficient resources, buffering a breeding population against those environmental disturbances that are either impossible or economically unviable to eliminate.

However, in a non-equilibrium perspective, complex dynamics are not externalised as 'disturbances' but integrated as structural forces in the system. Animals and environment are not separable but typically co-constructed in a circularity of causes and effects. Under these conditions, efforts to enhance the level of production – although still possible, as in the system run by the WoDaaBe – would not follow the familiar pattern of intensification.

The WoDaaBe do not wait for their cattle populations to 'adapt' to the changes in the environment: they have a sophisticated system in place to harness, enhance and even train their animals' individual and social capacity for niche construction. Through the animals' orchestrated and piloted life activities, their 'environment' is manipulated into patterns that favour the herders' production objectives. In this respect, the system is very modern and deals with issues – turning unpredictable variability into a resource – that are relevant also to other agricultural contexts.[30]

Instead of *sheltering* the animals from the rigour of the ecosystem and relying on external inputs to maximise peak production, the WoDaaBe engineer the animals' *encounter* with the ecosystem, through sophisticated knowledge/labour-intensive inputs, including a variety of instituted forms of mobility. The system also relies on 'high inputs other than labour' in order to secure an economically favourable (and constantly adjusting) match between the animals and their environment: social capital (in the form of networks for the circulation of animal resources); knowledge capital (in the form of knowledge that is embedded in herd management practices and social institutions); the historically tested configurations of extended inheritance within their breeding populations.

Intensification is frequently used in rural development policies as an indicator of rational exploitation or land development (the French *mise en valeur*). Definitions of rational and efficient use of resources on this basis, hinge on material investment in visible infrastructures and the physical transformation of the environment – for example, fencing, fodder cultivation, water collection, tree planting, 'modern' wells. Legal frameworks on land tenure in Sahelian countries rely on these notions of land development (cf. Hesse and Thébaud 2006). Full-time pastoralists, as such, are not typically eligible for land rights under these frameworks, on the basis of the view that, although they might use the land and maybe adapt to it, they do not transform or improve it for economic purposes. My findings make a case in the opposite direction. The WoDaaBe 'cultivate' their animals' complex capacity to construct the environment and, through their animals, the herders actively and strategically transform the land for economic purposes.

CONCLUSION

Work on complex dynamics in biology, ecology and economics over the last 30 years, together with applied research on animal behaviour, offers a well-developed base for a rethinking of animal breeding/production in the drylands, with significant implications for the current operational understanding of mobility. This work also offers new potential for a more effective integration of qualitative dimensions in non-equilibrium perspectives on range management. The orientation towards high reliability, in low-input livestock systems, should be at the centre of concern in pastoral development policy. That such livestock systems are tailored towards exploiting structural unpredictability needs to be fully understood and accepted with all its implications. Finally, rural de-

---

30. Brigitte Kaufmann describes similarly sophisticated forms of enhanced production in resource-poor livestock systems as 'information-intensive' systems under the umbrella of 'precision agriculture' (Kaufmann 2005).

velopment policies (for example in the Sahel) should recognise that mobile breeding systems using animals' extended inheritance are indeed an alternative way to construct an enhanced production environment (one capable of preserving high nature value). Such systems should therefore be granted full status as a type of land development. Specifically with regard to the WoDaaBe, given the substantial proportion of the livestock-related economy that, in Niger, relies on their Bororo cattle (meat consumers, butchers, restaurateurs, cattle traders, hide traders, market mediators, transporters, traditional-well builders and sellers of salt and straw amongst others), the reliability of their production/breeding system is to be seen as a benefit shared by many, well beyond the group of direct producers. Moreover, because of the system's focus on fostering variability within the breeding population (a variability structured into lineages), the herders constantly fine-tune domestic animal biodiversity, including economically crucial, extra-genetic diversity, at no cost to the state.

BIBLIOGRAPHY

Alimaev, I.I. 2003. 'Transhumant ecosystems: fluctuations in seasonal pasture productivity', in C. Kerven (ed.) *Prospects for Pastoralism in Kazakstan and Turkmenistan: From State Farms to Private Flocks.* London: Routledge-Curzon.

Alimaev, I.I. and Behnke, R.H. 2007. 'Ideology, land tenure and livestock mobility in Kazakhstan', in K. Galvin, R. Reid, R. Behnke R. and Jr N. Thompson Hobbs (eds.) *Fragmentation in Semi-arid and Arid Landscapes: Consequences for Human and Natural Systems.* Dordrecht: Kluwer Academic Publishers, Springer.

ALive 2006. *Investing in Maintaining Mobility in Pastoral Systems of the Arid and Semi-Arid Regions of Sub-Saharan Africa, an ALive Policy Note,* ALive Partnership for Livestock Development Poverty Alleviation and Sustainable Growth.

Anderies, J.M., Janssen, M.A. and Walker, B.H. 2002. 'Grazing Management, Resilience, and the Dynamics of a Fire-driven Rangeland System', *Ecosystems* **5**: 23–44.

Andom, G. and Omerw, M.K. 2003. 'Traditional cattle-husbandry systems in Eritrea: cattle–man relationships', *Journal of Arid Environments* **53**: 545–556.

AU 2010. *Pastoral Policy Framework in Africa: Securing, Protecting and Improving the Lives, Livelihoods and Rights of Pastoralist Communities,* Department of Rural Economy and Agriculture, African Union, Addis Ababa, Ethiopia, (5 June 2011) <http://www.celep.info/wp-content/uploads/downloads/2011/03/policy-framework-for-pastoralism1.pdf>

AU-IBAR 2010. *The Contribution of Animal Resources to Food Security in the Context of Climate Change Challenge in the EAC Region.* Background paper to the EAC Heads of State Retreat on Climate Change and Food Security on 2nd December 2010, Ngurdoto Mountain Lodge, Arusha, Tanzania, Interafrican Bureau for Animal Resources of African Union (AU-IBAR), (5 June 2011) <http://www.eac.int/environment/index.php?option=com_docmanandtask=doc_downloadandgid=146andItemid=186>

Saverio Krätli

Baars, T., Spengler, A. and Spranger, J. 2003. *Is there something like bio-dynamic breeding?*, paper presented at the workshop 'Initiatives for animal breeding in organic farming in Europe and evaluation for future strategies' 17–18 October 2003 (Driebergen, The Netherlands: Louis Bolk Institute).

Bailey, D.W. 1999. 'Influence of Species, Breed and Type of Animal on Habitat Selection', in K.L. Launchbaugh, J.C. Mosley and K.D. Sanders (eds.) *Grazing Behaviour in Livestock and Wildlife*, Pacific northwest Range Short Course, Station Bulletin No. 70. Moscow, Idaho: University of Idaho.

Bayer, W. 1986. 'Agropastoral herding practices and grazing behaviour of cattle in the subhumid zone of Nigeria', *ILCA Bulletin* J: 8–13.

—— 1989. 'Low-demand animals for low-input systems'. *ILEIA Newsletter* December: 14–15.

—— 1990 'Use of native browse by Fulani cattle in central Nigeria. International Livestock Centre for Africa, Subhumid zone programme, Kaduna, Nigeria', *Agroforestry Systems* **12**: 217–228.

Bayer ,W. and Waters-Bayer, A. 1995. 'Forage alternative from range and field: pastoral forage management and improvement in the African drylands', in I. Scoones (ed.) *Living With Uncertainty. New directions in pastoral development in Africa*. London: Intermediate Technology Publications Ltd.

Behnke, R.H., Scoones, I. and Kerven, C. (eds.) 1993. *Range Ecology at Disequilibrium: New Models of Natural Variability and Pastoral Adaptation in African Savannas* London: Overseas Development Institute.

Bennett, I.L., Finch, V.A. and Holmes, R.C. 1985. 'Time spent in shade and its relationship with physiological factors of thermo-regulation in three breeds of cattle', *Applied Animal Behaviour Science* **13**: 227–236.

Bennett, I.L. and Holmes, C.R. 1987. 'Formation of a feeding order in a group of cattle and its relationship with grazing behaviour, heat-tolerance and production', *Applied Animal Behaviour Science* **17**: 9–18.

Bernus, E. 1977. 'Les tactiques des eleveurs face à la sécheresse: le cas du sud-ouest de l'Aîr, Niger', in J. Gallais, J. (ed.) *Stratégies pastorales et agricoles des sahéliens durant la sécheresse 1969–1974*. Bordeaux, France: CEGET/CNRS.

—— 1981. *Touaregs nigériens: unités culturelles et diversités régionales d'un peuple pasteur*. Paris: ORSTOM.

Bertaudiere, L. and Djimadje, M. (1978), *Les Abbattages de Bovins à l'Abattoir Frigorifique de Farcha (N'djamena) en 1977*. Paris: IEMVT.

Boivin, X., Le Neindre, P. and Chupin, J.M. 1992. 'Establishment of cattle-human relationships', *Applied Animal Behaviour Science* **32**: 325–335.

Bonfiglioli (Maliki) A. 1981. *Ngaynaaka. Herding According to the WoDaaBe*, Niger Range and Livestock Project, Discussion Paper n. 2, Republic of Niger, Ministry of Rural Development and USAID/Niger, Tahoua, Niger.

——1988. *Dudal. Histoire de famille et histoire de troupeau chez un groupe de WoDaaBe du Niger*. Paris: Cambridge University Press, Editions de la Maison des sciences de l'homme.

Bonfiglioli, A.M., White, C., Loutan, L. and Swift, J.J. 1984. 'The WoDaaBe', in J.J. Swift (ed.) *Pastoral Development in Central Niger. Report of the Niger Range and Livestock Project*, République du Niger, Ministère du Développement Rural, Service de l'Elevage and USAID, Niamey.

Bouissou, M.F., Boissy, A., Le Neindre, P. and Veissier, I. 2001. 'The social behaviour of cattle', in L. Keeling and H. Gonyou (eds.) *Social Behaviour in Farm Animals*. Wallingford, United Kingdom: CAB International.

Bourn, D., Wint, W., Blench, R. and Wolley, E. 1992. *Nigerian Livestock Resources. Volume II: National Synthesis*. Federal Department of Livestock and Pest Control Services. Resource Inventory and Management Limited. Nigerian Livestock Resources Survey.

Boutrais, J. 1995. *Hautes terres d'élevage au Cameroun*, 2 vols, Institut Français de recherche scientifique pour le développement et la coopération, Collection Etudes et Thèses. Paris: ORSTOM Editions.

Breman, H. and De Wit, C.T. 1983. 'Rangeland Productivity and Exploitation in the Sahel', *Science, New Series* **221**, 4618: 1341–1347.

Brewer, T.K. 2005. *Livestock Grazing Distribution Patterns: Does Animal Age Matter?* (26 February 2006) <http://www.behave.net>

Burritt, E.A. and Provenza, F.D. 1997. 'Effect of an unfamiliar location on the consumption of novel and familiar foods by sheep', *Applied Animal Behaviour Science* **54**: 317–325.

COMESA. 2009. *Policy Framework for Food Security in Pastoralist Areas. Consultative Draft December 2009*, Common Market for Eastern and Southern Africa Comprehensive African Agriculture Development Programme (CAADP) Pillar III, (5 June 2011) <http://www. comesa.int/lang-en/component/content/article/326-comesa-drafts-policy-framework-for-food-security-in-pastoralist-areas-pffspa>

de Haan, C., van Veen, T.S., Brandenburg, B., Gauthier, J., Le Gall, F., Mearns, R., Siméon, M. 2001. *Livestock Development. Implications for Rural Poverty, the Environment, and Global Food Security*. Washington, DC: The World Bank.

de St Croix, F.W. 1972. *The Fulani of Northern Nigeria. Some General Notes*. Hants: Gregg International Publishers.

de Waal, F. 2002. *The Ape and the Sushi Master. Reflections of a Primatologist*. London: Penguin Press Science.

Diallo, A. 1978. *Transhumance: comportement, nutrition et productivité d'un troupeau de zébus de Diafarabé*, Thèse, Centre Pédagogique Supérieur, Ecole Normale Supérieure, Bamako, Mali.

Distel, R.A. and Provenza, F.D. 1991. 'Experience early in life affects voluntary intake of black-brush by goats', *Journal of Chemical Ecology* **17**: 431–450.

Distel, R.A., Villalba, J.J and Laborde, H.E. 1994. 'Effects of early experience on voluntary intake of low quality roughage by sheep', *Journal of Animal Science* **72**: 1191–1195.

Djariri, B. and Saley, M. with Dahiru, H.B. 2003. *L'adaptation des circuits de commercialisation des bovins nigeriens à l'evolution de la demande au Nigeria. Suivi des échanges transfrontaliers entre le Nigeria et les pays voisins*. Niamey: LARES and IRAM.

Dumont, B. and Boissy, A. 1999. 'Rélations sociales et comportement alimentaire au pâturage', *INRA Productions Animales* 12, **1** : 3–10.

Dupire, M. 1962. *Peuls nomades: étude descriptive des WoDaabe du Sahel Nigérien*, Travaux et Mémoirs 64. Paris: Institut d'Ethnologie.

Emmick, D. and Provenza, F. 2004. *Green Acres: Aiding dairy transition from confinement to pastures. 2004 Report*, (12 March 2007) <http://www.behave.net/projects/ pastures_dairy2004.html>

Saverio Krätli

Galaty, J.G. 1989. 'Cattle and cognition: aspects of Maasai practical reasoning', in J. Clutton-Brock (ed.) *The Walking Larder: Patterns of Domestication, Pastoralism and Predation*. London: Unwin Hyman.

Ganskopp, D. and Cruz, R. 1999. 'Selective differences between naive and experienced cattle foraging among eight grasses', *Applied Animal Behaviour Science* **62**: 293–300.

Grandin, T. 1987. 'Animal handling', in E. O. Price (ed.) 'Farm Animal Behaviour', *The Veterinary Clinics of North America: Food Animal Practice* **3**: 323–338.

Griffiths, P.E. and Gray R.D. 1994. 'Developmental systems and evolutionary explanation', *Journal of Philosophy* **91**, 6: 277–304.

—— 2001. 'Darwinism and Developmental Systems', in S. Oyama, P.E Griffiths and R.D. Gray (eds.) *Cycles of Contingency: Developmental systems and evolution*. Cambridge, Massachusetts: MIT Press.

—— 2005. 'Discussion: Three ways to misunderstand developmental systems theory', *Biology and Philosophy* **20**: 417–245.

Habou, A. and Danguioua, A. (supervised by Bloch P. and Keïta M.) 1991. *Transfert du Capital-Bétail au Niger (des Pasteurs aux autres Catégories Socio-Professionnelles). Illusion ou Réalité. Rapport Préliminaire de mission (21.12.90/26-01.91)*, University of Wisconsin and Secretariat Permanent du Comité National du Code Rural, Niamey.

Hesse, C. and Thébaud, B. 2006. 'Will Pastoral Legislation Disempower Pastoralists in the Sahel?' *Indigenous Affairs* **1** : 14–23.

Hiernaux, P. 2000. 'Fondements écologiques de la gestion des parcours au Sahel', in E. Tielkes, E. Schlecht and P. Hiernaux (eds.) *Elevage et gestion de parcours au Sahel, implications pour le développement. Comptes-rendus d'un atelier régional tenu à Niamey, Niger, du 2 au 6.10.2000*. Stuttgart, Germany: Verlag Ulrich E. Grauer.

Hinrichsen, J.K. 1979. 'Mensch-Tier-Beziehung bei afrikanischen Rindernomaden' [tr. Human-livestock interaction amongst African nomadic herders'], *KTBL-Schrift* **254**: 103–110.

Hodder, R.M. and Low, W.A. 1978. 'Grazing distribution of free-ranging cattle at three sites in the Alice Springs District, central Australia', *Australian Rangeland Journal* **1**: 95–105.

Homewood, K., Lambing, E.F., Coast, E., Kariuki, A., Kikula, I., Kivelia, J., Said, M., Serneels, S. and Thompson, M. 2001. 'Long-term changes in Serengeti-Mara wildebeest and land cover: Pastoralism, population, or policies', *Proceedings from the National Academy of Sciences* **98**: 12544–12549.

Howery, L.D., Provenza, F.D., Banner, R.E. and Scott, C.B. 1996. 'Differences in home range and habitat use among individuals in a cattle herd', *Applied Animal Behaviour Science* **49**: 305–320.

Howery, L.D., Provenza, F.D., Banner, R.E., Scott, C.B. 1998. 'Social and environmental factors influence cattle distribution on rangeland', *Applied Animal Behaviour Science* **55**: 231–244.

IIED and SOS Sahel. 2009. *Modern and Mobile. The future of livestock production in Africa's drylands*. Edited by Helen de Jode, International Institute for Environment and Development, and SOS Sahel International UK, London, (5 June 2011) <http://pubs.iied.org/pdfs/12565IIED.pdf?>

Imanishi, K. 2002. *A Japanese View of Nature. The World of Living Things*. London: Routledge Curzon.

Jablonka, E. and Lamb, M.J. 2005. *Evolution in Four Dimensions. Genetic, Epigenetic, Behavioral, and Symbolic Variation in the History of Life.* Cambridge, Massachusetts: MIT Press.

Joshi, N.R., McLauglin, E.A. and Phillips, R.W. 1957. *Types and Breeds of African Cattle*, FAO Agricultural Studies No. 37. Rome: Food and Agricultural Organization of the United Nations.

Kadzere, C.T., Murphy, M.R., Silanikove, N. and Maltz, E. 2002. 'Heat stress in lactating dairy cows: a review' *Livestock Production Science* **77**: 59–91.

Kaufmann, B.A. 2005. 'Precision livestock farming in developing countries: creating order where uncertainty prevails', in S. Cox (ed.) *Precision Livestock Farming 2005*. Wageningen, The Netherlands: Wageningen University Press.

Kerven, C., Alimaev, I.I., Behnke, R., Davidson, G., Malmakov, N., Smailov, A. and Wright, I. 2006. *Fragmenting Pastoral Mobility: Changing Grazing Patterns in Post-Soviet Kazakhstan*, USDA Forest Service Proceedings RMRS-P-39.

Krätli, S. 2007. *Cows Who Choose Domestication. Generation and management of domestic animal diversity by WoDaaBe pastoralists (Niger)*, Ph.D. thesis, Institute of Development Studies, University of Sussex, Brighton, United Kingdom.

—— 2008a. *Future Scenario Planning with WoDaaBe Herders in Niger. Preliminary report*, International Institute for Environment and Development, London.

—— 2008b. Animal Science and the Representation of Local Breeds: Looking into the Sources of Current Characterisation of Bororo Zebu, in K. Brown and D. Gilfoyle (eds.) *Healing the Herds: Essays on Livestock Economies and the Globalization of Veterinary Medicine*. Athens, Ohio: Ohio University Press.

—— and Schareika N. 2010. 'Living Off Uncertainty. The Intelligent Animal Production of Dryland Pastoralists', *European Journal of Development Research* **22**,5: 605–622.

Launchbaugh, K.L., Mosley, J.C. and Sanders, K.D. (eds.) 1999a. *Grazing Behavior in Livestock and Wildlife*, Pacific northwest Range Short Course, Station Bulletin No. 70. Moscow, Idaho: University of Idaho.

Launchbaugh, K.L., Walker, J.W. and Taylor, C.A. (1999b), 'Foraging Behavior: Experience or Inheritance?', in K.L Launchbaugh, J.C. Mosley and K.D. Sanders (eds.) *Grazing Behavior in Livestock and Wildlife*, Pacific northwest Range Short Course, Station Bulletin No. 70. Moscow, Idaho: University of Idaho.

Lazo, A. 1994. 'Social segregation and the maintenance of social stability in a feral cattle population', *Animal Behaviour* **48**,5: 1133–1141.

—— 1995. 'Ranging behaviour of feral cattle (Bos Taurus) in Donana National Park, S.W. Spain', *Journal of Zoology* (London) **236**: 359–369.

Lewontin, R.C. 1983. 'Gene, Organism and Environment', in D.S. Bendall (ed.) *Evolution From Molecules to Men*. Cambridge, Massachusetts: Cambridge University Press.

Loftsdóttir, K. 2000. *The Bush is Sweet: Identity and Desire among the WoDaaBe in Niger*, Ph.D. thesis, The University of Arizona, Tucson, Arizona.

Lott, D.F. and Hart B.L. 1979. 'Applied ethology in a nomadic cattle culture', *Applied Animal Ethology* **5**: 309–319.

Saverio Krätli

Macdonald, B.R and Mosley, J.C. 2006. 'Effect of Social Behavior on Habitat Selection of Cattle. Habitat Selection and Social Behavior: Influence of social rank on feeding sites and performance of free-ranging cattle', (12 March 2007). http://www.behave.net/projects/riparian_mosley2004.html

Mason, I.L. 1996. *A World Dictionary of Livestock Breeds, Types and Varieties*, 4th edition, CAB International, Wallingford, United Kingdom.

Mesnil, J.G. 1978. *Rapport Succinte d'Activité. Zootechnie – Agrostologie*, République du Niger, Service de l'Elevage, Niamey.

Morand-Fehr, P. and Doreau, M. 2001. 'Ingestion et digestion chez les ruminants soumis à un stress de chaleur', *INRA Productions Animales* **14**,1 : 15–27.

Mornet, P. and Koné, K. 1941. 'Le zébu peulh bororo', *Bulletin des Services Zootechniques et des Epizooties de l'Afrique Occidentale Française* **4**, 3 and 4: 167–180.

Niamir-Fuller, M. (ed.) 1999. *Managing Mobility in African Drylands. The Legitimisation of Transhumance*. London: IT Publications.

Oba, G., Stenseth, N.C. and Lusigi, W. 2000. 'New perspectives on sustainable grazing management in arid zones of sub-Saharan Africa', *Bioscience* **50**: 35–51.

Odling-Smee, F.J., Laland, K.N. and Feldman, M.W. 2003. *Niche Construction: The Neglected Process in Evolution*. Princeton, New Jersey: Princeton University Press.

O'Reagain, P.J. and Schwartz, J. 1995. 'Dietary selection and foraging strategies of animals on rangeland. Coping with spatial and temporal variability', in M. Journet, E. Grenet, M-H. Farce, M. Theriez. and C. Demarquilly (eds.) *Recent developments in the nutrition of herbivores. Proceedings of the 4th International Symposium on the nutrition of herbivores*, Clermont-Ferrand, France.

Oyama, S. 1985. *The Ontogeny of Information: Developmental Systems and Evolution*. Cambridge, Massachusetts: Cambridge University Press.

Oyama, S., Griffiths, P.E. and Gray, R.D. (eds.) 2001. *Cycles of Contingency: Developmental Systems and Evolution*. Cambridge, Massachusetts: MIT Press.

Prins, H.H.T. 1996. *Ecology and Behaviour of the African Buffalo: Social Inequality and Decision Making*. London: Chapman and Hall.

Provenza, F.D. and Balph, D.F. 1987. 'Diet learning by domestic ruminants: theory, evidence and practical implications', *Applied Animal Behaviour Science* **18**: 211–232.

Provenza, F.D. and Cincotta, R.P. 1993. 'Foraging as a self-organisational learning process: Accepting adaptability at the expense of predictability', in R.H. Hughes (ed.) *Diet Selection*. London: Blackwell Sci. Publ. Ltd.

Provenza, F.D. and Launchbaugh, K. 1999. 'Foraging on the Edge of Chaos', in K.L Launchbaugh, J.C. Mosley and K.D. Sanders (eds.) *Grazing Behavior in Livestock and Wildlife*, Pacific northwest Range Short Course, Station Bulletin No. 70. Moscow, Idaho: University of Idaho.

Rass, N. 2006. *Policies and Strategies to Address the Vulnerability of Pastoralists in Sub-Saharan Africa*, PPLPI Working Paper No. 37, Pro-Poor Livestock Policy Initiative. Rome: Food and Agriculture Organization of the United Nations.

Robbins, C.T., Hagerman, A.E., Austin, P.J., McArthur, C. and Hanley, T.A. 1991. 'Variation in mammalian physiological responders to a condensed tannin and its ecological implications', *Journal of Mammology* **72**: 480–486.

Roe, E., Huntsinger, L. and Labnow, K. 1998. 'High-Reliability Pastoralism Versus Risk-Averse Pastoralism', *Journal of Environment and Development* 7, 4: 387–421.

Roe, E. and Schulman, P.R. 2008. *High Reliability Management. Operating on the edge* Stanford, California: Stanford Business Books, Stanford University Press.

Rushen, J., De Passillé, A.M. and Munksgaard, L. 1997. 'Fear of people by cows and effects on milk yield, behavior and heart rate at milking', *Journal of Dairy Science* 80, suppl.1: 202.

Salthe, S.N. 1993. *Development and Evolution: Complexity and Change in Biology*. Cambridge, Massachusetts: MIT Press.

—— 2000. *Regaining the Riches of a Lost Heritage. Developmental Systems Theory and natural philosophy*, ISSS Paper, (13 November 2007). http://www.isss.org/2000meet/ papers/20065.pdf

Schareika, N. 2003. *Know to Move, Move to Know. Ecological Knowledge Among the WoDaaBe of South Eastern Niger*. Rome: Food and Agriculture Organisation of the United Nations, (26 October 2004). http://www.fao.org/DOCREP/006/ Y5115E/Y5115E00.HTM

Schareika, N., Graef, F., Moser, M. and Becker, K. 2000. 'Pastoral Migration as a Method of Goal-oriented and Site-specific Animal Nutrition among the Wodaabe of South-eastern Niger', *Die Erde* **131**: 312–329.

Schlecht, E., Hiernaux, P. and Turner, M.D. 2000. Mobilité régionale du bétail: nécessité et alternatives?', in E. Tielkes, E. Schlecht and P. Hiernaux (eds.) *Elevage et gestion de parcours au Sahel, implications pour le développement. Comptes-rendus d'un atelier régional tenu à Niamey, Niger, du 2 au 6.10.2000*. Stuttgart, Germany: Verlag Ulrich E. Grauer.

Seabrook, M.F. 1972. 'A study to determine the influence of the herdsman's personality on milk yield', *Journal of Agricultural Labour Science* **1**: 45–49.

—— 1994. 'Psychological interaction between the milker and the dairy cow. Dairy Systems for the 21st Century', in R. Bucklin (ed.) *Dairy Systems for the 21st Century*. St. Joseph, Michigan: ASAE.

Seabrook, M.F. and Bartle, N.C. 1992. 'Human Factors', in C. Phillips and D. Piggins (eds.) *Farm Animals and the Environment*. Wallingford, United Kingdom: CAB International.

Stenning, D. 1959. *Savannah Nomads*. London: Oxford University Press.

SZE – Pécaud G. 1933. *Rapport annuel 1932*, Colonie du Niger, Service Zootechnique, Niamey.

Uphoff, N. Ball, A.S., Fernandes, E., Herren, H., Husson, O., Laing, M., Palm, M., Pretty, J. and Sanchez, P. 2006. *Biological Approaches to Sustainable Soil Systems*. Boca Raton, Florida: CRC Press.

Van de Vijer, G., Salthe, S.N. and Delpos, M. (eds.) 1998. *Evolutionary Systems. Biological and Epistemological Perspectives on Selection and Self-Organisation*. Dordrecht, The Netherlands: Kluwer Academic Publishers.

Vetter, S. 2005. 'Rangelands at equilibrium and non-equilibrium: recent developments in the debate', *Journal of Arid Environments* **62**: 321–341.

Waiblinger, S., Menke, C., Coleman, G. 2002. 'The relationship between attitudes, personal characteristics and behaviour of stockpeople and subsequent behaviour and production of dairy cows', *Applied Animal Behaviour Science* **79**: 195–219.

Saverio Krätli

Waiblinger, S., Boivin, X., Pedersen, V., Tosi, M-V., Janczak, A.M., Visser, E.K. and Jonesg, R.B. 2006. 'Assessing the human–animal relationship in farmed species: A critical review', *Applied Animal Behaviour Science* **101**, 3 and 4: 185–242.

Williamson, G. and Payne, W.J.A. 1978. *An Introduction to Animal Husbandry in the Tropics*, 3rd edition. London and New York: Longman.

3

DISENTANGLING 'FORCED DISPLACEMENT' FROM PASTORAL MOBILITY: RECOVERY AND RECONSTRUCTION IN THE SAHEL AND IN SOUTH SUDAN.

Salem Mezhoud

Independent Scholar and Consultant

Clare Oxby

Institute of Social Anthropology, University of Bern, Switzerland

INTRODUCTION

Forced displacement in many cases involves livestock keepers, herders, pastoralists, agro-pastoralists; we shall use the term 'pastoralist' to include all those people who rely on domesticated livestock – camels, cattle, sheep and goats, or yaks – for a major part of their livelihood.[1] Pastoralist displacement implies involuntary movement to locations beyond the usual waterpoints and grazing grounds of the particular herding group. Displacement may be the result of drought, famine, insecurity or war. In this paper we discuss both people who are displaced within their countries of origin, usually referred to as Internally Displaced Persons or IDPs, and those displaced beyond international frontiers to other countries – that is, refugees. Forcible displacement has affected herders in many places throughout the world; these include Sudan, Somalia, the Sahel, Afghanistan and North West Pakistan.

This paper is an account of ongoing research in two of these areas, South Sudan and the Sahel. The research compares these two African situations of displacement – one, South Sudan, a very publicised key example of protracted conflict, at least until the

---

1.   It is rare that pastoralists rely only on herding for a livelihood: herders are usually also traders, exchanging livestock and livestock products for the goods that they need; many hunt and collect wild leaves, fruits and seeds; others engage in seasonal agriculture; a growing number engage in seasonal paid labour or support their families from abroad by sending remittances.

2005 Comprehensive Peace Agreement and excluding the Darfur conflict; the other, the Sahel, less well known and long considered as a successful settlement. In this paper we outline some of the similarities between these two situations, both in their nature and in terms of their specific needs, and we will explore explanations for the failure of international assistance to provide adequate and long lasting solutions.[2] The research has a policy orientation, which is to learn from previous experience in the Sahel and to apply the lessons in South Sudan in the context of return and reintegration of displaced herders. The next stage of the work would involve the drafting of a blueprint for the reintegration of herders and agro-pastoralists; the rehabilitation of their pastoralist livelihoods; and the formulation of sustainable reconstruction policies in areas with large numbers of livestock keepers. This blueprint would be applicable to other parts of the world inhabited by livestock keepers. This paper sets the scene and presents a few basic issues central to any policy formulation and programme development.

The Sahelian focus begins with the aftermath of the 1989–90 rebellion in Niger and Mali, in which thousands of persons, mainly Tuareg, fled to neighbouring countries and many were hosted in refugee camps in Algeria, Mauritania and Burkina Faso (WFP 1999). Thousands more were displaced internally within the national territories of Mali and Niger. In 1992, a National Pact was signed between the Malian Government and Tuareg rebels (see République du Mali 1992) and, in 1995, a peace treaty was signed in Niger with the Tuareg rebellion (République du Niger 1995). Promises for economic, social and political improvements were made, which opened up the possibility of voluntary returns as well as repatriation of refugees. By March 1997, it was estimated that about 100,000 Malian refugees had returned home, either spontaneously or with UNHCR assistance.

Despite international efforts and Government promises, droughts and food shortages have continued to threaten the survival of the northern populations of Niger and Mali – mostly Tuareg – who once again felt abandoned by central governments (Mezhoud 1992). In June 2005 there was a state of alert in response to widespread hunger following the failure of the previous year's rains throughout the Sahel. Again, the discontent provoked by a perceived inadequate response of the central authorities to the plight of the inhabitants of the pastoral zones of Mali and Niger, has led to regular outbreaks of rebellion in the northern parts of both countries since January 2006, with raids on *gendarmerie* (rural police) posts and confiscation of vehicles and weapons. The Niger Movement for Justice (Mouvement Nigérien pour la Justice – MNJ) was formed in February 2007 and by January 2008 clashes between rebels and government troops had resulted in a number of deaths. In neighbouring Mali too, a rebellion has flared up again. In both countries, the rebels have declared among their objectives to be greater autonomy from the states of Niger and Mali, which they feel do not adequately serve their interests.

---

2.   This paper does not take into account any developments taking place after the 2011 referendum on self-determination and the subsequent independence of South Sudan. These constitute the very situation that the comparative analysis and lessons learned from it purport to educate.

The second area of focus is South Sudan. Despite the referendum on self determination in South Sudan, there was a general feeling that the success of the landmark 2005 Comprehensive Peace Agreement (CPA) was not assured; and the subsequent independence of South Sudan on 9 July 2011 has not allayed all the fears of renewed conflict. The CPA, signed in Kenya in 2005, ended a civil conflict responsible for nearly two million deaths and the displacement of an estimated four million South Sudanese. Since 2005 over two million refugees and IDPs have returned to their homes, often with the assistance of the UN and other organisations, in the midst of a large international effort for the reconstruction of a devastated South Sudan.

Our fundamental observation is that international humanitarian assistance to forcibly displaced herders is often inappropriate because of the failure to distinguish their special livelihood needs from those of other displaced persons, in particular crop farmers. This failure is obvious when one takes into consideration other cases of reconstruction, such as that following the 2004 tsunami in Aceh, Indonesia, which did take into account peoples' previous livelihoods: here the priority was to assist fishermen to restart their previous livelihood by distributing fishing equipment and newly built boats to them (Cossée *et al.* 2006).

In this article we shall explore the reasons for this inadequacy in relation to herders and suggest that it is linked with, firstly, the official invisibility of herders and the difficulty for outsiders to distinguish between herders on the move and displaced herders; secondly, the insufficient recognition of the land rights of herders in open access grazing lands, in contrast with farmers in the agricultural zone; and thirdly, misconceptions about the nature of pastoralism, in particular the identification of mobility with absence of roots or solid link to land or territory and the belief that herding is an outdated and inappropriate mode of life – misconceptions which persist over the decades and continue to be used in order, among other things, to justify inappropriate assistance packages.

We shall explore the gap between the real needs of displaced pastoralists and the assistance provided to them and look at alternative ways of addressing pastoralist displacement, from a holistic approach which includes political representation, land rights and other human rights and the protection of traditional livelihood patterns. The final section will explore international instruments for the protection of herders' right to enjoy the lifestyle and livelihood of their choice.

DISPLACED HERDERS AS 'INVISIBLE'

Difficulty of Identifying Herder Displacement

A group of Tuareg nomads in central Niger, women perched high upon camels, donkeys laden with tent posts and varied containers, men walking fast to guide the livestock – a familiar sight no doubt… but are they on 'normal' seasonal migrations or are they 'displaced' and heading for unfamiliar destinations? Not such an easy question for outsiders to answer. This is quite clear, however, to those on the move, who would use

Tamasheq (Berber) words with different linguistic roots to distinguish ordinary travel – *tezrek* – undertaken by herding families who are moving camp, from exceptional travel or 'flight' – *tegheriz* – to which groups of herders resort during times of drought or other emergencies (Khamed Attayoub 2002, 163; personal communication 2009).

People with mobile lifestyles such as herders, pastoralists, agro-pastoralists are not as easily recognised, when displaced, as other groups with clear, fixed bases, such as those who cultivate demarcated crop fields. It is much easier for outside observers to notice a displaced farmer who has left his well-delimited fields behind, than a herder who was forced to abandon his regular grazing grounds. The herder may well know the geographical boundaries of his annual grazing grounds intimately; to the unfamiliar outsider, however, these zones may appear as undefined, open access communal lands. Whether out of ignorance or lack of sympathy for this way of life, officials may like to think of herders on the move as if they were on normal migrations, even when they leave their grazing lands forcibly.

Mobile herders may have to cross international boundaries to be recognised as displaced (i.e. become 'refugees'); even when they do so, however, there may be problems in distinguishing them from herders on regular seasonal migration, since many pastoralists live in peripheral areas close to frontiers and regularly cross these.[3] The Tuareg of Niger and Mali, displaced as a result of the rebellion in the early 1990s, had to cross the international boundaries of Algeria to the north, or Burkina Faso to the south, in order to receive official recognition, under international law, as refugees. Many, who did not fill all the UNHCR (United Nations High Commission for Refugees) criteria, were without status in neighbouring countries. Often, the lack of status would lead either to their expulsion or to their being left in vulnerable, unprotected situations. Their counterparts who stayed within their national borders remained largely invisible, unrecognised and unassisted. When the Tuareg crisis flared up in 1989–90, the nascent concept of internal displacement was neither applied, nor envisaged as a legal mechanism of protection for displaced Tuaregs. This resulted in large migrations of Malian and Nigerien Tuareg to peripheral urban areas, where they attempted to survive and make a living in what were often totally alien circumstances for pastoralists.

Whereas the growing phenomenon of internal displacement in Sudan (four million out of nearly 40 million, before the CPA, excluding Darfur where IDPs number nearly three million) and other places (Angola, Somalia) forced the international authorities to improvise new forms, frameworks and mechanisms of both humanitarian assistance and legal protection to the newly dubbed 'IDPs', internally displaced persons in the Sahel were ignored for much of the decade. Only in the 2000s, with the concept now established in other parts of the world, have international and local organisations begun to mention the existence of IDPs in the region. The absence of an internationally recognised legal status for internally displaced persons, however, cannot alone explain

---

3.   The regular crossing of frontiers puts herders in a vulnerable legal position and in a situation of potential statelessness, as is described by Aukot (2009) for the Ateker, a nomadic pastoralist group straddling four countries: Sudan, Ethiopia, Kenya and Uganda.

this 'neglect'. Arguably, had the displaced Tuareg been agriculturalists and therefore more obviously recognisable as displaced, they might have received more attention.

Because the official invisibility of displaced herders is due partly to their mobile lifestyle, other mobile groups who are not herders may find themselves in a similar situation. In the case, for example, of the Karen shifting cultivators in forested regions of Burma, like pastoralists, their displacement may be confused, either through ignorance or deliberately, with their normal livelihood-related movements. Since the recognition of internally displaced persons depends to a certain extent upon government cooperation, the extent to which the plight of internally displaced peoples is known outside their country varies considerably and the Karen case demonstrates continued difficulties in the recognition of the full extent of the IDP emergency.[4]

Even in Sudan, where the extent of the IDP problem has been acknowledged by the government, the volume of assistance given to IDPs is subject to limitation by internal government policy. Operation Lifeline Sudan, at one time the largest humanitarian operation in the world, was set up as a tripartite agreement between the United Nations (represented by UNICEF, the instigator), the Government of Sudan (GOS) and the 'rebel' movement, the Sudan People's Liberation Movement (SPLM). Because the UN was bound by its Charter (especially Article 2) to respect Sudan's national sovereignty, even operations within the territory controlled by the SPLM could not take place without express agreement from GOS. Indeed that privilege was used to effect by Khartoum which, on countless occasions, denied the UN humanitarian flights access to certain areas, depriving thousands of IDPs of assistance in the process.

To sum up, the invisibility of displaced herders in the Sahel and in South Sudan is compounded by: the lack of government support to the internally displaced – pastoralists share this with all IDPs whatever their livelihood; the mobility involved in this way of life – this is common also to non-herders leading mobile lifestyles, such as shifting cultivators; and by general ignorance about the herding way of life – a condition familiar to herders worldwide.

Misconceptions Justify Policies which Disinherit Herders

Misconceptions about the land rights of people who lead mobile lifestyles are common (Capot-Rey 1961) and still survive today – statements such as 'they roam around with no fixed territories' and 'they move within a no man's land' continue to be heard. Over the decades these misconceptions have not disappeared as one might expect when con-

---

4.   Cross-border assistance entails numerous diplomatic problems as well as problems relating to international sovereignty, and for a long time Karen populations have suffered both from the absence of international organisations within their territory and from the inability and/or reluctance of those in Thailand to undertake cross-border assistance. Cross-border assistance was prohibited by the Myanmar Government and infringements can result in imprisonment or even death at the hands of the Burmese military. It was only in March 2007, that the UK government and its foreign aid branch, the Department for International Development, DFID, changed its policy and allowed its funding to go to cross-border assistance from Thailand (House of Commons Select Committee on International Development, HC Deb, 5 March 2007, col. 117WS).

fronted with detailed studies confirming the precise territorial movements of particular social groups.[5] On the contrary they have persisted through time and provide renewed justification for the implementation of certain policies that progressively disinherit and disempower mobile peoples. 'No man's land' too easily becomes 'unoccupied land' or 'vacant land', and thus land previously used for seasonal grazing gets officially allocated to other purposes, and herders become displaced.

The exploitation of mineral resources is one use of pastoralist land that has caused the displacement of herders in both Niger and Sudan. Niger is a world producer of uranium and the exploitation of oil resources is just beginning in the northeast of the country; all the sites involved represent the homelands of herders who have been and continue to be dispossessed to allow the exploitation.

In Sudan large swathes of pastoralist lands in Western Upper Nile have been cleared to make way for oil exploration (Mezhoud 2006). From mid-1998 to 2004, the GOS armed forces mounted vast operations involving aerial bombings, helicopter gunship raids, infantry attacks and sometimes boat raids, to systematically empty the region of its people (UN 1999). The GOS denied any wrongdoing by claiming, in particular in the context of an international human rights lawsuit, that the entire area was a no man's land, traditionally devoid of inhabitants. The oil area was in fact the seasonal dwelling of Nuer pastoralists who, after being displaced, relocated into grazing lands away from the oil.[6]

Displacement in pastoralist and agro-pastoralist areas has resulted from a wide range of causes: drought, conflict, mineral exploitation, the development of game parks and natural reserves and the allocation of grazing land to alternative production systems such as irrigated agriculture or ranching; but whatever the cause, there is one common feature, the lack of clear allocation of land rights to nomadic herders which helps to hide their dispossession and makes it officially invisible and inexistent.

Loss of Land Rights: Livestock Keepers More Vulnerable Than Crop Farmers

So what are the land rights that allow such dispossession? In the Sahel there is a clear distinction between land rights in the 'agricultural zone' and land rights in the 'pastoral

---

5.   In relation to different Nigerien communities, many volumes were published by ORSTOM Paris and IRSH Niamey in the 1970s and 1980s, see for example Bernus 1981 on the Tuareg of Niger. In relation to pastoralists and agropastoralists in Sudan, the Sudanese ESRC published several volumes about the seasonal movements of different social groups during the same period, see Ahmed 1976; this has now been expertly updated, see Casciarri and Ahmed 2009.

6.   Although clearly the result of the conflict between GOS and the southern populations, this example of forced displacement also present aspects of what can be termed 'development-induced displacement', especially since GOS claimed oil exploitation would bring wealth to the region. The argument is reminiscent of the controversial Jonglei Canal project of the 1970s which, if completed, would have increased the Nile water flow in northern Sudan and Egypt, but would have drained the marshes (known as the Sudd) which were the grazing lands of the largely pastoralist Dinka, Nuer and Shilluk populations in the south. These flood plains are the most vital component of a livelihood system based on seasonal livestock herding and thus the entire ecosystem was at risk of destabilisation.

zone'. The division between these two categories was established under the French co-lonial government and the dividing line was drawn on the map as the rough northern limit of crop cultivation as it was at that time. Population densities were lower then, there was no acute shortage of land such as that which exists today and land rights and land access did not have the importance they have today.

However, the 1993 *Code Rural* in force in Niger today largely reproduces the same division, and is being applied to a very different current situation along the north-ern limit of cultivation, namely of intense population pressure and competition over access to land. The law formalises a clear distinction between the rights of inhabitants in the two zones. People living in *communes* (the smallest administrative units) that lie in the 'agricultural zone' enjoy secure rights to the land they farm, to the exclusion of other users; their exclusive rights to their clearly demarcated fields are defended by local leaders at the head of whom is an elected mayor; and formal private tenure agreements are increasingly common.

By contrast, the inhabitants of *communes* within the 'pastoral zone' do not enjoy any exclusive rights to their land. According to the *Code Rural*, 'traditional users' have priority use over other potential users. But since the grazing resources are used jointly and are usually unfenced, in practice their leaders cannot easily deny access to other users, particularly around any government built water points. Even their mayors do not have the authority to prevent other first time users from settling around water or grazing resources and monopolising their use; and they cannot curb the increasingly common practice of town-based individuals arriving by truck to cut and remove grass in order to sell it to intensive livestock farmers based in other areas. There are, equally, no means of stopping migrant farmers from other areas attempting to farm in the so-called 'pastoral zone'.

Furthermore, in connection with development projects, sections of grazing land may be fenced off for ranches or plantations which do not benefit local herders; as an illustration, one particular World Bank-funded project (Niger Agro-Pastoral Export Promotion Project) involved, among other things, the creation of seven fenced gum arabic plantations, some of them as large as 200–300 ha, in what was previously graz-ing land used by local herders. The mid-term review of this project carried out in 2004 confirmed that this land had been acquired; in other words, it had been permanently removed from the grazing resources available to herders. The result is a gradual and systematic encroachment by outsiders onto community grazing lands and increasing pressure on local herders.

RECOVERY AND RECONSTRUCTION: HERDING UNDERVALUED

Conflict Involving Herders Dismissed as 'Tribal'

Negative and derogatory terminology is recurrent among planners and officials where lifestyles appear different, as with nomadic pastoralists and other herders up and down Africa. Political insecurity in livestock-keeping areas is dismissed as 'intertribal raiding', in other words something localised and insignificant, even when the issues at stake concern the relationship between the local population and local government or the state.

In South Sudan, the Khartoum government has made ample use of the particular characteristics of the pastoralist way of life to justify its actions and distance itself from internationally unjustifiable acts. For example, the supply train from northern Babanusa to the southern garrison town of Wau, in the Bahr el Ghazal province, was often protected by 'Arab' tribesmen who accompanied it on horseback and fanned out to attack all southern villages in the vicinity of the railroad – killing, looting and taking slaves in the process (UN 1999). To counter international protests the GOS has claimed that the perpetrators were Arab pastoralists, who were traditional neighbours of the also pastoralist Dinka victims, and that the conflict between them was the result of ancient rivalries over pastures and cattle and had no relation to Government policy. The same argument of pastoralist rivalry over livestock was also used on numerous occasions to deny any responsibility in the raids perpetrated on Dinka and Nuer villages by government-armed and funded militia in Bahr al Ghazal and other provinces such as Western Upper Nile. Thus the downgrading of insecurity involving pastoralists as 'inter-tribal' fighting has been largely used by government to dismiss any claims of GOS interference (via militia) and accusations of attacks and direct responsibility for displacement.

Peace Agreements: Herding Subsidiary, Herders Absent

Unlike the protracted civil war in South Sudan, the conflicts in Mali and Niger have been mostly episodic alternating flare-ups and peace agreements. The latter were either temporary arrangements and ceasefires or full blown 'National Covenants' or pacts, such as the Malian *Pacte National* of 11 April 1992 (cf. Introduction above), an ambitious document which purports to achieve a permanent peace in the North as well as 'national reconciliation between all Malians' (Title 1, article 1). Brokered by Algeria, the Pact quite predictably dwells a great deal on security issues and military matters. Reconstruction is dealt with (Article 11) with the proposal of two funds for the benefit of displaced persons and other victims of the armed conflict in northern Mali. The first fund would provide financial support and compensation for military and civilian victims, while the second is a development fund designed to encourage the creation of 'small and medium size industries' and 'small and medium size companies' (PMI and PME, see République du Mali 1992). In a conflict involving herders, no provision of any kind is made for the reconstruction, preservation, rehabilitation or rebuilding of livestock herds.

The Pact gave rise to much hope, however, because of one innovation (Title III) the granting of a special status for the northern (Tuareg) region. In an area with a predominance of herders, this would be ground-breaking as it would entail livestock keepers themselves making all the major decisions that affected their lives. In a wide-ranging medley of provisions which include economic but also social and cultural commitments such as the promotion of local languages, the document provoked much excitement, especially as it also provides for power sharing through the creation of local communities and elected representatives (Title III, Article 15, 16 and 17). This would, if implemented, pioneer integration of livestock keeping communities into the larger national context.

The Tuareg conflict in Niger followed a similar path to that of Mali and has taken place simultaneously. Several flirtations with democracy in the 1980s and 1990s did not achieve much in the road to peace. In Niger, the early 1990s rebellion was concentrated in the Azawad (Azaouad) region – a pastoral region to the west of the country. Support was drawn in large part from young herdsmen who knew only the way of life based on the care of camels and other livestock: '*Ces jeunes forces touarègues sont composées en grande majorité de bergers qui ne connaissent pas les villes … Bref il s'agit des gens du peuple de l'intérieur, des nomades qui habitent dans leurs vallées*'[7] (Ouray ag Wanayer 1996, 128). But the peace agreements were negotiated by Tuareg leaders and mediators who came from rather different urban and French language educated backgrounds and, if one examines these agreements for the livelihood strategies proposed for these pastoral zones, few details can be found and the strategies are not clear.

The Ouagadougou agreement of 1994 mentions the need for new 'projects' in the areas touched by the conflict, but with no details (Article 9). The final agreement, the Ouagadougou Agreement of 15 April (République du Niger et Résistance Touarègue 1995) was facilitated by France and Algeria one year later; like its Malian counterpart, it provides for power-sharing in the northern regions (Articles 7 and 8), assistance to returnees, as well as 'reintegration sites in which adequate socio-economic activities will be created' (Article 19). It itemises the proposed rural development activities, which include development of animal production and crop cultivation, in particular new techniques of irrigated horticulture for market oriented production. The animal production focus, however, is on livestock and its commercialisation; livestock keepers are largely ignored and livestock keeping livelihoods and lifestyles are nonexistent in the document (*ibid.* para. A: Rural Development).

Algeria has been and still is the main mediator in most of the peace talks between the governments of both countries and the Tuareg rebels, particularly through its ambassadors in Bamako and Niamey. Algeria has a great deal at stake and sees links between the Tuareg rebellion and many aspects of its domestic policies, regional economy and border security.[8] Until the 1970s, Algeria led an active policy of sedentarisation of its own nomadic and more particularly its own Tuareg populations. The constant

---

7. 'Most of these young Tuareg fighters are herdsmen who are not familiar with towns... In brief they belong to peoples of the interior, nomads who live in their valleys.'

8. From the 1960s, the Tuareg of Mali and Niger, who have traditional links to the Tuareg of Algeria, were seen by the Algerian government as a threat to its economic and political stability. In 1963, barely one year after achieving independence, Algeria helped Mali to ruthlessly put down a Tuareg rebellion. The new government also handed over to the Malian government certain Tuareg leaders who had found shelter in Algeria. Although cooperation between the two countries did not always reach this degree of complicity, Algeria maintained enough close contacts with both Mali and Niger to ensure that its views on the Tuareg rebellions not only counted but often prevailed.

presence of other nomads from neighbouring countries posed a threat, in the eyes of the Algerian government, to this policy. Cooperation between states seemed therefore necessary, and the richest of the three, Algeria, could wield enormous influence on the way this cooperation worked. Rather than settling the Tuareg into agricultural lands, which, in the Sahara, are in short supply, the Algerian government tried to attract them into employment in tourism and in the large oil, gas and mining industrial complexes.

The lesson was learned in particular by Niger, which is replicating this pattern of development in its northern uranium mines. Besides a similarity of domestic political interests, Mali and Niger are also not indifferent to Algerian economic participation in large regional projects which affect them both, such as the trans-Saharan road, the trans-Saharan oil pipeline and the Nigerian gas pipeline. A further major reason for Algerian interests in the Tuareg rebellion in Mali and Niger is the perceived potential threat to its security, in particular through a political convergence or an alliance between the northern Kabyles and their Berber cousins, the Tuareg.[9]

The final peace agreements, resulting from such discussions overshadowed by national level economic and security issues, reveal no clear livelihood strategy for the ordinary people trying to make a modest living in the pastoral zones of northern Mali and Niger, nor do they refer to the herding way of life characteristic of these zones. In this they are quite consistent with national government policy, which has systematically neglected to support and develop pastoralism, the main livelihood in the central and northern parts of both countries and which has persisted in looking to introduce alternative livelihoods (Walentowitz 2000, 37–40; Oxby 1999, 227).

Repatriation: Retraining in Other Livelihoods, No Assistance to Herding

Provisions for Tuareg returnees followed the same logic; standard repatriation packages for rural dwellers in Africa are designed to answer the basic needs of settled farmers: shelter, monthly rations, seeds and tools (see for example Bakewell 2000, 369 on UNHCR provisions for Angolan refugees returning from Zambia). This is justified where returnees were previously farmers and want to return to their previous lifestyle. However, it is often assumed that this type of horticulturally oriented package is also appropriate where rural dwellers were not previously farmers. In fact repatriation is often seen by policy makers as an opportunity to encourage and engineer a planned change of livelihood, for example to irrigated agriculture (see for example Haug 2002

---

9. See Mezhoud 1993: since the birth of the Berber nationalist movement in the late 1960s, the Algerian government feared, and tried very hard to prevent, a political convergence or an alliance between the northern Kabyles and their southern Berber cousins, the Tuareg. It did not take lightly the idea of any renewed alliance with nationalists cum separatists from the South. With Libya at one time arming Tuareg rebels, Algeria had grounds for fearing the destabilisation of the region; limiting Tuareg movements was one way of decreasing the danger to security. The Tuareg's intimate knowledge of the terrain makes them invaluable as guides not only to the tourism industry, scientific or economic exploration, but also to infiltrators like, recently, Islamist combatants such as those of the so-called Al Qaeda in the Maghreb (AQIM), transporting arms and supplies into northern Algeria, and more recently, southern Algeria, northern Mali, and Niger.

on the rehabilitation of displaced Hawaweer pastoralists in new desert locations in northern Sudan). This type of repatriation moves us into what, for the returnees, is a huge step; it involves retraining in a new way of life – 'livelihood reconstruction'. The extent to which this is a voluntary choice on the part of returnees is not always clear, particularly as there may be no other viable alternative solutions available to them.

In the Sahel, a repatriation programme was launched in 1997 to assist the return of Malian and Nigerien refugees (not IDPs) back to their homelands. UNHCR appealed for US$17.6 million for Mali and Niger. By March 1997, it was estimated that about 100,000 Malian refugees had returned home either spontaneously or with UNHCR assistance. Among the cost effective reintegration projects to accompany repatriation, US$1.1 million was to go towards income generating projects. The World Food Programme (WFP) prepared follow up activities to meet the needs of 'victims of conflict' in northern Niger and Mali; in 2002 they were estimated at US$5.1 million for Mali and US$12.6 million for Niger. Following are examples of repatriation packages. Table 1 shows what was distributed to Tuareg refugees in Mauritania, Burkina Faso and Algeria returning to their home country Mali. Most of these people had been brought up in the herding way of life, and the care of livestock was their expertise. As can be seen, the assistance involves food and water, loans for gardening and handicraft projects. There was no support or assistance to livestock keeping, the only livelihood many of these people really knew. Table 2 illustrates recent repatriation assistance in South Sudan and describes packages distributed to refugees and IDPs.

According to Sperl (2000, 8–9), a major constraint in the design of the programme concerned the decision not to support measures to help in the rehabilitation of livestock for the pastoralist communities. He quotes some returnees in Tessalit, Mali, who state this clearly: 'the only thing we really lack is our animals ... we would have preferred receiving sheep and goats rather than all the other benefits.' Sperl explores why this decision was taken: lack of knowledge of the herding way of life was given as

Table 1. UNHCR and WFP assistance package distributed to Malian returnees 1995–99

To returnees only:
3 months food rations
To all community members where returnees had settled:
Complementary food rations or vulnerable groups
Distribution of non-food items (soap, blankets, tarpaulins)
Food for work programmes
Water provision (repairing / digging wells, drilling boreholes, installing water pumps)
Loans for small projects in a variety of sectors (but not animal production), especially market gardening and crafts

Source: Sperl 2000.

Table 2. Examples of assistance package to Sudanese returnees

Repatriation from Central African Republic
UNHCR Briefing Notes, 13 April 2007: 1,300 returned refugees received an aid package from humanitarian agencies containing a three-month food ration, seeds, agricultural tools and basic household items
Repatriation from Uganda
UNHCR News Stories, 23 April 2009: 20,000 returnees received packages containing agricultural tools, seeds, plastic sheeting, kitchen utensils and food for three months
Returned refugees from Uganda
UNHCR 10 February 2009: Received reintegration assistance including funding for wells, schools and medical clinics.
Repatriation from Ethiopia
UNHCR Briefing Notes, 4 April 2006: Received package of non-food items, including blankets, sleeping mats, plastic sheets, guinea-worm filters, kitchen sets and soap.

Source: UNHCR website 2006–2009.

the main reason but the author suggests that the underlying reason is that this way of life is thought of as outdated and inappropriate.

It was felt that this was a long term development challenge for which the humanitarian agencies at hand did not have the necessary expertise. As a result, the assistance measures provided by the programme favoured sedentarisation at the expense of pastoralism despite the fact that this had been the traditional occupation of many beneficiaries. Implicit in this policy may have been the assumption that sedentarisation was the complement of an inevitable process of modernisation which the programme was there to support and consolidate. However, the policy also went to the detriment of the many semi-nomadic and newly sedentarised communities whose livelihood still depends on animal husbandry, as the soil conditions in this arid zone rarely lend themselves to sustained agricultural production. (*ibid.*)

This example shows the way herding is poorly understood by planners and how decisions are affected by negative assumptions about the herding way of life: that it is inappropriate, outdated, not 'modern' – when clearly, in the absence of major and continued capital investment in alternative livelihood strategies, it is the only sustainable livelihood in many dry areas. Even if the official reason given is lack of experience on the part of aid agencies, the effect is to promote the message that herding is not a way of life to be supported; therefore it is downgraded officially in contrast to a more acceptable option like market gardening which is given official backing.

Life after Camps: Assumption of Sedentarisation

A 2003 follow-up study of nomadic and semi-nomadic herders who left Mali for Mauritania during the rebellion of the early 1990s, and returned in the late 1990s to settle in Western Mali, near the Mauritanian border, investigated livelihood strategies and trends in sedentarisation. The study found that 'having been in a refugee camp is by far the most important factor predisposing to sedentarisation' (Randall and Giuffrida 2006, 450). After a long history of unsuccessful planned attempts on the part of the French colonial government and the independent government to sedentarise Tuareg and other nomadic herders around schools and other services provided in new settlements in the vicinity of outlying administrative posts, the rebellion and repatriation process seemed at first to have succeeded in transforming the way of life of much of this population.

However, the longer-term trends are not clear. Sedentarisation appeared as part of a process facilitating access to development funds: 'Most of the development agencies … fund activities which are much better adapted to a sedentary lifestyle, often including construction of infrastructure. The only intervention which would contribute towards facilitating a return to a mobile lifestyle – herd reconstitution – is rare.' (Randall and Giuffrida 2006, 459). Some people owned absent herds, and many relied on remittances from relatives in Bamako and Libya, but the reliance on external development resources appeared fundamental to the subsistence of these communities and the authors wondered whether this sedentarisation, like other episodes in the history of this region, might be transient.

Sperl's 2000 study of the rehabilitation and reconstruction needs of returnees and others in northern Niger, five years after the final peace agreement, noted the lack of substantial commitment or detailed plans to support or relaunch either herding or agricultural activities in general. The main emphasis was on small loans for urban projects such as crafts for the tourist industry, *boulangeries* and restaurants. Moreover, the author did not notice any general trend towards sedentarisation or aid dependency. Indeed another survey of needs around the same time mentioned that many of the returnees from Algerian camps were keen to build upon their experiences there and consolidate their newly acquired networks in order to develop transport and trading activities between the two countries; a group of them had joined together to buy a truck for that purpose (Walenowitz 2000, 88).

CONSTRAINTS AND OPPORTUNITIES FOR POLICY REFORM

Representation and Participation: A Pastoralist Deficit

The pastoralist lifestyle, almost by definition, lacks representation in central government; the government is at the centre, livestock keepers at the periphery, geographically, economically, culturally and politically. This distance results in a number of deficits, many of which have given rise to a rich literature.[10] The Tuareg and the Southern Sudanese are good examples of the downside of this territorial and political position.

Arguably, much of the current situation in both cases is a legacy of colonial rule. However, disturbance in the economic and political balance in transitional areas was not adjusted at independence and post-colonial governments inherited colonial prejudices and assumptions about pastoralist societies and economies with no intention of correcting them; this, at best, was through lack of understanding, but often with strikingly similar interests and aims to those of colonial administrations. The peripheral (hence marginal) pastoralists tend to benefit least from the largesse of central government and often have no other recourse than rebellion to wrest a fairer share of resources and power.

This situation prevailed in the Sahel after independence; and, in Sudan, it could be said that there was never any rupture between the colonial and the post-colonial periods. The almost continuous civil war in Sudan was fought around the demarcation line inherited at independence in 1956, which constituted the boundary between the Anglo-Egyptian Sudan in the north, and the territory secured by the British, as a result of their nineteenth-century colonial rivalry with the French and Belgians, in the south. It is estimated that the population of the south is made up of 80 per cent pastoralists,[11] a feature which undoubtedly is used to justify much of the northern derogatory depiction of southerners as backward.

Both geography and prejudice still contribute to the increased marginalisation of pastoralists in Sudan and especially in the Sahel. One way this manifests itself is through the lack of provision of education to the livestock-keeping communities.[12] In Niger and Mali, Tuareg access to education has always been hindered by their distance from settlement centres, their nomadic lifestyle and their comparatively small numbers. The situation is gradually changing, however, and there are now small but increasing numbers of Tuareg with university qualifications.[13] In South Sudan a contributing element to the desirability of education is the presence of active church groups with strong links to powerful organisations abroad, especially the US. For a number of reasons, these groups have attempted to improve schooling and education in the south. Their success may be due in part to GOS' own introduction of an educational system designed to further the Arabisation – and islamisation – of the southerners.

During the civil war, education was near impossible to provide in the south, because of constant, repetitive displacement and the dearth of teachers. Many teachers

---

10. In relation to the Tuareg, see Claudot-Hawad 2006. More generally, see Chang and Koster 1994; Flintan 2006; Li *et al.* 2002.

11. SNV Netherlands Development Organisation website March 2009. The term 'pastoralist' would include those often known as agro-pastoralists.

12. For studies on the provision of education to pastoralist societies see Aikman and Unterhalter 2005; Aikman and El Haq 2006; Oxfam 2003, 2005.

13. It is clear, for instance, that northern Berbers in Morocco and especially in Algeria realised the value of education since colonial times, and access to better education was always part of nationalist demands during the struggle for independence.

joined the rebellion and existing schools were frequently torched along with entire villages during attacks. In IDP camps, basic education was sometimes provided, mostly by international organisations. Even in camps, however, IDPs could be further displaced, as was the case in Khartoum;[14] this led inexorably to the under-education of southern children, thus considerably undermining the reconstruction effort.

Post Peace Agreements: Opportunities for Increased Representation of Herders

The intermittent character of the conflict in Mali and Niger, in contrast with the Sudanese civil war, often carried hope and promise in the form of peace agreements; these sometimes appeared like genuine signs of a new beginning. The reality on the ground, however, is more complex. In Mali, the promises of the *Pacte National* failed to materialise and the Malian population largely ignored it. The Pact did not bring peace to the country and hostilities continued until another agreement, the Algiers Peace Accord, was signed in July 2006. This too is considered precarious.

As in Mali, the peace agreement in Niger is slow to come into force. In spite of what was often considered as token participation of the Tuareg in government, the peace was continuously interrupted by renewed clashes between the Nigerien armed forces and Tuareg rebel groups throughout the late 1990s and again in the early 2000s and in particular during 2007. One main reason was that the peace accords were not being implemented; the other was the continued Tuareg demands for a greater share of the profits from the uranium mined in their territory, which have only partially been met. This pattern repeats itself in neighbouring Mali, now the third producer of gold in Africa, where the claims of livestock keepers against the mining industry are equally neglected.

The Niger peace agreement of 1995, and especially the provision for the decentralisation of political and administrative life, power sharing and local participation in the implementation of economic projects, remains the main instrument for improving the plight of livestock keepers and preventing further conflict. Administrative reforms in Niger have led to the creation of *communes* (see above) each headed by an elected mayor. These mayors theoretically have the same power and authority in both agricultural and pastoral zones,[15] but the increasingly deteriorating security situation in many parts of the pastoral zone threatens to undermine the position of mayors representing livestock-keeping communities, a fact seized upon by the government for not allocating more development assistance to these communities. This, in turn, gives

---

14. A notorious conflict continued for over a decade between the international community and the GOS, to prevent these further displacements in Khartoum IDP camps. The GOS, through the Office of the Governor of Khartoum, undertook systematic destruction of IDP homes under the pretext of an urban development plan for the capital. The destruction was conducted without warning and during the worst possible period, the rainy season, when IDPs were unable to rebuild homes elsewhere.

15. Though in practice the *Code Rural* and, in particular, the division of land into pastoral land and agricultural land, means that the powers of mayors in relation to the protection of community grazing lands are severely restricted.

rise to further resentment and deterioration of the situation. It is worth noting that, although the governments of both Niger and Mali have held negotiations with Tuareg rebels and signed several peace agreements, the overwhelming reason for this may be simply external pressure,[16] especially from Algeria, for reasons of security and regional stability; and from France, the most important partner in uranium mining in Niger, with equally large economic and political interests in Mali. Whatever the motives, both internal and external, the results of political negotiations and the structure of the agreements are heavily influenced by industrial exploitation of the pastoralist regions. What is always lacking are long term vision, sustainable solutions and holistic approaches to the development of these territories with livestock keeping as the centrepiece of the edifice, for historical, sociological, legal and ecological reasons.

In Sudan, the presence of oil in the south has been the single most important stumbling block to the demarcation of north–south boundaries. The reluctance of GOS to relinquish some transitional regions and recognise them as being part of South Sudan has resulted in the creation of special zones – the Three Areas – in addition to the South proper, with the aim of securing part of the oil regions for GOS. In spite of their otherwise immense differences, GOS and GOSS, however, have in common a desire to control the natural resources in the disputed territories.

Unlike Niger and Mali where central government was always charged with implementing agreements, in Sudan the southern populations were fortunate to have their own regional government with a large degree of autonomy and a natural interest in the region, their own. With regard to the exploitation of resources, however, GOSS policies are not very different from those of GOS; the former's main interest concerns more particularly the size of the share of the proceeds of the oil industry it would receive. Most of the revenue spent on the reconstruction effort is used to finance and create an urban-based economy, and rural economic potentials have, so far, received very little attention.

Even if a large number of southerners voluntarily abandon livestock keeping as a form of livelihood, having both lost their livestock and become accustomed to a more sedentary lifestyle after many years of displacement, livestock keepers will still represent a large proportion of the population and will play a part in southern reconstruction. Even the oil industry will not guarantee success; in recent months the number of returnees has decreased with the fall of oil prices and loss of revenue for the South. Refugees International recently claimed that 'the Government of Southern Sudan (GOSS) and international agencies have not shifted their focus to the reintegration of returnees'. It deplored the fact that the only existing livelihood opportunities were 'limited to subsistence agriculture and small commerce which fail to guarantee adequate food security … [resulting] in non-sustainable returns and drift towards urban areas'

---

16. The Malian and Nigerien majority settled populations, not usually consulted on these accords, are on the whole hostile to them. Political parties have taken advantage of the lack of consultation to agitate against 'selling out' to the Tuareg and for defending the 'territorial integrity' of their respective countries against so-called secessionist claims from the Tuareg.

and called for a 'holistic reintegration strategy ... to help the millions of people who have returned rebuild their lives, obtain basic services and access livelihoods' (Refugees International 2009).

The context of the independent Republic of South Sudan is potentially favourable to livestock-keepers. Since pastoralists constitute an overwhelming majority of the population of South Sudan – and are therefore massively represented in government – they are in a position to expect from the new government an economic, social and cultural system which is based on, or takes considerably into account, livestock-keeping values and lifestyle.

Human Rights of Herders: the Right to Maintain their Traditional Lifestyle

Pastoralists in general and displaced pastoralists in particular, are not only physically vulnerable and perpetually subjected to the effects of drought, development policies, territorial and land encroachment, as well as conflict, but also institutionally and legally vulnerable. Unlike agriculturalists, they lack title to their land and, in contrast with refugees, as displaced persons they do not benefit explicitly from international legal protection, although this has changed significantly in recent years.

Pastoralism as an economic, social and cultural system is very rarely designated as a subject of international protection and international human rights. Livestock keepers benefit from the protection afforded them as individuals on a par with their fellow countrymen. This, however, does not mean that pastoralists are totally deprived of legal protection. Although there is no specific system or framework of protection tailored specially for pastoralists, livestock keepers can claim protection from numerous other mechanisms depending on their particular context.

In recent years, the Tuareg have placed their conflict with the governments within the context of their human rights. To do this, they have to distinguish their rights from those of other groups within their countries. Apart from their rights as individuals guaranteed by the International Bill of Human Rights (i.e. the Universal Declaration of Human Rights – UNDHR – and the two Covenants), their rights as pastoralists are determined by a number of standards dealing with group rights.

Where individual rights, those which they share with all their fellow countrymen, fail them, pastoralists may find legal protection as members of a minority, although in the context of the Sahel a minority is a difficult concept which can be claimed by many. In addition, international legal standards deal mainly with national, religious and linguistic minorities and not social, economic, livelihood or lifestyle minorities. The International Covenant on Economic, Social and Cultural Rights (ESCR) and the International Covenant on Civil and Political Rights (CCPR) in their common Article 1, provide that 'all peoples have the right of self-determination and ... they freely determine their political status and freely pursue their economic, social and cultural development'. As it has been argued that Article 1, common to both covenants, deals with the rights of entire 'peoples' (the populations of nation-states) and not specific components of a people, in response common article 1 has been incorporated into the

UN Declaration of the Rights of Indigenous Peoples (UNDRIP) as its Article 3. The Declaration is not a binding instrument, but since both CCPR and ESCR are binding they lend authority to Article 3 of UNDRIP.

As a minority, livestock keepers can invoke both Article 27 of CCPR and the Declaration on the Rights of Persons Belonging to National or Ethnic, Religious and Linguistic Minorities (DRM). The jurisprudence of the Human Rights Committee (HRC) has upheld both the cultural traits and livelihoods of minorities as constituting rights to be protected under Article 27: 'culture manifests itself in many forms, including a particular way of life associated with the use of land resources, especially in the case of indigenous peoples. That right may include such traditional activities as fishing or hunting and the right to live in reserves protected by law' (HRC, General Comment no 23). The HRC has taken inspiration from the DRM and has acknowledged the rights of indigenous peoples in the process. UNDRIP for its part, deliberately shuns a definition of what constitutes an indigenous people and relies largely on self-definition (E/CN.4/Sub.2/AC.4/1996/2/Add.1, 10 June 1996, paras. 2 and 3). This was taken up by the Tuareg and other African pastoralists (Maasai, Samburu, WoDaaBe) as the basis of their claims.

The rights of nomadic peoples are specifically protected by ILO Convention C169 especially insofar as labour and land rights are concerned. In Article 14, C169 provides that 'the rights of ownership and possession of the peoples concerned over the lands which they traditionally occupy shall be recognized. ... Particular attention shall be paid to the situation of nomadic peoples and shifting cultivators in this respect.'

Stronger protection may be available to pastoralist children under the Convention on the Rights of the Child (CRC). Apart from a wide scope of issues, most notably health (Article 24) and education (Articles 28 and 29), the CRC singles out the rights of children of both minorities and indigenous peoples. Its jurisprudence has extended its interest explicitly to nomadic children.[17]

Unlike refugees, IDPs, until the late 1990s, did not enjoy special protection under international law and did not have a specialised agency, such as UNHCR, to advance their cause or defend their rights. However, the phenomenal growth of the IDP problem worldwide put pressure on the international community to develop a system of international protection. This took several forms including an expanded role for UNHCR in IDP protection. As IDPs, pastoralists can, therefore, claim increased rights.

---

17. CRC, Concluding Observations: Algeria /Recommendations (CRC/C/15/Add.76): 18 June 1997. Para. 30: 'The Committee recommends that further steps be taken to ensure that nomadic children have access to education and health-care services through a system of specifically targeted education and health-care schemes which will allow these children to enjoy their right, in community with other members of their group, to their own culture, as stipulated in article 30 of the Convention.'

CONCLUSION

Herders, including pastoralists and agro-pastoralists, have been the victims of forced displacement worldwide and, because of lack of understanding and prejudices about their lifestyle, they have remained largely invisible and above all vulnerable. Their mobility has often thrown a veil on their plight when they are forcibly displaced, as governments and institutions fail or refuse to distinguish between the two. This occurs more particularly when pastoralists remain within their national borders as IDPs and do not cross international frontiers to qualify as refugees.

Herders' geographical remoteness, their deficit in formal education and the ensuing lack of access to international mechanisms, together with the complexity of these mechanisms, have usually prevented them from claiming and defending their rights. There is, nevertheless, a body of international human rights law and international mechanisms that may be put to use for that purpose. They can, most importantly, demand and defend their right to remain livestock keepers and keep their pastoralist way of life and chosen livelihood.

Livestock keeping constitutes arguably the most sustainable form of livelihood in certain areas and, with climate change and global warming, these areas may increase significantly in number. It is the right of livestock keepers to continue to enjoy all aspects of their way of life; this right is guaranteed by international human rights law. Governments and institutions engaged in post-conflict reconstruction or development initiatives should make this right the basis of all their efforts. In many cases, livestock keeping may represent the most viable option in the pursuit of reconstruction and development goals. Governments may be slow or resistant to understanding this, but livestock keepers are, for their part, already beginning to make it reality.

BIBLIOGRAPHY

Ahmed, Abdel Ghaffar M. (ed.) 1976. *Some Aspects of Pastoral Nomadism in the Sudan*. Khartoum: Sudan National Population Committee and Economic and Social Research Council.

Aikman, S. and El Haq, H. 2006. 'EFA for Pastoralists in North Sudan: a Mobile Multigrade Model of Schooling', in A.W. Little (ed.) *Education For All and Multigrade Teaching: Challenges and Opportunities*. Amsterdam: Springer.

Aikman, S. and Unterhalter, E. (eds.) 2005. *Beyond Access: Transforming Policy and Practice for Gender Equality in Education*. Oxford: Oxfam GB.

Aukot, E. 2009. 'Am I Stateless because I am a Nomad?' *Forced Migration Review* **32**: 18.

Bakewell, O. 2000. 'Repatriation and Self-Settled Refugees in Zambia: Bringing Solutions to the Wrong Problems', *Journal of Refugee Studies* **13**, 4: 356–73.

Bernus, E. 1981. *Touaregs Nigériens. Unité Culturelle et Diversité Régionale d'un Peuple Pasteur.* Harmattan: Paris.

Capot-Rey, R. 1961. 'Note sur la Sédentarisation des Nomades du Sahara', *Annales de Géographie* **70**, 377 : 82–6.

Casciarri, B. and Ahmed, Abdel Ghaffar M. (eds.) 2009. *Pastoralists under Pressure in Present-Day Sudan*, Special issue, *Nomadic Peoples* **13**, 1: 10–22.

Chang, C. and Koster, H.A. (eds.) 1994. *Pastoralists at the Periphery: Herders in a Capitalist World*. Tucson: University of Arizona Press.

Claudot-Hawad, H. 2006. 'A Nomadic Fight Against Immobility: the Tuareg in the Modern State', in D. Chatty (ed.) *Nomadic Societies in the Middle East and North Africa entering the 21ˢᵗ Century*. Leiden and Boston: Brill.

Cossée, O., Hermes, R. and Mezhoud, S. 2006. 'Real Time Evaluation of the FAO Emergency and Rehabilitation Operations in Response to the Indian Ocean Earthquake and Tsunami'. Consultant's Report. Rome: FAO.

Flintan, F. 2006. 'Combating Marginalisation of Pastoralist Women: SOS Sahel's Experience in Ethiopia', *Gender and Development* **14**, 2: 223–33.

Haug, R. 2002. 'Forced Migration, Processes of Return and Livelihood Construction among Pastoralists in Northern Sudan', *Disasters* **26**, 1: 70–84.

Khamed Attayoub, A. 2002. 'Les Mots du Voyage: Quelques Eléments Lexicologiques en *Tsetserret* Chez les Touaregs Ayttawari Seslem (Azawagh)', in H. Claudot-Hawad (ed.) *Voyager d'un point de vue nomade*. Paris: Paris-Mediterranée.

Li, Y., Johnson, D.L. and Marzouk, A. 2002. 'Pauperizing the Pastoral Periphery: the Marginalization of Herding Communities in the World's Dry Lands', *Journal of Geographical Sciences* **12**, 1: 11–14.

Mezhoud, S. 1992. '*Murder of a Romantic Myth. The Tuareg*', *Anti Slavery International Report* **8**: 106–10.

Mezhoud, S. (Kusyel Tissas) 1993. 'Truly Indigenous: the Berbers of North Africa', *IWGIA Newsletter* Copenhagen. April/May/June No. 2.

Mezhoud, S. 2006. Expert Witness Account. Presbyterian Church of Sudan v. Talisman Energy Inc., New York, United States District Court, Southern District of New York.

Ouray ag Wanayer. 1996. 'Moi, Jeune Combattant Révolutionnaire de Base' in: H. Claudot-Hawad and Hawad (eds.) 'Touaregs – Voix Solitaires sous l'Horizon Confisqué' Ethnies Documents 20–21. Paris: Peuples Autochtones et Développement.

Oxfam GB. 2003. 'Achieving EFA through Responsive Education Policy and Practice for Nomadic and Pastoralist Children: What can Agencies do?' Unpublished Report. Oxford: Oxfam GB.

Oxfam GB. 2005. 'Beyond the Mainstream Education for Nomadic and Pastoralist Girls and Boys' *Education and Gender Equality Series, Programme Insights* December 2005: 3. Oxford: Oxfam GB.

Oxby, C. 1999. 'Mirages of Pastoralist Futures. A Review of Aid Donor Policy in Sahelian Pastoral Zones', *Review of African Political Economy* **80**: 227–37.

Randall, S. and Giuffrida, A. 2006. 'Forced Migration, Sedentarisation and Social Change: Malian Kel Tamasheq', in D. Chatty (ed.) *Nomadic Societies in the Middle East and North Africa entering the 21ˢᵗ Century*. Leiden and Boston: Brill.

Refugees International. 2009. 'South Sudan: Urgent Action Needed to Avert Collapse' *RI* [website], (updated 26 March 2009) http://www.refintl.org/policy/field-report/south-sudan-urgent-action-needed-avert-collapse, accessed 20 May 2009.

Disentangling 'Forced Displacement' from Pastoral Mobility

République du Mali et Mouvements et Fronts Unifiés de l'Azawad. 1992. 'Pacte National Conclu entre le Gouvernement de la République du Mali et les Mouvements et Fronts Unifiés de l'Azawad Consacrant le Statut Particulier du Nord du Mali', Fait à Bamako, le 11 avril 1992.

République du Mali, Gouvernement du, et Alliance Démocratique de la République du Mali du 23 mai 2006 pour le Changement. 2006. 'Accord d'Alger pour la Restauration de la Paix, de la Sécurité et du Développement dans la Région de Kidal', Fait à Alger, le 4 juillet 2006.

République du Niger et Résistance Touarègue. 1995. 'Texte des Accords Définitifs entre la Résistance Touarègue et l'État du Niger. Accord établissant une Paix Définitive entre le Gouvernement de la République du Niger et l'Organisation de la Résistance Armée (ORA). Accords de Ouagadougou, 15 avril 1995.

Sperl, S. 2000. 'International Refugee Aid and Social Change in Northern Mali', *New Issues in Refugee Research*, Working Paper 22. Geneva: UNHCR.

Walentowitz, S. 2000. 'Programme Niger-Nord. Soutien a la Paix. Document de Référence pour la Définition des Stratégies d'Intervention et de Concertation du Projet', Consultant's Report. GTZ : Bonn.

WFP. 1999. Summary Report of Evaluation of Pro-Mali 5804.00. Executive Board Second Regular Session, Rome, 13–14 May 1999.

UN. 1996. 'Standard-setting Activities: Evolution of Standards Concerning the Rights of Indigenous People' Working Paper by the Chairperson-Rapporteur, Mrs. Erica-Irene A. Daes, on the concept of 'indigenous people'. Doc. E/CN.4/Sub.2/AC. 4/1996/2, 10 June 1996. Geneva: United Nations.

UN. 1999. 'Situation of Human Rights in the Sudan' Report of the Special Rapporteur on the Situation of Human Rights in the Sudan (Leonardo Franco), Commission on Human Rights Fifty-fifth session Agenda item 9. Doc. E/CN.4/1999/38/Add.1, 17 May 1999. Geneva: United Nations. [Report prepared by Salem Mezhoud]

UN OCHA. 2009. 'Consolidated Appeals Process (CAP): Mid-Year Review of the United Nations and Partners 2009 Work Plan for Sudan'. Geneva: United Nations.

4

PASTORALISTS AT CROSSROADS: COMMUNITY RESOURCE GOVERNANCE IN THE CONTEXT OF A TRANSITIONING RANGELANDS TENURE SYSTEM

Stephen S. Moiko

Department of Anthropology, McGill University

INTRODUCTION

The territoriality, land-tenure and livelihood conditions of most pastoral societies in Sub-Saharan Africa have undergone extensive transformations over the past decades. The changes can be attributed, in general, to the shifting dynamics of a rapidly expanding human population and of a biophysical environment strained by global climate change but also to state-led land tenure transformations that have facilitated the fragmentation and annexations of pastoral rangelands. In Kenya, state-introduced land tenure policies that sought to create private, liberal property rights systems to replace communal customary systems have in particular extensively transformed rangelands, landscapes and livestock based livelihoods. In many instances, the land tenure transitions have resulted in the disintegration of communal pastoral resource systems, created inequity and insecurity in land ownership and made vulnerable the resilient pastoral livelihoods systems that the rangelands support.

Commencing during Kenya's colonial era, pastoral communities have progressively lost vast territories and vital pasture and water resources, resulting in strained livestock husbandry conditions. The cause of these territorial constrictions has mainly been land acquisition by the state, initially to accommodate incoming colonial settlers and later for purposes of biodiversity conservation, tourism and industrial mining. Also contributing to the land fragmentation and losses have been encroachments into rangelands by cultivating communities, land takeovers by large-scale commercial farming entities and seizures by individual pastoral elites and corrupt officials. The emergent constrained livelihoods conditions present circumstances for range degradation and environmental mismanagement, which existing conditions of global climate warming now exacerbate, making even more precarious the fragile rangelands ecologies in the semi-arid landscapes. As a result pastoralists in the region have in recent times routinely experienced severe droughts, famines, and floods, all transpiring at a time when their customary institutions and ecosystems are least structured to cope with the crises.

Pastoralists have also faced challenges emanating from prejudiced political regimes and incongruous development strategies, both of which have restricted vital infrastructural development and extension of services to marginalised rangelands. Pastoralists, across the region, must incessantly surmount significant systemic and structural obstacles in order to effectively participate and become competitive in mainstream national commerce and economies (Kituyi 1990; Ndeng'e *et al.* 2003). Accordingly, they have weak economic and political leverage and exhibit poor poverty and socio-economic indicators relative to dominant cultivating communities and economic sectors. Despite the challenges, pastoralists have, nevertheless, proved to be resilient and dynamic herders and entrepreneurs, as exhibited by the range of diversified livelihoods activities and innovative herding systems now practiced across the region. Livestock rearing remains the least risky livelihood option for many pastoralist families but one that must also be now supplemented with incomes from employment, trade or investments to meet household needs. Resultant from and linked to all the above is a predicament posed by a gradual dissipation of robust governance institutions customarily employed by pastoral communities to regulate human–environmental interactions in communal socio-ecological systems.

Inhabiting a territory adjacent to Kenya's largest metropolitan area, the Maasai pastoralist society has in particular faced the brunt of the challenges posed by state-introduced reforms to pastoral and customary land tenure systems. Introduced processes of land reform transformed many parts of traditional Maasai territories into formal communal group ranches and subsequently into registered individual land holdings, many of which, in the process, were acquired by non-locals and elite individuals through fraudulent acquisitions and, in recent years, through rampant land sales. The policy-derived individuation, enclosure and fragmentation of the rangelands poses severe challenges for a pastoral livelihood system at a period when dryland ecologies are severely strained and when livestock require greater mobility to cope with the increasing vagaries of climate change. In the face of government ideologies that undermine communal ownership and governance of natural resources and promote sedentarisation and individuation over nomadic lifestyles, and confronting mounting territorial and livelihood insecurity, many pastoral communities are at a crossroads. The communities are cognisant of the ownership security and 'collateral' prospects that formal land registration provides, yet, on the other hand, have witnessed widespread land losses and fragmentation, limitations on livestock mobility and increasing livelihood vulnerability, all occasioned by individual land titling and the gradual dissipation of robust communal socio-ecological land use systems.

This chapter examines the transformational experiences, in land tenure, of the Maasai pastoral community in Kenya and discusses the challenges and responses that livestock herders in Sub-Saharan Africa face regarding the governance of their livelihoods,

Stephen S. Moiko

Figure 1: Maasai children playing at Olkiramatian, Southern Kenya.

property rights and land. Specifically, it employs the case of the Maasai community in Olkiramatian Group Ranch to discuss the dilemmas that many pastoral communities in the region's rangelands face regarding their livelihoods and land tenure. It highlights the important roles that land and property rights systems that are attuned to local cultural, ecological and institutional conditions can play in facilitating sustainable productivity and security in land ownership, while allowing for the flexibility necessary to counter emerging threats on production related to global climate warming.

The chapter also makes the point that while customary and communal systems of land and resource ownership and management are commonly targeted for tenure transformations, pastoral communities still rely on these systems and institutions as functional strategies for secure livelihoods and sustainable management of resources. Further, since privatisation and state control models of resource governance have already been largely shown to be unsuitable for most rangeland environments (Amanor and Moyo 2008; Besteman 1994; Bruce 1988), more attention should be given to functional local pastoral systems and institutions of resource management. Therefore, rather than seek to abolish or transform customary tenure systems, policy makers and land reformers should aspire to build upon various aspects of existing traditional tenure systems to develop tenure paradigms that promote sustainable livelihoods and enhance resource security in pastoral rangelands.

CONTEXTUAL BACKGROUND OF LAND TENURE REFORMS IN PASTORAL RANGELANDS

Beginning at the turn of the nineteenth century, during the onset of colonialism, and escalating in post-independence years, many countries in Sub-Saharan Africa engaged in concerted land-tenure reform processes. In large, the reforms aimed to replace customary land holding systems with formal state-control or market models of land tenure and property rights (Amanor and Moyo 2008; Okoth-Ogendo 1976; Smith 2003; Toulmin and Quan 2000). Private and individual ownership of land, in contrast to communal traditional models, were portrayed, in the reforms, as crucial means for empowering and modernising rural dwellers to achieve efficiency in agricultural production and for propelling national economic growth. Indigenous communal tenure systems, which the modern-day models sought to replace, were conversely presented as inherently lacking the security of ownership necessary for the promotion of investment, intensification of productivity and conservation of land; and thus incompatible with capital-intensive agriculture and the attainment of rapid social-economic progress (De Soto 2000). Further, it was asserted that customary tenure encourages land fragmentation and limits the emergence of vibrant land markets, since land in customary systems is seen to be embedded in local social systems (Barlowe 1953; Dorner 1972).

Consequently, widespread reforms have been undertaken across Sub-Saharan Africa despite growing evidence questioning the effectiveness of land registration and formalisation processes in directly promoting investment or land productivity (Bruce and Migot-Adholla 1994; Migot-Adholla *et al.* 1991) and underscoring the versatility of indigenous customary tenure (e.g. Berry 1993). Although not always lacking support from pastoral populations (e.g. Mwangi 2005), land tenure reforms undertaken in pastoral rangelands have nevertheless been predominantly founded on received wisdoms, myths and misreading or misapplication of scientific models, which misinterpreted the nature and complexity of tropical rangeland socio-ecological systems (Bromley and Cernea 1989). Most notable in these narratives is Garret Hardin's popular thesis on the 'Tragedy of the Commons' (Hardin 1968), which describes pastoral commons as open-access systems inherently destined to degradation through overstocking and overgrazing. Equally influential has been the misreading of perceived episodes of 'desertification' and 'degradation' through the application of equilibrium theories to Africa's rangelands based on models of 'carrying capacity', 'linear succession' and 'climax vegetation' developed in temperate Western environments (Behnke *et al.* 1993; Scoones 1994).

While tenure systems based on individual and private ownership of land have been shown, by neo-liberal scholars, to be crucial in stimulating economic growth in market economies (De Soto 2000), the same has not been the case for developing economies in sub-Saharan Africa, where land-use, social networks, ecologies and cultural institutions remain intricately linked (Berry 1993). This is particularly so in pastoralists' commons, where ecological imperatives require that communities manage and use resources jointly (Bromley 1989). In many rural settings in Sub-Saharan Africa,

Stephen S. Moiko

tenure transformations and land formalisation have not succeeded in consolidating land rights into forms of exclusive control comparable to western notions of private property (Berry 1993). Rather, the individual's ability to exercise claims to land has remained linked to membership in social networks and participation in both formal and informal political and cultural processes.

Contrasted with customary tenure systems employed by agrarian societies in arable tropical zones, where ecological conditions and land-use practices are more amenable to land privatisation and individuation, communal rangelands utilised through mobile livestock husbandry naturally pose hindrances to land individuation reforms (Lesorogol 2005; Seno and Shaw 2002). To avoid the possible detrimental outcomes of inequitable land allocation and creation of land units of sub-economic size, hybrid tenure systems that confer private property rights to communities rather than individuals were recommended in some countries. The resultant land tenure model subsequently became commonly referred to as the group ranch system. First implemented in Kenya and Chad, under the World Bank's stewardship (Sandford 1980, 1981, 1983), the resulting communal 'private' land holdings are most aptly distinguished not from 'private' property *per se*, but from 'individual' ownership and state ownership, since they constitute communal lands registered under a 'private' collective title

Figure 2. A section of a Maasai homestead (*enk-ang*), Kenya.

granted to communities residing on the land (Bromley and Cernea 1989). In Kenya, the group ranch system of land tenure was first pioneered in the Maasai Districts of Kajiado and Narok and subsequently implemented across other semi-arid rangeland districts. Olkiramatian Group Ranch, the case study of this paper, is a product of this tenure reform process but one which, as will be demonstrated shortly, has followed a different trajectory from the majority of other ranches to craft its own local land use and governance system.

Nonetheless, where state programmes have focused on property rights and land-tenure reforms in pastoral rangelands, notably where the group ranch system was implemented in Kenya, pastoral commons have inescapably undergone the mutually reinforcing processes of land sub-division, privatisation and individuation. These, in turn, have generated, driven and exacerbated rangeland fragmentation and enclosure (Galvin 2008, 2009). While pastoralist communities have not essentially been hostile to rangeland tenure reform, and indeed commonly demanded it (e.g. Lesorogol 2005, 2008), the alterations have had severe implications for the sustainability of rangelands' socio-ecological systems and pastoral livelihoods.

The rangelands tenure reforms in Kenya are largely typical of land reforms elsewhere across Africa. State-led rangeland tenure reforms in most of the continent have, in general, experienced failure in their stated objectives (Okoth-Ogendo 1976; Toulmin and Quan 2000). In the majority of cases, tenure reforms have made possible the loss of rights to key resources by their indigenous land-users, exacerbated tenure insecurity and intra-group conflict and entrenched inequitable distribution of property rights across genders, social units and age-sets (Galaty 1994a; Kimani and Pickard 1998; Rutten 1992; Talle 1988). Moreover, they have had outcomes that facilitate the fragmentation and incursion of pasturelands by external groups, and hence constrain human and livestock mobility, both necessary for the efficient use of spatially variable rangeland resources (Kimani and Pickard 1998). As a result, they have contributed to making pastoralists' livelihoods and nutrition vulnerable (Fratkin and Roth 2005; Hogg 1980), and undermined indigenous institutions customarily used in governing pastoral land and natural resources (Mwangi and Ostrom 2009; Swallow and Bromley 1995).

Conversely, however, property rights and land-tenure changes could be credited with creating opportunities and conditions under which some desirable socio-economic transformations have occurred in Kenya's rangelands. In some instances, land registration seems to have provided, in the context of ominous pastoral land expropriation, forms of political security for landowners. Indeed, the goal of enhanced tenure security, Galaty (1980) contends, fundamentally motivated Maasai adoption of the group ranch land-tenure reforms in Kenya.

Stephen S. Moiko

THE MAASAI GROUP RANCHES: TOWARDS RANGELANDS' FRAGMENTATION

Typical of rangeland environments elsewhere across the globe, semi-arid pastoral land-scapes in Kenya posed challenges to policy makers pushing for the land privatisation and individuation models of land tenure. Ecological imperatives in arid environments demand that land users are flexible and mobile to access and effectively utilise sparse resources. Nomadic and transhumant pastoralism allows temporally and spatially distributed pasture to be used opportunistically, effectively turning the scarce resources into useful sources of nutrition and livelihoods for human communities (Behnke *et al.* 1993; Swallow 1995). To address the challenge of rangelands tenure reform, the government of Kenya and its then international development partners designed the above mentioned group ranch system and conferred private land ownership rights on pastoral communities rather than individuals (Galaty 1980, 1994b; Rutten 1992).

The group ranch system, first implemented in 1968 in Maasai areas close to Nairobi, sub-divided customary pastoral territories to create smaller group ranches with rigid boundaries enclosing a designated community of registered members. Upon demarcation and registration of the land a formal title deed was produced in the name of a group ranch. A management committee, elected from the registered members, was mandated to head the group ranch and make decisions regarding infrastructural development, land investment, and the use of land and other resources (Galaty 1980; Rutten 1992). The pivotal feature of group ranches was the conversion of communal land under customary tenure and with flexible access to resources, to formal group tenure with confined legally enforced boundaries and membership (Lane 1998).

The logic behind the group ranch enterprise was the perception that pastoral communal land tenure systems provided no impetus for improvements on land maintenance, pasture management, and stock upgrading (Rutten 1992). Paradoxically, however, a few individual ranches, which had previously been created on the fringes of the semi-arid districts to address these issues, had by then already proved to be non-viable for pastoral production systems that inherently 'necessitated periodic movement of stocks and people over large areas' (*ibid.*). In a sense the planners hoped to convert 'open access' property regimes, which they believed the pastoral rangelands to be operating under, into 'common property' regimes. The difference between the two is that the latter has a limited membership, known boundaries and rules regulating access and use of resources, while the former regimes are open to a limitless user base that is not bound by any resource use regulations (Bromley 1989; Hardin 1968; Ostrom 1990).

The group ranches were expected to meet a number of objectives. First, it was hoped they would create some form of 'responsibility' towards land on the part of pastoralists and address the perceived problem related to the individual ownership of livestock in freely accessible lands ('tragedy of the commons') (Rutten 1992). The restriction of livestock movement was expected to reduce stocking levels and encourage market off-take. Second, group ranches were expected to create a framework through which the government could extend basic services such as education, health services and veterinary care to the Maasai (Galaty 1980). In this way, the group ranches were expected to facilitate government efforts to curb the spread of livestock diseases and improve livestock breeds. Third, the government wanted to turn the Maasai and other pastoralists into commercial producers of meat and improve their participation in the national livestock economy. Munei (1991) points out that there was a general feeling that 'the pastoral economy was falling down' both in supporting itself and promoting national development, adding that government surveys had consistently identified pastoralists as among the poorest in the country. Finally, a 'long term and seldom stated' objective of the group ranches was the removal of 'the relatively large portion of land, adjacent to the highly populated Kenyan highlands and the urban centre of Nairobi', from communal control of the Maasai and bringing it into the lively real estate market in Kenya (Galaty 1994a, 190). This process would facilitate the transfer of land through market mechanisms to those who were 'most suited to use it', and also indirectly meet the high demand for land then experienced in the adjacent high density demographic zones (*ibid.*).

It can, therefore, be argued that the development of group ranches was necessitated by the government's expectations relating to pastoral rangelands and supported by its perception that the pasturelands, especially the sprawling and watered Maasai reserves around Nairobi, were underutilised, contributed little to the national economy, lagged behind in 'development' and were in real danger of being converted into wastelands through overstocking and overgrazing. The resettlement and economic needs of the government, and not those of the pastoralists *per se*, thus emerge as a motive for the creation of group ranches. This assertion is clearly supported by an examination of the context under which the group ranch concept was hatched, the top-down nature of its design and implementation, the inherent 'contempt' for pastoral indigenous knowledge systems that existed among planners and the minimal consultation the 'target group' received during the process. The group ranch concept was the answer to the 'how' element of the government problem of tapping the economic potential of the rangelands and integrating it into the framework of the national economy, rather than a strategy primarily seeking to address the livelihood needs of pastoral peoples. In the group ranches, the government and its development partners had found a 'wagon' for hitching pastoral rangelands and communities to the 'capitalisation' train, aimed at conveying the country towards economic progress and development.

Unsurprisingly, the majority of Maasai group ranches failed to meet government expectations and disintegrated soon after their formation. Few, if any, group ranches had ecologically self-sufficient territories capable of sustainable pastoral production for their membership. In addition, internal wrangles, poor governance and unsuccessful projects diminished members' enthusiasm for the enterprise. Facing external political pressure from a market oriented political elite, and lacking crucial financial support, many ranches resolved to abandon the tenure model and subdivide. By 1990, barely two decades after inception, almost 80 per cent of the Maasai group ranches had decided to do away with the group ranch structure and convert into individual land holdings. At present only a handful of group ranches, including the case study area Olkiramatian, remain un-subdivided.

The subdivision and individuation of Maasai group ranches has been a mainly irregular, corrupt process that has signified 'elite capture and distribution of spoils' (Mwangi 2007). Aided by a vague legal framework, land individuation has ended up concentrating land in the hands of a few, creating non-viable units of land and allocating land rights to outsiders. Moreover, collective ownership of land was lost, since subdivision vested ownership of land to individual, mainly male, family heads. With their names on title deeds, such individuals could then legally transact in land, including selling it, without consent from others. In recent years, high demand for land linked to demographic expansion around the Nairobi metropolis has precipitated uncontrolled loss of key pastoral resources, through land sales, from the Maasai. This not only threatens to permanently dispossess the pastoralists and create widespread landlessness, but also endangers their cultural heritage, which is intricately linked to a pastoral livelihood. This is despite many studies indicating that a mobile pastoral land use system is the most efficient livelihood strategy for the semi-arid rangelands (e.g. Sandford 1983; Scoones 1994).

OLKIRAMATIAN GROUP RANCH: OBSERVATIONS IN THE STRATEGIC GOVERNANCE OF A PASTORAL COMMONS

The majority of studies conducted in the past on Maasai land topics have focused on processes of land fragmentation and their impact on the political and socio-economic dynamics of Maasai communities. Less attention has been given to some few remaining intact communal group ranches, such as Olkiramatian Group Ranch, which despite tremendous internal and external pressure to fragment, resiliently continue to provide socio-ecological environments for the pursuance of a pastoral livelihood by the rural poor. Such communal pastoral landscapes, it is often observed, are the last frontiers through which marginal Maasai communities are now engaging in collective action to manage their environment and natural resources and to adapt to rapidly changing socio-economic conditions.

Like other Maasai communities, the residents of Olkiramatian embraced the group ranch system largely because of the opportunity it then offered for socio-economic development, but also for the security against external land annexations promised by the title deeds. Olkiramatian was registered as a group ranch in 1978 and has remained one to the present. The group ranch is located in the northwest part of Magadi Division of Kajiado County in southern Kenya. It is bordered to the east by Magadi Soda Company concession area, a mining facility that has appropriated land and water resources from the community but which also provides a much-needed source of economic diversification to the community through employment. To the west, Olkiramatian is bounded by the Nguruman escarpment, which forms part of the western border of the Rift Valley. Olkiramatian Group Ranch covers an area of about 21,612 hectares and hosts a population of approximately 15,000 people. The residents of Olkiramatian are predominantly Maasai livestock keepers of the Loodokilani section, one of the several autonomous territorial groupings that constitute the larger Maasai society. The livelihoods of community members, while largely dependent on their cattle, sheep and goats, have also been progressively diversifying to include incomes from trade, cultivation, employment and more recently ecotourism and wildlife conservation. Minority populations of non-Maasai ethnic groups are also found in the agricultural and trading centres areas of the group ranch. These include Kikuyu, Kamba, Luo, Somali and the agri-pastoral Sonjo from Tanzania. These migrants are largely government employees, immigrants working in irrigation farms or business people resident in the few trading centres within Olkiramatian.

Figure 3. Livestock watering along Ewuaso-ngiro River, Olkiramatian.

Olkiramatian has two slightly differing climatic zones, a sub-humid to semi-arid climate (rainfall between 400 and 800 mm per year) along the escarpment and a dry and semi-arid to arid climate in the open plains in the east (rainfall of less than 400 mm per year). The Ewuaso-ngiro River, which roughly dissects Olkiramatian into these two ecological zones, is the main lifeline of the group ranch. The river and two other smaller streams (Oloibortoto and Sampu) provide water for year-round irrigation and for domestic and livestock use. The availability of a year round supply of river water has traditionally presented a unique opportunity for economic diversification from pastoralism into cultivation for residents of Olkiramatian. For decades, the community has explored this alternative and practised irrigation cultivation, hence the name *Ilkurman* (the cultivators) often sarcastically used by other Maasai communities in reference to Olkiramatian residents. In recent years, some members of Olkiramatian community have engaged in transnational trade as growers of horticultural crops for European markets. Global currency fluctuations and competition from elsewhere have, however, since dampened a promising economic alterative in international horticultural trade. The potential for profitable economic returns from irrigation farming have, nevertheless, steadily attracted the above mentioned immigrants into Olkiramatian. The ensuing ethnic mix and a steadily rising educated Maasai population are inevitably causing socio-economic change among the indigenous Maasai. Significantly, perceptions that the value of land has changed have heightened awareness regarding land tenure, and the community is particularly sensitive regarding the ownership security and management of its land resource.

Rainfall in Olkiramatian follows a bi-modal annual pattern but, in general, it is low and erratic, hence a short growing season with high evaporation. In recent years, climate change has made the rainfall even more unpredictable and highly unreliable in the area. Droughts have become regular occurrences and cultivation is only possible in the ranch through irrigation. These particular climate and ecological constraints in Olkiramatian, determining land-use potentials, have over time, combined with the possibilities presented by the communal nature of land tenure in the group ranch to gradually give rise to a dynamic institutionalised local system for managing land and natural resources. Inimitably, the Olkiramatian community has responded to this mix of challenges and opportunities (in particular the triple factors of a communal land-tenure system, the culturally and ecologically dictated pastoral livelihood, and need for adaptation and economic diversification) by creating a dynamic institutional framework for local resource governance.

Livelihood adaptation and diversification and resource management in Olkiramatian are now achieved through an innovative local institutional system composed of semi-autonomous decision-making organs, locally referred to as committees. The committees constitute a functional dynamic local framework for the collective management of community resources in the Ranch. Since they borrow elements from both modern formal governance structures and the customary Maasai institutions, these local committees are a unique and innovative hybrid of the Maasai customary gerontocractic system and the formal land-tenure system prescribed by the Group Representative Act 1968, the statute that governs the group ranches. In addition, and complementing the local institutional governance system, the community has strategically divided the group ranch into three distinctive land-use zones as dictated by their ecological suitability. Further, it has empowered the committee structures to govern and monitor the use of resources and community affairs within the land-use zones.

Livestock Zone

Taking up most of the ranch's land is the pastoral grazing zone (*Emurrua e-ramatare*), which comprises the more arid grassland plains lying east of the Ewuaso-ngiro River. It is largely open plains and receives less rain but has rich pasture that grows and deplete fast. The zone is the wet season grazing area for the community. Livestock only migrate away from the zone when pastures are depleted there, or when access to Ewuaso-ngiro waters becomes too far for livestock. The community has set up a local grazing committee to oversee the use of pasture and movement of livestock to and from the zone. No livestock are allowed to migrate from the zone into the dry season pastures (conservation zone) west of the Ewuaso-ngiro River before the committee convenes a public meeting to make a collective decision to authorise a migration. Monitoring of pasture use in the zone is, therefore, the collective duty of all community members but the committee spearheads the undertaking of this obligation, including ensuring that appropriate penalties are imposed on offenders. While land within the zone is communally owned and pasture use negotiated, individual families can also appropriate portions of land within for personal livestock needs, such as for young, sick or weak animals. The community also refers to the zone as the 'permanent' area since it is the preferred settlement area where permanent settlements are located.

Agricultural Zone

The second land-use zone is the cultivation area (*Il-chambai*), where uninterrupted irrigation cropping is made possible by permanent river waters, warm temperatures and rich alluvial soils deposited down from the Nguruman escarpment. It is located in the northwest section of the ranch and is crucial for its food security. In the dry season, herders commonly drive in their livestock to graze on crop stubbles and riverine pastures, also making the zone an important dry season pasture resource. A significant portion of Olkiramatian's population, including those with settlements in the pastoral zone, have land portions in this zone, where the community has informally allocated land pieces for cultivation to most registered members. A 'demarcation committee' manages land allocation issues and related disputes.

Most Maasai families with land holdings in the zone cultivate the land them-selves, but a significant number hire migrant labour to work the land for them. In contrast to land individuation elsewhere, the community in Olkiramatian has refrained from formalising the land sub-division in the zone to individual landholders. Lack-ing formal land title deeds, landowners can therefore only use land for production but cannot individually engage in the rampant land selling as witnessed elsewhere in formally individuated land holdings in Maasailand. In recent years, demand for fruits and horticultural crops in urban and international markets has provided a useful source of income to Olkiramatian's farmers, expanding opportunities for livelihood diversification but also encouraging an influx of immigrants into the zone. A number of local 'irrigation committees' oversee and make decisions regarding water distribution

Stephen S. Moiko

Figure 4. An irrigation farm in Olkiramatian.

to individual farms, the maintenance of irrigation canals and the punishment of those infringing water distribution rules.

Conservation Zone

Lying in the southwest end of the ranch, west of the Ewuaso-ngiro River, the conservation zone (*ol-ale loo nguessi*)[1] is the traditional dry season pasture area for livestock herders. It is woody with dense vegetation and harbours large herds of buffalo, giraffe and elephant. Due to its bountiful wildlife, acacia woodlands and tall grass, it is designated for wildlife conservation and tourism activities but also as a dry season grazing bank for livestock. No permanent human settlement is allowed in this zone but 'temporary' cattle camp settlements are set up annually during the dry season. While the seasonal use of the area for grazing is a long established tradition, conservation practices have only been adopted recently with the encouragement and support of external conservation agencies and enterprising local leaders and individuals. With donor funding, the community has set up a tourism facility in the zone, the Sampu Lodge, which it is struggling to develop and make profitable.

---

1.   Literal meaning: 'The wildlife enclosure'.

The conservation zone is under the stewardship of the community's 'conservation committee', which is responsible for the development of the lodge, for collection of tourism revenue and for working closely with the Kenya Wildlife Service (KWS) in wildlife conservation. Pasture use or human occupation in the zone is, however, controlled by the powerful herding committee, which determines, at the onset of a dry season, the date from which herders can start to cross the boundary-marking Ewuaso-ngiro River into the conservation zone and, at the onset of rains, the dates by which livestock and people must vacate the temporary homesteads and return to the pastoral and permanent settlement zone east of the River. Herding rules, since they are collectively made, are typically uncontested and monitoring to prevent shirking is also a collective responsibility. In cases of non-compliance, gatherings called by the relevant committee deliberate on transgressions and mete out warnings and fines. The setting aside of a huge chunk of land for conservation purposes definitely has enormous opportunity costs for the community. The strategy is, however, made with livelihood diversification in mind. It is also an attempt to emulate other communities in the region that have pursued conservation ventures with considerable success. The Maasai herders seem to tolerate the wildlife well, so long as they can access the area for dry season pasture.

DISCUSSION

In the absence of effective policy structures for managing communal resources and facing pressure from proponents of models of land privatisation and state control, pastoral communities in Sub-Saharan Africa, such as Olkiramatian, are in a dilemma. They crave the security of tenure that private land titles create yet they are aware of the flexibility and resilience which communal socio-ecological environments provide in the pursuance of secure pastoral livelihoods, especially against the increasingly unpredictable droughts and weather vagaries associated with global climate change. The Olkiramatian community responded to this dilemma by devising local institutions, organised on the basis of Maasai cultural institutions and incorporating elements of formal group ranch laws, to manage land and natural resources in their communal land holding. These local institutional structures, in the form of local organisational committees, have enabled the community to create its own localised rules to outline acceptable land-use practices, control access to resources, mete out sanctions to non-conformers and define rules of inclusion and exclusion, all of which are hallmarks of a functional self-governing common property system (Bromley and Feeny 1992; Bromley and Cernea 1989; Dolsak and Ostrom 2003). Useful in this process of collective self-governance, for Olkiramatian Group Ranch, have been a combination of enabling factors that include a varied rangelands ecosystem (that exclusively demands complementary use of pockets of resources), a permanent river system (which makes alternative year-round irrigation possible) and a relatively homogenous community involved in customary livestock husbandry. The community adopted the group ranch system at inception but soon informally modified its structure to create a localised resource management system that has since enabled it to manage its land and natural resources in accordance with local ecological and cultural demands.

While land ownership is communal at the collective group ranch level, the community has informally demarcated a section of its land, the cultivation and irrigation zone, into individual units but has, up to now, reserved to the collective Olkiramatian community the right to authorise any land sales and transfers. Individuals can therefore utilise land within the zone for personal production but cannot engage in land selling without the authorisation of the broader community. In the livestock rearing and conservation land use zones, land use and access are dynamically monitored and regulated to coordinate livestock and wildlife movements and to ensure year-round availability of pasture for the majority pastoral residents. The localised system of land management in Olkiramatian, which is only partly supported by formal laws, is, moreover, facilitating the pastoral community to pursue livestock rearing while diversifying into other viable economic opportunities. The collective management of land, wildlife and pasture enables strategic use of land for cultivation, trade, pastoralism and tourism and has made possible improved food and livelihood security for the community.

CONCLUSION

Several decades ago, Robert Netting observed that when well-endowed peasants with substantial sovereignty to devise their own regulations inhabited and utilised land in two environmental zones, they developed two distinct forms of property rights systems (Netting 1972, 1976). This observation, I argue, was relevant then and is still valid now. Netting's observation underscores the importance of devising property rights systems that are congruent to local ecological systems and recognising that indigenous land users who have sustainably exploited land for long periods of time have useful lessons to offer in the development of policies for sustainable natural resource management and livelihoods in rural settings. As demonstrated by the case of disintegrating Maasai group ranches in Kenya, rather than being the norm, communal pastoral property regimes functioning through collective institutions are increasingly under threat in Sub-Saharan Africa. The trend is occurring at a time when privatisation and state models of land tenure and resource governance have been shown to be not always suitable for all environmental and land-use conditions (Bruce and Migot-Adholla 1994). Moreover, the present adverse circumstances of global climate change and high demand for natural resources by an exponentially growing population, demand innovative land tenure strategies to guarantee equity and efficiency in accessing and utilising land and production resources. Rather than seeking to abolish and transform customary tenure systems, development policies and tenure reforms should aspire to build upon the positive aspects of functional local systems to create secure and equitable systems that work in tandem with local ecologies and customary livelihoods systems.

Finally, radical transformations in customary tenure, such as the case of the Maasai group ranches, are fundamentally altering the context of common resource use in the developing world (Toulmin *et al.* 2004). Institutionally regulated patterns of resource use in stable, communal, relatively homogenous social units are even becoming rare. Conversely, highly differentiated socio-economic contexts, in which 'the commons' are used by the rural poor as a last defence against poverty, and by the economic elite to advance processes of capital accumulation, have become increasingly evident. Notwithstanding ongoing tenure changes, Maasai herders are simultaneously resisting, innovating and adapting to the new conditions of land and resource scarcity (Kimani and Pickard 1998). Although they remain resilient in sustaining pastoral livelihoods, they are also dynamically engaging with new socio-economic imperatives through diversification into trade, formal employment, community tourism and formal education. Paradoxically, to address challenges posed to their livelihood by landlessness, Maasai small landowners are falling back on proven communal strategies of land use and pool their land holdings together through kinship or neighbourhood networks (Galaty 1980). They are also adapting new technologies, such as trucks and cell phones, and expanded social networks, formed though trade and school networks, to migrate further with their livestock during seasons of drought and mitigate increasingly erratic rainfall patterns.

Not surprisingly, and having observed the risks associated with land individuation, the few still intact Maasai group ranches, such as Olkiramatian, are even more cautious of tenure changes that seek to individuate their commons. Rather than seeking to subdivide their land to create individual property rights, as expected by proponents of liberal economic ideologies, the herders are relying on institutions 'that resemble neither the market nor state models' (Agrawal 2003), to pursue their livelihoods under common property resource systems. A policy framework and tenure system that allows sustainable land use systems to function in the context of a peoples' socio-cultural system, such as the localised institutional system in Olkiramatian, I argue, would go a long way in sustaining secure livelihoods, promoting local economic growth and reducing poverty and landlessness in rural sub-Saharan Africa. The process of land individuation in semi-arid rangelands, it has become evident, has high environmental and socio-economic costs and has failed to provide the incentives it promises for improvements in investment in land and national economic growth.

BIBLIOGRAPHY

Agrawal, A. 2003. 'Sustainable Governance of Common-pool Resources: Context, Methods, and Politics', *Annual Review of Anthropology* **32**: 243–62.

Amanor, K. and S. Moyo (eds.) 2008. *Land and Sustainable Development in Africa*. London: Zed.

Barlowe, R. 1953. 'Land Reform and Economic Development'. *Journal of Farm Economics* **35**, 2: 173–187.

Behnke, R.H., Scoones, I., and Kerven, C. 1993. *Range Ecology at Disequilibrium: New Models of Natural Variability and Pastoral Adaptation in African Savannas*. London: Overseas Development Institute.

Berry, S. 1993. *No Condition is Permanent: the Social Dynamics of Agrarian Change in sub-Saharan Africa*. Madison, Wis.: University of Wisconsin Press.

Besteman, C. 1994. 'Individualisation and the Assault on Customary Tenure in Africa: Title Registration Programmes and the Case of Somalia'. *Africa* **64**, 4: 484–515.

Bromley, D.W. 1989. 'Property Relations and Economic Development: The Other Land Reform', *World Development* **17**, 6: 867–77.

Bromley, D.W. and Cernea, M.M. 1989. *The Management of Common Property Natural Resources: Some Conceptual and Operational Fallacies*. Washington, D.C.: World Bank.

Bromley, D.W. and Feeny, D. 1992. *Making the Commons Work: Theory, Practice, and Policy*. San Francisco: ICS Press.

Bruce, J.W. 1988. 'A perspective on Indigenous Land Tenure Systems and Land Concentration', in R.E. Downs and S.P. Reyna (eds.) *Land and Society in Contemporary Africa* (p. xiii, 383 p.) Hanover: Published for University of New Hampshire by University Press of New England.

Bruce, J.W. and S.E. Migot-Adholla. 1994. *Searching for Land Tenure Security in Africa*. Dubuque, Iowa: Kendall/Hunt.

De Soto, H. 2000. *The Mystery of Capital: Why Capitalism Triumphs in the West and Fails Everywhere Else*. New York: Basic Books.

Dolsak, N., and Ostrom, E. 2003. *The Commons in the New Millennium: Challenges and Adaptation*. Cambridge, Mass.: MIT Press.

Dorner, P. 1972. *Land Reform and Economic Development*. Harmondsworth: Penguin Books.

Fratkin, E. M. and E.A. Roth. 2005. *As Pastoralists Settle : social, health, and economic consequences of the pastoral sedentarization in Marsabit District, Kenya*. Studies in human ecology and adaptation. New York : Kluwer Academic Publishers.

Galaty, J.G. 1980. 'The Maasai Group Ranch: Politics and Development in an African Pastoral Society', in P.C. Salzman and E. Sadala (eds.) *When Nomads Settle : processes of sedentarization as adaptation and response* (pp. 157–172). New York: Praeger.

Galaty, J.G. 1994a. 'Ha(l)ving Land in Common: the Subdivision of Maasai Group Ranches in Kenya'. *Nomadic Peoples* **34-35**: 109–122.

Galaty, J.G. 1994b. 'Range land Tenure and Pastoralism in Africa', in E. Fratkin, K. Galvin and E.A. Roth (eds.) *African Pastoralist Systems : an integrated approach*. Boulder, Colo.: L. Rienner Publishers.

Galvin, K. 2008. *Fragmentation in Semi-arid and Arid Landscapes : consequences for human and natural landscapes*. Dordrecht, the Netherlands: Springer.

Hardin, G. 1968. 'The Tragedy of the Commons'. *Science* **162**: 1243–1248.

Hogg, R. 1980. 'Pastoralism and Impoverishment – the Case of the Isiolo Boran of Northern Kenya'. *Disasters* **4**, 3: 299–310.

Kimani, K. and J. Pickard 1998. 'Recent Trends and Implications of Group Ranch Sub-Division and Fragmentation in Kajiado District, Kenya'. *The Geographical Journal* **164**, 2: 202–213.

Pastoralists at Crossroads

Kituyi, M. 1990. *Becoming Kenyans : socio-economic transformation of the pastoral Maasai*. Drylands research series. Nairobi, Kenya: Acts Press.

Lane, C.R. 1998. *Custodians of the Commons: Pastoral Land Tenure in East and West Africa*. London: Earthscan.

Lesorogol, C.K. 2005. 'Privatizing pastoral lands: economic and normative outcomes in Kenya'. *World Development* **33**, 11: 1959–1978. doi:10.1016/j.worlddev.2005.05.008

Lesorogol, C.K. 2008. *Contesting the Commons: Privatizing Pastoral Lands in Kenya*. Ann Arbor: University of Michigan Press.

Migot-Adholla, Shem E., P. Hazell, B. Blarel and F. Place 1991. 'Indigenous Land Rights Systems in Sub-Saharan Africa: A Constraint on Productivity?' *The World Bank Economic Review* **5**, 1: 155–175.

Munei, K.O. 1991. *Study on Sub-division of Group Ranches in Kajiado District*. Nairobi: Livestock Production, Department Kajiado District.

Mwangi, E. 2005. 'The Transformation of Property Rights in Kenya's Maasailand: Triggers and Motivations'. CAPRi Working Paper No. 35.

Mwangi, E. 2007. *Socioeconomic Change and Land Use in Africa*. Palgrave Macmillan.

Mwangi, E. and E. Ostrom 2009. 'Top-Down Solutions: Looking Up from East Africa's Rangelands'. *Environment* **51**, 1: 34–45.

Ndeng'e, G., CBS, C. Opiyo, J. Mistiaen and P. Kristjanson. 2003. *Geographic dimensions of well-being in Kenya where are the poor?* [Nairobi]: Central Bureau of Statistics Ministry of Planning and National Development.

Netting, R.M. 1972. 'Of Men and Meadows: Strategies of Alpine Land Use'. *Anthropological Quarterly* **45**, 3: 132–144. doi:10.2307/3316527

Netting, R.M. 1976. 'What Alpine Peasants Have in Common: Observations on Communal Tenure in a Swiss Village'. *Human Ecology* **4**, 2: 135–146.

Okoth-Ogendo, H.W.O. 1976. African Land Tenure Reform. *Agricultural Development in Kenya ? An Economic Assessment* (p. 371). Nairobi ?: Oxford University Press.

Ostrom, E. 1990. *Governing the Commons: the Evolution of Institutions for Collective Action*. Cambridge / New York: Cambridge University Press.

Rutten, M.M.E.M. 1992. *Selling Wealth to Buy Poverty : the process of the individualization of landownership among the Maasai pastoralists of Kajiado District, Kenya, 1890–1990*. Saarbrücken and Fort Lauderdale: Verlag breitenbach Publishers.

Sandford, S. 1980. 'Pastoral Production and Society – Proceedings of the International Meeting on Nomadic Pastoralism, Paris 1–3 December 1976 – Equipe-Ecologie-Et-Anthropologie-Des-Societes-Pastorales'. *Third World Quarterly* **2**, 3: 580–581.

Sandford, S. 1981. *Review of World Bank Livestock Activities in Dry Tropical Africa*. Washington D.C.: World Bank, Agriculture and Rural Development Department.

Sandford, S. 1983. *Management of Pastoral Development in the Third World*. Chichester: Wiley.

Scoones, I. 1994. *Living with Uncertainty: New Directions in Pastoral Development in Africa*. London: Intermediate Technology Publications.

Seno, S.K. and W.W. Shaw. 2002. 'Land tenure policies, Maasai traditions, and wildlife conservation in Kenya'. *Society & Natural Resources*, **15**, 1: 79–88.

Smith, R.E. 2003. 'Land tenure reform in Africa: a shift to the defensive'. *Progress in Development Studies* **3**, 3: 210.

Swallow, B.M. 1995. 'Mobile Flows, Storage, and Self-Organized Institutions for Governing Common-Pool Resources: Comment', *Land Economics* **71**, 4: 537–8.

Swallow, B.M. and D.W. Bromley. 1995. 'Institutions, governance and incentives in common property regimes for African rangelands'. *Environmental and Resource Economics* **6**, 2: 99–118.

Talle, A. 1988. *Women at a Loss : changes in Maasai pastoralism and their effects on gender relations.* Stockholm Studies in Social Anthropology, 19. Stockholm: Dept. of Social Anthropology, University of Stockholm.

Toulmin, C. and Quan, J. (eds.) 2000. *Evolving Land Rights, Policy, and Tenure in Africa.* London: DFID / IIED / Natural Resources Institute.

Toulmin, C., Quan, J. and Fei Tan, S. 2004. *Land in Africa: Market Asset or Secure Livelihood.* London: IIED / Natural Resources Institute.

~ 5 ~

BOOKING AND GRABBING LAND: STRATEGIES OF APPROPRIATION IN LOITA MAASAILAND, KENYA

Angela Kronenburg García

Wageningen University

INTRODUCTION[1]

In September 2008 I visited the site where a Loita Maasai family had recently started constructing a new homestead.[2] As we walked towards the new homestead I noticed lines of cut branches laid down all over the landscape that had not been there two weeks before. These lines had been placed by neighbours who were 'booking' a piece of land for a homestead and functioned as the boundaries of the patch they claimed. It had all started a week before when two family heads, including the family I visited, who previously shared larger homesteads with other families, started demarcating a piece of land for the construction of their own individual homesteads at quite a distance from the cluster of homesteads of the area. Others in the area, seeing the favourable locations they had picked and fearing they would remain behind, panicked, and in a matter of days about fifteen individuals rushed to 'book' their own chunks of land as well. This rush to stake out land was not particular to this area but had become a widespread phenomenon during my field research. This paper explores the strategies of appropriation employed by Loita Maasai families during this land rush and places them in their socio-historical context.

1. This paper is based on fieldwork carried out in Loita Maasailand, Kenya for a period of 18 months in 2007 and 2008 in the context of my Ph.D. research at the Wageningen University in the Netherlands. Funding was provided by the Dutch Organisation for Scientific Research (NWO–MaGW) and the Prins Bernhard Cultuurfonds. I am very grateful to my supervisors, Han van Dijk and Sabine Luning for their helpful comments, as well as to Scott Matter, Maarten Onneweer and Jos Kronenburg and to the participants of the IUAES congress in Kunming, China where I presented a first draft of this paper. Special thanks go to the Loita Maasai for their confidence and hospitality throughout fieldwork.

2. 'Loita' refers both to the Loita Maasai people, one of the sections of the larger Maasai community, and the territory they inhabit. The Loita Maasai live on both sides of the Kenya–Tanzania border, in the highlands west of the Rift Valley. In Kenya, Loita is located in Narok District.

Loita is one of the remaining Maasai areas of Kenya where land has not been formally demarcated and registered into either group or individual holdings. However, the need to secure land for livelihood activities and a general belief in the inevitability of formal land demarcation slowly led people to start demarcation in their own way over the past decade. During my field research, this culminated into a rush to 'book' and 'grab' as much land as possible. This paper explains the current strategies of appropriation that typify this land rush and describes the translocal and local processes of change that shaped them. I address what Sikor and Lund call the 'grey zone' between access and property: 'between what people have rights to and what they merely have access to' (2009, 2). This paper will show how Loita endeavour to secure their gained access to land as recognised individual property by inscribing their claims onto the landscape in anticipation of imminent formal land demarcation.

THE GREY ZONE BETWEEN ACCESS AND PROPERTY

Ribot and Peluso (2003) developed a theory of access to natural resources (also see Ribot 1998; Peluso 1992; and Berry 1989). They define access as 'the ability to benefit from things' (153, 155), the 'thing' discussed in this paper being land in Loita. They differentiate between 'access control', 'access maintenance' and 'gaining access'. Gaining access refers to 'the more general process by which access is established' (159). Access control and access maintenance go together, because access maintenance involves efforts like expending resources or investing in a social relationship 'to keep a particular sort of resource access open' (159) that is controlled by another actor – be it an individual, a group of people or an institution. Access control, then, is defined as 'the ability to mediate others' access' (158). This paper describes how Loita families gain access to land for settlement and for cultivation that previously had been used in common for seasonally grazing cattle. Gaining access to land involves strategies of appropriation that aim to exclude others from using the land. In other words, people also attempt to control access. Strategies of appropriation in Loita are thus employed both in the process of gaining and controlling access to land.

In Loita, appropriative strategies convey claims of individual property over the accessed land, advancing the family head as owner of the land. I follow Sikor and Lund's (2009) understanding of property as 'legitimatized claims, in the sense that the state or some other form of politico-legal authority sanctions them' (4). The difference between property and access is that while property requires legal or social legitimisation, access does not, because access refers to *all* ways by which people can benefit from resources, including legal ways (such as property) and illegal ways such as through theft or by using violence. Access thus encompasses property (Ribot 1998, 310–12, 335–6; Ribot and Peluso 2003, 155–161) or at least they overlap partially (Sikor and Lund 2009, 4–6). This paper addresses this overlap, or, as Sikor and Lund (2009, 1) call it, the 'grey zone' of access and property. In post-colonial and post-socialist countries this 'grey zone' is characterised by a 'central dynamic ... created by people's attempts to secure rights to natural resources by having their access claims recognized as legitimate property by a politico-legal institution' (1). This paper discusses the strategies of appropriation that Loita employ when seeking to turn their gained access to land into recognised individual property.

The process of appropriation in Loita takes the form of what I call 'grounding claims', because it involves inscribing the land with visible markers that are socially understandable in Loita. Grounded claims can be used as justifications when property claims to particular pieces of land are challenged or when formal demarcation takes off. As long as the grounded claims by a particular family over a piece of land go unquestioned by others, they may be seen as socially legitimised claims. When grounded claims are challenged, for example by a neighbour, the issue is normally laid before a land dispute meeting to be mediated and resolved by the elders. The resolution reached by the mediating elders, who in this case function as the politico-legal authorities enacting Loita Maasai law, will either grant or reject, or adjust, a particular claim to land, thereby sanctioning landed property in Loita. It is generally believed in Loita that if one's property claims to land are socially accepted or have been legally acknowledged by the elders, one's chances of having those claims recognised by state law when formal land demarcation starts will be greater. Strategies of appropriation may continue even after a counterclaim has been dismissed by the elders; to strengthen the claim in preparation for formal demarcation or to enlarge the land base even more. This paper describes a period in Loita when strategies of appropriation were in full swing and individual property in land was not (yet) formalised legally according to state law. It was only a year after I completed my field research that the first boundaries were being drawn to start the process of formal land demarcation in Loita.

'THE LAND IS BECOMING SMALLER'

The rush for land was repeatedly explained to me by Loita Maasai as a response to the 'fullness' of the land: the land has become full, I was told, because people have become many, settling at places that before were used exclusively for grazing cattle, which in turn is making the land to become 'smaller' for cows to graze. In fact, the increase of the Loita population is perceived as having far-reaching consequences for the viability of pastoralism in the long run.[3] Because of population growth and subsequent dispersal of settlements there is not enough pastureland left for the cattle to graze, which is why 'even in the rainy season they remain thin, and die in the dry season', as one elder explained. This general sense, that 'cows are finishing' (i.e. pastoralism) due to population increase, is what led many and is leading still more to pay serious attention to the 'work of fields' (cultivation).[4] Indeed, decreasing land availability seems to

---

3. Population in Loita grew from an estimated 6,500 in 1969 (Kronenburg 1986, 16) to 10,303 20 years later (Legilisho-Kiyiapi 1999, 7). According to the 2009 Kenya census there are 22,873 inhabitants in Loita Division.

4. Maundu *et al.* (2001, 26) also ascribe agricultural expansion in Loita to population growth.

be a central dynamic influencing the way people engage with land. I will first discuss translocal factors that affect or threaten land availability in Loita. Then I will examine the local processes of change that developed in mutual interaction with a diminishing land base. This historical review of translocal and local processes provides the context for understanding current strategies for booking and grabbing land. It roughly covers the last 50 years.

Purko Maasai Encroachment, the Naimina Enkiyio Forest Conflicts and the Legal Battle over Kamorora Group Ranch

Loita territory is shrinking literally.[5] The Loita Maasai have lost large tracts of land to encroaching Purko Maasai ever since the Purko arrived in the area during the Maasai Moves, when they were displaced from their land for white settlers in the colonial period (Hughes 2006, 106; Waller 1990, 95). Larger in numbers and well represented in district politics, they took over the vast Loita Plains, confining the Loita further south to the Loita Hills. This encroachment continues up to date and leads to incidental violent clashes between warriors of both groups. More recently, Purko have successfully settled the northern tip of Loita territory next to the Naimina Enkiyio forest in the Loita Hills. The loss of land to Purko Maasai restricts Loita pastoral mobility in Kenya, forcing them to expand southwards into Tanzania, clashing with other Maasai and non-Maasai communities there.

Another form of loss of access to land happened on the Nguruman escarpment beyond the Naimina Enkiyio forest. Kamorora, as the area is called, is inappropriate for settlement because of the presence of the tsetse fly that affects the cattle herds, but was shared by Loita and Loodokilani Maasai for grazing in times of drought. In the 1970s a group of Maasai, most of them Loita, applied for the formation of a group ranch during the land demarcation programme (see below) and became the owners of the Kamorora Group Ranch. They subsequently leased the area to a number of individuals. The last of these lessees, a man of European origin who has been there for the last three decades, now claims ownership of the land. The group ranch members dispute this, and they are currently embroiled in a bitter legal case to win back the land.[6]

Fears of further land loss also developed with a growing outside interest in the Naimina Enkiyio forest in the east of Loitaland, a critical resource for Loita livelihood and ceremonial life (see Kronenburg García 2003). As early as the 1970s the forest had already been identified as a potential site for the development of tourism. But it was not until the local authority, the Narok County Council, announced its plans for turning the forest into a Nature Reserve for tourism purposes in the early 1990s that

---

5.   The government administrative Loita Division, formerly coinciding with Loita territory, is estimated to be 1718 km2 (Legilisho-Kiyiapi 1999, 4), but in 1998 only 900 km2 was occupied by Loita Maasai (Voshaar 1998, 102).

6.   The history of this case and the way it is currently unfolding will be discussed in my Ph.D. dissertation.

such an interest took a concrete form. A decade later, the World Conservation Union (IUCN) initiated a community-based management project for the protection of the forest's biodiversity. Both initiatives failed after the emergence of complex conflicts that articulated with political struggles for power at local, district, and national level.[7] Underlying conflict and failure was local resistance fed by a fear (whether real or imagined, politically instigated or not) of losing access to the forest.

The encroachment of Purko Maasai, the experience with the Naimina Enkiyio forest and the Kamorora Group Ranch feed a desire for formal land demarcation as a way to stop further land loss and secure tenure of Loita territory for the Loita Maasai. When in the late 1960s the Kenyan government implemented a land demarcation and registration programme that aimed to provide security of tenure in Maasailand by turning communally held areas into group ranches with legal title (Mwangi 2007a and 2007b; Kimani and Pickard 1998; Galaty 1992 and 1994; Rutten 1992), the Loita Maasai submitted a proposal to convert Loita into a single group ranch (Kronenburg 1986, 51). This proposal was rejected by government officials, because the group ranch was considered too large and unviable. Subsequent attempts to turn Loita into two or three group ranches also failed, this time due to unresolved disputes of where the boundaries would pass, both internally and between the Loita and the Purko (see also Kronenburg 1986, 51, 52; Voshaar 1998, 112). Loita interviewees blame the Purko for continuously and deliberately boycotting the demarcation of the Loita–Purko boundary because this would put a stop to their encroachment on Loitaland. Thus, despite a willingness to formally demarcate Loita on the side of the Loita Maasai, formal land demarcation failed due to unresolved boundary disputes, a point also made by Kronenburg (1986, 50–52) and Voshaar (1998, 106).[8] Despite the fact that the creation of group ranches resulted in debatable land tenure security in Kamorora and elsewhere in Maasailand and this exercise was eventually abandoned,[9] Loita eagerness for formal land demarcation

---

7.　A discussion of these conflicts is beyond the scope of this paper, but they are addressed in depth in my forthcoming Ph.D. dissertation. See Ngece *et al.* 2007; Zaal and ole Siloma 2006; ole Siloma and Zaal 2005; Karanja *et al.* 2002; Kantai 2001; Peron 2000; LNECTC 1994 for descriptions of the Narok County Council conflict. For references to this conflict, see Maundu *et al.* 2001, 25–6; Shelley and Lempaka 1999, 14, 15. See for references to the IUCN conflict: Ngece *et al.* 2007, 179 and ole Siloma and Zaal 2006, 11.

8.　Other authors interpret the failure of formal land demarcation as resistance to government intervention, see Ngece *et al.* 2007, 178; Karanja *et al.* 2002, 4, 19, 21; Kantai 2001, 41; Peron 2000, 386; LNECTC 1994, 2. During interviews this is also sometimes the first response.

9.　There is a general consensus in the literature that the privatisation of land into group ranches and the individualisation through subdivision that ensued has been to the detriment of the majority of the Maasai and favoured instead a few, Maasai and non-Maasai alike, who acquired vast tracts of prime land through land grabbing (both prior and during subdivision) and through the purchase of fragmented plots, mostly by migrant non-Maasai cultivators. This left many former group ranch members with either individual ranches in the marginal areas, with unviable small land units or without land at all.

as the best available option to stop further land loss was clearly apparent during my field research and was often discussed during Loita leaders' meetings.[10]

The general expectation, especially of the better-informed Loita, is that Loitaland will be first divided into five areas that correspond to the current government administrative locations. The land of a location will then be subdivided, allocating all eligible male residents of that area an individual plot. This expectation takes its precedent from the experience of the government-led land demarcation programme described above, with the areas in Loita mirroring the group ranches that were later subdivided to its registered members who were largely men. This expectation is important because it will explain why some of the Maasai families have deliberately 'booked' and 'grabbed' land in different locations. This is because individualisation of land will take the eligible male residents of a location as a point of departure and not the eligible male residents of the whole Loita area. Thus, if one has acknowledged claims in different areas/locations one can double or triple the total land allocated during formal land demarcation.

Anticipation of formal land demarcation seems, of late, to be an important motive for booking and grabbing land in Loita. This process, however, also springs from different concerns that stem from different sources. In the next sections, I turn to local history to describe the changing ways of using the land that gave rise to these concerns. I will start by a description of pastoral strategies of land use to give a glimpse of how Loita Maasai livelihood looked around 40 years ago, before cultivation was adopted in Loita. The new ways of using land will help explain why the Loita are claiming individual property in land from a situation where land was previously held in common.

Land and Pastoral Use

Loita distinguish three landscapes that are significant for their pastoral strategies: *olpurkel*, *osupuko* and *olaiparak*. From west to east, ascending in elevation towards the Naimina Enkiyio forest, one finds first *olpurkel*, the lowland, characterised by its rolling plains of abundant grass. *Olpurkel* is the land that 'likes' goats and sheep in particular, because the grass that grows there, typical for open spaces, although short, forms a thickly interwoven mass on which small-stock grow very big. The openness of *olpurkel* further prevents the goats and sheep from getting lost in the bush or being taken by thieves or leopards, and *olpurkel* is considered to be disease-free for small-stock. When water is available, *olpurkel* also provides good pastures for the cattle because it offers plenty of open space to graze. In short, provided there is water, at *olpurkel* the herds become healthy and multiply.

Olpurkel gradually gives place to *osupuko*, the highland. The trees grow taller and more frequent, inverting the balance of grassland and bush found in *olpurkel*. *Osupuko* culminates with the Naimina Enkiyio forest in the east after which the landscape drops

---

10. In the beginning of 2010, after my field research, Loita leaders actively approached reluctant government officials to initiate formal land demarcation in Loita. They went so far as to organise a Loita-wide obligatory monetary contribution to pay the government boundary surveyor to do his job.

sharply along the Nguruman escarpment into the Rift Valley floor at the height of Lake Magadi. The third landscape distinguished in Loita is called *olaiparak*. *Olaiparak* is the area between lowland and highland, where it is not clearly *olpurkel* or *osupuko*. It adds more nuance and detail to the Loita landscape than the *olpurkel–osupuko* duality most commonly mentioned in the literature (see for instance Lamprey and Waller 1990, 23). The difference between *olaiparak* and *osupuko* lies in the height of the vegetation: *osupuko* has a 'long forest' (*entim seur*), i.e. with many tall trees while *olaiparak*, also forested, has short trees or bush land (*osero*). The difference between *olaiparak* and *olpurkel*, on the other hand, lies in the availability of water. Until recently, most parts of *olpurkel* did not have permanent water sources. Seasonal rivers filled with the rains of the wet season would progressively dry up as the dry season advanced. *Olaiparak* on the other hand stretches along the main permanent river of Loita whose tributaries originate in the forest and join to form a river that flows roughly in a north–south direction and almost parallel to the forest edge until it enters the forest again in the southern tip and drains into Lake Natron in Tanzania. Along the river are various saltlick areas used by both livestock and wildlife.

About 30 to 40 years ago Loita Maasai settlements were exclusively located in the *olaiparak* area where people and animals had ready and year-round access to water. Located between *osupuko* and *olpurkel*, it offered the best of both landscapes for cattle rearing; it did not lack in water as *olpurkel* did during the dry season and unlike *osupuko* it offered enough open pastures where the cattle could feed on the nutritious grass. Moreover, the numerous saltlicks along the river ensured that the animals got their necessary mineral intake. Large homesteads of several families were built on the natural open spaces on both sides of the river. The few plains located in *osupuko* that profited from the first rains coming from the forest were the places where people would take their herds at the beginning of the wet season during the short rains (November–December) to take advantage of the new grass that grew after controlled burns. Eventually, the rains would proceed to *olpurkel*, which was then used as wet season grazing during the long rains (March–May). The herds would follow the showers at *olpurkel* to profit from the fresh shoots of grass as far as the Loita Plains, an area that is now inaccessible to the Loita because Purko Maasai have settled there.[11] Grazing at *olpurkel* was only possible until the water dried up, after which the herds would be moved to *olaiparak* until the next rainy season when they would be taken again to the highland plains. A movement back and forth to *olpurkel* and *osupuko* from a base at *olaiparak* typified Loita Maasai pastoral use of the land. Today, however, as a result of mounting pressure on the land resources due to growing numbers of people and fields, the forest area of *osupuko* has become an important additional pastoral resource. During prolonged dry seasons and droughts, like the 1993, 2000–2001 and 2005–2006 droughts, when grazing is exhausted elsewhere the herds are driven inside the forest

---

11.   The Loita Plains were a highly valued *olpurkel* area because of the saltlick there, something lacking in the other *olpurkel* areas.

to exploit the numerous streams and springs and the open patches of grassland found here and there and along the swamp area (see Zaal and ole Siloma 2006, 4; Kantai 2001, 42; Peron 2000, 387; LNECTC 1994, 3, 5). In cases of severe drought, like that of 2000–2001, the leaves of the trees are used to feed the animals as a last resort.

This seasonal use of the pastoral resources of the Loita landscape and the movement it implies is called transhumance and used to apply to the bulk of the herds and the people who herd them. Today, though increasingly constrained, people still strive to practice this form of transhumance, as will be discussed later. The settlements in *olaiparak* were permanent in that most people remained behind, usually women, old people, and small children, with enough milking cows for domestic use. Those who left in search of water and good grass for the cattle, usually warriors and older boys, set up temporary cattle camps (*ronjo*) that could be shared by several herds. The herd and the herders would stay at the cattle camp for as long as it was necessary and possible; in *olpurkel* until water got finished and in *osupuko* until it rained again at *olaiparak* or beyond. Today in Loita, only two areas are still used for temporary grazing because these are the last areas that remain uninhabited. Typically located at the edge of Loitaland both of these are also contested areas. Oldoinyo Sampu (in Tanzania) is claimed by Loita Maasai and Sonjo (an enclave of Bantu-speaking irrigation agriculturalists on the Nguruman escarpment), and saw the arrival of Kisongo Maasai in 2008 after their relocation by the Tanzanian government from the Ngorongoro area. Kisinande, also on the Nguruman escarpment but across the Naimina Enkiyio forest, claimed by Loita Maasai to be theirs, is slowly being appropriated by the neighbouring Kamorora estate. During the prolonged dry season of 2008–2009 both areas were used for temporary grazing by Loita but their continued use in future remains uncertain.

Economic Diversification and Changing Settlement Patterns

The Introduction of Goats and Sheep

The immediate trigger for the introduction of goats and sheep to Loita seems to have been a disease outbreak that 'finished cows' in the late 1960s called *lipis*.[12] The outbreak was particularly harmful because it not only killed animals but also appeared to have affected the fertility of the surviving stock. With no medication available, it took exceptionally long to recover and build up the herds again. The fact that cows could not calve is important, because this meant that the supply of milk, the Maasai staple food, also diminished. People would usually cope with periodic decreases in milk supplies, like during dry seasons and periods of drought, by selling oxen and using the money to buy ground maize (*posho*) for food at shops ran by non-Maasai traders. Maize could also be obtained through trade with Kipsigis (called Ilumbwa by Maasai). When maize supplies were exhausted, the families who shared a homestead would in

---

12. McCabe (1997, 60) and McCabe *et al.* (1992, 357) recorded a drastic increase of small-stock numbers in the Kisongo Maasai herds and carefully describe this as a response to significant cattle losses due to disease.

turn contribute oxen for slaughter to feed the people of the homestead with its soup and meat. This was done until the shops or the Kipsigis had supplies of maize again. During and after the disease outbreak the only way of acquiring money to buy maize flour was by selling the skins of the dead animals to Indian traders. Some enterprising Loita elders then also traded skins of cattle for goats and sheep with Kipsigis, and when this business turned out to be a success others soon followed their example. Although individual Loita elders appear to have had flocks of goats and sheep in the plains and beyond Loita territory these were never brought to the Loita heartland and the introduction of goats and sheep at this period appears to have constituted the first step towards the diversification of the economy in Loita. The shift to small-stock in Loita followed an earlier trend in Maasailand that started during and after the droughts of the early 1930s (Lamprey and Waller 1990, 24). Goats and sheep, whose reproduction rate is higher than that of cattle, could now be slaughtered to feed the people especially when supplies of maize flour ran short, sparing the cattle herd, and allowing it to grow again. When another cattle disease (*oltikana*) struck the herds again, the Loita Maasai economy was further diversified. The reason was the same; cultivation was adopted as a means to spare the herds and ensure their recovery.

Cultivation

The cultivation of crops was not unknown in Loita because trading partners like the Kipsigis and neighbouring communities like the Sonjo engaged in agriculture. In the 1950s, settlements associated with the irrigation agriculturalists of the Nguruman escarpment extended into what today comprises Loitaland (see Maundu *et al.* 2001, 26). By that time agriculture was also practised sporadically inside Loita by individual *Ilkokoyo* immigrants who acquired cattle and 'became Maasai'.[13] These agricultural immigrants are different from later Kikuyu immigrants in that they cultivated in the Loita heartland and were accepted as Maasai. The Kikuyu immigrants who arrived during the Emergency (1952–1959),[14] on the contrary, established two colonies on the northern fringes of Loitaland and sought relationships with the Loita through patronage, and most likely also marriage, but maintained their own social identity by clinging to their language and livelihood.[15] When they started to prosper and their numbers grew, and the size of the land they tilled increased, their relationship with the Loita soured. Eventually, they moved away and settled outside Loita.

---

13. I am not sure whether these immigrants really were of Kikuyu origin, because the word *Olkokoyo* (plural *Ilkokoyo*), although clearly derived from the word Kikuyu, is commonly used for any non-Maasai cultivating stranger.

14. The Emergency (1952–1959), when Kikuyu were systematically rounded up and forcibly moved into fenced policed villages by the colonial authorities in a bid to control the Kikuyu Mau Mau rebellion, created streams of Kikuyu refugees all over Kenya (Berman 1990, 347–76).

15. These two different forms of immigration, of the Kikuyu 'acceptee' and the Kikuyu 'alien', follow a familiar pattern of Kikuyu immigration across Maasailand (see Waller 1993).

But long before Kikuyu cultivation took place in Loita, Maasai cultivation occurred in isolated and intermittent cases. One very old lady, originally a Siria Maasai, claimed to have been the first Maasai in Loita to have cultivated the land, something she had learned from the Kipsigis before she settled in Loita. Another case is that of an old man, who used the local development project's tractor in 1972 to plough a piece of land. Eventually, he had to abandon that field because he met fierce opposition from the local community and not the least from his own father; agriculture was seen as a 'dirty' practice that reduced the space for the cows to graze. The perception that using the land for agriculture undermined pastoralism touched a sensitive nerve; some neighbours accused him of wanting to grow wheat and, as some had seen elsewhere, wheat was known to 'take a lot of land'. Taking up cultivation by this development-minded elder was not out of necessity. This necessity was only felt a few years later, by many, and taking up cultivation in this latter instance was expressed to me as a way of 'finishing the drought' because cows alone could no longer sustain the growing numbers of people, especially during dry seasons and droughts.[16]

This became clear after the hard time people had during and after the cattle disease *oltikana* that affected the herds in Loita. *Oltikana* broke out 'when Ilkitoip were warriors' (somewhere between 1973 and 1985) and it is precisely this age-group that commenced to take up cultivation en masse after they graduated from warriorhood and became junior elders (around 1980).[17] These young men who were now allowed to marry had a bad start as upcoming family heads and independent herd owners. During their warriorhood, cattle raiding, the traditional way to build up an economic base in preparation for family life, had become more and more problematic due to government interference. Because of this and the reduced herds as a result of the disease, they found themselves with too few animals to provide for their families' needs, especially those who also had to take care of their mothers and siblings. Cultivating maize (and later beans) secured food for their families during the dry seasons and droughts without need to sell or slaughter the surviving livestock for food and by engaging in livestock trade they could slowly build up the herds again. It was also this young generation of men that increasingly attended the workshops of the new Ilkerin Project (Kronenburg 1986, 21), officially initiated in 1973, who responded to the new interest in agriculture accordingly (also see Maundu *et al.* 2001, 26). It also appears that by that time, the Loita from Tanzania had already turned to agriculture (see McCabe *et al.* 1992, 362)

---

16.   In a survey carried out by ter Schegget and Schoenmakers commissioned by the Ilkerin Project the main motivation behind crop growing was explained as 'to fill the stomach during milk shortage', that is, during dry seasons, by 88 per cent of the interviewed respondents (1988, 52).

17.   A similar experience seems to have happened earlier to the Maasai further south in Tanzania: 'During the early 1960s, an outbreak of east coast fever killed a large number of cattle and many of the poorer Maasai families found themselves depending on the grain they produced. According to O'Malley (2000), enough Maasai had begun cultivating by the early 1960s for this period to constitute the first of three waves of agriculture by Maasai in the Loliondo Division of Ngorongoro District' (McCabe 2003, 104).

and all these factors together influenced the Loita in Kenya to adopt agriculture. Those 'poor' living in north Loita, who were already familiar with crop agriculture because of previous Kikuyu presence there, seem to have been the first to take up cultivation.

Although at first fields were small, they spread all over Loita and by 1988, according to a survey commissioned by the Ilkerin Project, 93 per cent of the respondents' families grew crops (ter Schegget and Schoenmakers 1988, 52). With every subsequent age-group graduating to junior elders and starting their own families, the fields increased in numbers. But with the growth of cultivation developed a tension over how land should be used, a tension between two different and, so it was felt, competitive modes of using land, because occupying land for fields implied a loss of pastureland for cows. This tension was evident in the elders' vigilant monitoring of the sites and the sizes of new fields. When a family head wanted to clear a field, something that coincided more and more with the establishment of a new and smaller-sized homestead (see next section), he first had to announce this in a local meeting. The local elders would then allocate the requester a place for a homestead and mark an area for the field, carefully chosen so that it would not obstruct areas used by people or livestock. In this way, settlement patterns and field clearing were to a certain degree controlled by the elders. However, these restrictions would soon be loosened. If Maasai cultivation spread in Loita due to the effects of the cattle disease *oltikana*, it grew dramatically after the experience of the 2000–2001 drought. According to many, this drought was one of the worst in living memory.

Immediately before the drought, most Loita already had small family fields where they grew maize. However, as the drought advanced, a serious maize shortage developed in Loita by the end of 2000. Wild vegetables and fruits gathered in the forest were the only food many could eat. The drought was all over the region and some areas in Kenya were receiving relief food but Loita only got relief food when it started to rain again, heavily, in March 2001. The rain created another problem: the trucks with the relief food could not enter Loita because they could not cross the sand river that marks the boundary between Loita and Purko. Thus people had to travel from where they lived to receive their ration of maize. This journey could take up to four days. The distributed relief food was not enough. People continued to suffer from food shortage, though things were a bit better because now they could add milk to their diet of wild vegetables and fruits, if milking cows had survived at all. I was told that this period was especially hard because the fields needed to be prepared for the next harvest. When the rains were delayed in 1993, the Loita received plenty of relief food and thus they didn't suffer from hunger as was the case in the 2000–2001 drought. The experience had not been severe enough to force the reluctant majority to embrace agriculture in earnest. However, after the experience of the 2000–2001 drought the attitude of the elders in particular towards tilling the land changed dramatically and cultivation was seen as key to prevent food shortage in future. Restrictions on field making by the elders relaxed significantly.

The importance of cultivation in Loita is evident today in that every married man has a field, sometimes several fields according to the number of wives, and the size of the fields is becoming bigger and bigger. Sometimes even unmarried men clear a field and sell the maize and beans to raise cash for the bridewealth in preparation for marriage. Elders today, the same men that adopted agriculture in the 1980s, deplore that the young generation are more interested in having their own separate homestead with their own field than in keeping cows, while they in their day had only taken up cultivation in relation to pastoralism, i.e. so as not to sell and slaughter cows for food during the dry seasons and thus be able to grow the herd.[18] Over the years the attitude towards pastoralism as an economic activity changed, with the accent tilting more and more towards cultivation. This is especially so for the younger generation of Loita Maasai.

Settlement Patterns

It is difficult to ascertain how many permanent homesteads there were and where they were located in 1970 but from interviews it can be deduced that they were 'very few', 15–20 in the whole of Kenyan Loitaland. Some would be inhabited by as many as 40 families. Population growth as well as the spread and intensification of agriculture coincided with a break-up of these large homesteads. Consequently this led to the dispersal of settlements first over the *olaiparak* area and then into *osupuko* and *olpurkel*. In the 1970s, the large homesteads started to break up. This dispersal is said to have accelerated in the 1980s. The overcrowding of people in a homestead was one reason for the disintegration of the large homesteads. But also the growing importance of having their own field played a key role for families to move away. A homestead typically consisted of several families whose houses were built in a circle; the family herds that were herded separately during daytime would mix in the centre to spend the night. The homestead was fenced and each family would have its own entrance and its own fenced section within the homestead. Homesteads build in this style are still found in Loita, especially in the sparsely inhabited areas of *olpurkel*, but usually accommodate no more than six families. Initially, individual families would clear small fields attached to the outer fence of the homestead. But as more families started to clear fields the fields started to block the passage of people and livestock to and from the homestead. As a result, fields were cleared further away and with time the families would also move there, triggering in the process disintegration of the large homesteads. The break-up of the large homesteads was thus a result both of population growth and of the search for space for fields.

The local processes of change described (population increase, the introduction of small-stock and cultivation, the disintegration of the formerly large homesteads) combined with translocal processes of land loss and resulted in an increased demand

---

18.   Compare McCabe (2003, 106): 'It may seem counterintuitive that people would adopt agriculture to maintain a pastoral identity, but many Maasai respondents told me that the principal reason they began farming was to save the livestock'.

for land. At the same time, these changes stimulated a transformation of land tenure more appropriate to a more sedentary and dispersed settlement pattern of smaller agro-pastoral homesteads comprising one or two families. This transformation becomes apparent in the current claims of individual property on land that had been used formerly for common grazing. The following section draws on a longitudinal study of six families to show how strategies of appropriation developed to substantiate these claims of individual property.

STRATEGIES FOR THE APPROPRIATION OF LAND

Strategies for booking and grabbing land are usually planned and carried out by the male family head or herd-owner for the benefit of his family.[19] Strategies of wealthy stockowners differ from the strategies of small herd-owners, as we shall see below. Roughly speaking, the number of cattle owned by the large stockowners described in this section range from 100 to 300. Cattle owned by the small herd-owners range from 10 to 20 head. In general, large herd-owners have more than one wife, while small herd-owners have only one.

The Wealthy Stockowning Elite I: Dispersing Wives

The break-up of the large homesteads into smaller units and the increase of fields along the *olaiparak* area meant a reduction in space for grazing cattle, a change whose effects were first felt by large herd-owners. My material suggests that the lack of space for their large herds drove wealthy stockowners to 'follow cows' to where space and grass was, thereby pioneering settlement beyond *olaiparak*. Erecting a new homestead beyond *olaiparak* was only attractive if one could maintain a stake in the locality (*emurua*) one left in *olaiparak*, because although becoming congested with people and fields it still provided (and provides) the benefits of permanent water and saltlicks, as well as shops, markets and schools. The way out was to leave one wife behind and take another one to the new homestead. The swamp area of the forest and the plains of *osupuko* seem to have been the first choice, because they provided space and grass, and crucial year-round water.

Ole Reson pioneered settlement in one of the highland plains around 1983.[20] With time many others followed his example and today the area is congested with homesteads, fields, livestock, shops and a school. The plain itself is continuously overgrazed, and grass is only available in far and inaccessible places. And thus according to ole Reson the same reason that had pushed him away from *olaiparak* – i.e. because of the 'work of grass' as he phrased it – had also pushed him away more recently from *osupuko*. Around the year 2000 he pioneered – again – settlement in a particular area of

---

19. An exploration of the role of women in land appropriation, and the gendered use of land more broadly, will be undertaken in my dissertation.

20. I use pseudonyms.

olpurkel, whose vast grassy plains offered exactly what he needed. Permanent settlement had been made possible because of the construction of a mechanised borehole in the vicinity. But although the 'work of grass' pushed him out of the populated *osupuko,* the 'work of the field' pulled him back. *Osupuko* turned out to be an excellent area for growing maize and beans and as the importance of subsistence cultivation had grown, he was reluctant to give up his field, because when you move from a locality you give up the rights over land you have in that place. The abundant harvests of *osupuko* in comparison to the rest of Loita are attributed to its fertile red soil and high rainfall in comparison to *olpurkel's* black cotton soil that does not retain the low and erratic rainfall long enough for the crops to mature. *Osupuko's* suitability for rainfed agriculture was once more confirmed when the meagre short rains of 2008–2009 resulted in poor or failed harvests all over Loita, except for those in the *osupuko* area.

Another reason for ole Reson's unwillingness to leave *osupuko* despite its reduced importance for pastoralism was because of the local primary school; all his school-going children were living there with his senior wife so as to attend school. Having a school in the area adds value to a certain locality and thus plays a role in making the decision to establish a new homestead or remain in an existing one there. For ole Reson then, *osupuko* is the ideal place for taking care of the people (*eramatare oo ltunganak*) because the field provides food for his family and the school, education for his children. *Olpurkel* on the other hand is best for taking care of the livestock (*eramatare oo nkishu*) including goats and sheep, because of the space to graze and the availability of permanent water made possible by the borehole. His reluctance to leave *osupuko* and his eagerness to move to *olpurkel* was solved by marrying a third wife who was taken to live at a new homestead in *olpurkel.*

Ole Reson knew the plain at *osupuko* and the plains at *olpurkel* because these were places where he used to go to for temporary herding (*ronjo*), even before the time he separated from his father and became an independent herd-owner. Establishing temporary cattle camps at these places is no longer possible because they are now settled, with defined rules of access and use that discriminate between residents and non-residents. Having dispersed his wives over the three landscapes of *osupuko,* *olaiparak* and *olpurkel,* he can continue practising transhumant pastoralism, and in addition profit from the agricultural productivity of *osupuko.* And whether he consciously dispersed his wives or just found himself in a favourable situation, he is in one of the best positions to face formal land demarcation, because he has already 'booked' three sites where he has a socially acknowledged claim. With some luck, and manipulation by fellow wealthy stockowners on how Loita will be divided, or more precisely, on where the first boundaries of the areas to be subdivided will pass, he could obtain legal title for three different sites. He hopes that this will allow him to continue practising transhumant pastoralism for as long as is possible. More generally, it will allow him to continue benefiting from the diverse natural and social resources that *osupuko,* *olaiparak* and *olpurkel* offer to ensure the reproduction of his family's livelihood.

The Wealthy Stockowning Elite II: Spacing Wives

Wealthy stockowners are in a position to marry several wives and disperse them because they have the means to pay bridewealth and maintain a large family across several homesteads. Although initially it was their large herds in need of space and grass that spurred them to settle beyond *olaiparak*, today anticipated formal land demarcation has become an important additional motive for dispersing wives. Ole Kosiom for instance, married to three wives, has one homestead in *olaiparak* and another one in the swamp area of *osupuko* next to the forest. During my fieldwork period in Loita he was constructing a third homestead for one of the two wives that lived at the *osupuko* homestead. Instead of building the third homestead in *olpurkel* to benefit of its pastoral resources as ole Reson had done, he decided to build it in an unexpected site close to his existing *osupuko* homestead. Separated from his *osupuko* homestead by a steep ascent and a small forested area he started by fencing a cattle enclosure in an unlikely open space on top of the hill. The place was unexpected because of the absence of grazing space; half of the open area was occupied by another homestead, and the other sides were blocked by a patch of forest that would make clearing for space a hard job and a very steep and stony slope. Moreover, the added value of having two homesteads in the same ecological zone raises questions in the light of ole Reson's (and with him many others) strategy of dispersing wives over different ecological zones to benefit from the different pastoral resources they provide, even more so because ole Kosiom's herds already had access to that particular area. But a closer look reveals a very strategic reason for locating the new homestead at exactly that site. Ole Kosiom's intention is not only to 'book' new land and to gain legitimate rights over it, but also to block the expansion of the other homestead into the direction of his homestead down at the swamp. Moreover, by spacing the new homestead in such a way in relation to his other homestead he is not only blocking his neighbour but also, more importantly, discouraging others from claiming the land in between, thus in the process obtaining extra land. In other words, the distance between both homesteads is just little enough to discourage other people from settling in between (they would have little space and no prospects of expansion) and large enough for him to 'win' land beyond the claim-able land. Ole Kosiom is even taking this strategy a step further. During my visit at the onset of the 2008–2009 drought, he expressed to me his intention of constructing a temporary cattle camp (*ronjo*) across the swamp towards the forest, creating in effect a line of three homesteads in *osupuko*. The reason for this, he claimed, was to have his cows reach the grazing and water resources inside the forest more easily during the dry season. He added that if after a while people had not complained of his move he would 'take a wife' there. Indeed, I later learnt that he was in talks for marrying a fourth wife.

An important reason for ole Kosiom to do the spacing of his wives in *osupuko* and not in *olaiparak* is first because there is still space available in *osupuko* that permits this, and second because having worked as a tourist guide in the forest he realised the forest's tourist potential. With this in mind, he has already identified scenic spots on his land for putting up campsites. Tourism potential can now be added to the list of benefits provided by the swamp area of *osupuko*, such as year-round water, evergreen pastures and the irrigated agricultural potential opened up by the wet margins of the swamp.

Ole Kosiom and others who apply this method for appropriating land are accused of being 'land-grabbers'. But although the name has a negative connotation it also evokes admiration because nowadays many aim to grab as much land as possible. Variations on the two discussed strategies, i.e. dispersing wives over different ecological zones, and spacing wives in the same area, abound in Loita. At times, a widowed mother, instead of a wife, is used by a son to claim permanent settlement at a certain locality, and sometimes the wives of married sons or occasionally a married daughter are used by their father to disperse claims. Sometimes both strategies are used at once, as in the case of ole Okuluo who spaced his three wives over two homesteads to claim parts of a plain and a hill in *olaiparak*. A plot he owns at the nearby trading centre further completes his claim on almost the whole hill, because his field lies in between the plot and one of his homesteads. He also has a homestead at *olpurkel* and another one at *osupuko* where the wives of a married son reside.

Small Herd-owners I: Tying Stock-friendships

For small herd-owners, the situation is different and so are their possibilities and their choices. Like large herd-owners, small herd-owners also try to find ways to continue practising transhumant pastoralism. Ole Turuni lives at *olaiparak* and because his herd is small it remained there during the dry seasons of 2007 and 2008, since it had rained sufficiently during the rainy seasons and grass was enough. However, when by early 2009 the short rains had not yet come he requested a friend to allow his herd to join his friend's (larger) herd at his homestead in *osupuko* during the dry spell, to profit from the water and pasture resources available there. The friend accepted and by doing so, he sealed the beginning of a relationship based on mutual assistance in livestock management and characterised by the asking and granting of favours and counter-favours. I call this a 'stock-friendship'.

Before, ole Turuni used to go for temporary grazing (*ronjo*) to *osupuko* and *olpurkel*; however, since these places have become occupied localities exclusively exploited by the inhabitants and can no longer be used for temporary grazing, requesting access from a resident friend is the last alternative open to him to continue using the pastoral resources of *osupuko* and *olpurkel*. Stock-friendships are initiated on the basis of an existing relationship. In the case of ole Turuni and his friend their stock-friendship was made possible because they belong to the same clan. Moreover, they have a bond based on the age-groups they belong to[21] and they developed a close relationship that stems from his friend's previous friendship with ole Turuni's deceased father. Both

---

21.   The stock-friend is what is called an *olpiron* elder to ole Turuni, because the stock-friend's age-group ceremonially initiated the age-group to which ole Turuni belongs. Also he is categorically his father because he belongs to the same age-group as ole Turuni's late father.

large and small stockowners use stock-friends to place their herds or parts of them in distant homesteads according to the needs of their livestock or to the season of the year. Stock-friendships in Loita may also crosscut communities like the Purko and Ilkunono Maasai.

Stock-friendships are reciprocal relationships. Ole Turuni's friend's underlying motive for giving in to ole Turuni's request became clear when their combined herd was moved to ole Turuni's homestead in *olaiparak* when it started to rain again in March 2009. The friend, who also has a homestead at *olaiparak* but in a different locality, had already expressed his wish to abandon that homestead (including the rights of use of the resources of that particular locality) and bring all his wives to live in the *osupuko* area. However, he can only permit himself to do so when he is assured of continued access to *olaiparak* during wet seasons. The stock-friendship with ole Turuni opens this possibility.

Their stock-friendship also opens the possibility for ole Turuni to settle in *osupuko*. By having brought his animals to that particular locality in *osupuko*, and visited them regularly, he had initiated a first 'booking' for future settlement. Both ole Turuni and his friend have been discussing ole Turuni's chances to settle in *osupuko* in the future. Taking his cattle is a first step, the next step would be taking his wife to his friend's homestead and, after having gathered enough support from other inhabitants in the locality, they could call a meeting and request the locality to give him his own place to live. Alternatively the stock-friend might agree to give ole Turuni a piece of his own land, which would save him the uncertain way of going through a locality meeting. Ole Turuni does not intend to marry a second wife, because he cannot afford it but also because he is (primary school) educated and considers this an outdated practice. To maintain a claim on his current homestead at *olaiparak* he is discussing with his close brother (who is likewise educated, married and does not wish to marry a second wife) the possibility of splitting up so that one would remain at their currently shared homestead at *olaiparak* and the other one would move to *osupuko*. Their bond as full brothers, the fact that they belong to the same age-group and the small size of their combined herds guarantees them both future pastoral access to each other's locality. In the present situation where almost the whole of Loita is divided up into localities exclusively exploited by their inhabitants, access for settlement can only be achieved by asking formal permission during locality meetings. As in the case of ole Turuni, to enhance chances of success this is usually done through the patronage of an inhabitant who will promote the newcomer during the meetings and by additionally cultivating friendships in the locality to ensure support. At times, a patron gives some of his acknowledged land to the newcomer and in that case there is no need to go through the official way of calling for a locality meeting.

That ole Turuni has now expressed a desire to settle in *osupuko* is remarkable because he could as well just bring his cattle to his stock-friend in times of need. Yet his interest in settling there springs from a need to secure dry season grazing in a time when rumours of imminent land demarcation exist in Loita that create an unclear and uncertain future that might decrease mobility of livestock. Thus, just like wealthy stockowners who are spreading claims by dispersing wives in anticipation of land demarcation, ole Turuni is similarly trying to stake out claims in diverse ecological zones by tying a stock-friendship to gain access to a new area, *osupuko* in this case, and by mobilising his brother (or more precisely his brother's wife) to maintain access to his current home at *olaiparak*.

Small Herd-owners II: The Field-cum-*olokeri*

Cultivation is practised by large and small herd-owners alike but my material suggests that small herd-owners put more effort and have more hope in the 'work of the field' in comparison to large herd-owners. The fact that small herd-owners have more to lose during disease and dry spells than large herd-owners, who would be assured of the survival of a sufficient number of animals to acquire foodstuffs and rebuild their herds, certainly plays a part. For small herd-owners, ensuring enough food production for their own consumption counteracts the adverse situation of losing the little means of acquiring food (i.e. livestock) when other sources of income fail. Ole Keko experienced such an adverse situation in 1992 when as an unmarried man and living with his parents and six siblings they were left with only one cow to provide the needs of the entire family. It is no surprise, then, that afterwards ole Keko concentrated on working and expanding his field, being able to profit from selling the maize surplus he harvested in good years. Ole Keko's contrasting slow and uncertain progress in increasing the herd and relative success in cultivation resulted over the years in a solid conviction of the value of expanding his land for cultivation. His actions and the problems he faced as a result of them underscore this stern conviction.

Early 2007, when ole Keko unscrupulously doubled his field, by clearing bush and fencing the perimeter with it, he entered into an intense argument with a neighbour, his father's brother, who accused him of 'grabbing the land' and 'suffocating' the locality. The discussion escalated and reached a point where they actually fought. A meeting was called to resolve the matter and in the end it was decided that ole Keko could keep the land he had demarcated but, because he had committed a serious cultural offence by fighting with somebody from an older age-group, who was not only a clansman, but also categorically his father, he had to surrender six head of cattle in total to restore the various cultural rules that he had breached, an enormous sacrifice on ole Keko's part.[22] His field extension had cost him a very high price but nevertheless he considers

---

22. Ole Keko was fined two heifers by his clan; one for fighting with a clansman, and another for fighting with a clansman who is categorically his father. Breaking somebody's bone during a fight is traditionally punished with a fine, and because ole Keko broke his uncle's finger during the skirmish he had to give him a heifer. And lastly, as the junior of the two he had to give his uncle a heifer, blankets and beer to obtain his blessing during a final ceremony to restore the peace between the two of them. To afford the blankets and the beer ole Keko had to sell a calf, and a second calf was further sold to pay for his uncle's transport, as he was too weak to come to the ceremony by foot.

that it was worth the loss because as he put it: 'over time your herd can grow but not so your land'. Ole Keko's demarcated field is the largest I have come across in Loita.

Ole Keko's search for new ways of improving his livelihood makes him one of the trendsetters in Loita of what I call the field-cum-*olokeri*. An *olokeri* is a common grazing area set aside within a locality for the dry season. An *olokeri* is officially 'opened' during a locality meeting when the rest of the grazing areas of the locality are left without grass towards the end of the dry season. During closed periods, only the young, sick and draught animals may graze there but it is closed for the bulk of the herd. Trespassers caught in a closed *olokeri* were severely punished by the locality; hence the system was pretty much respected. However, since 2005, reports of increasingly (open) transgressions and the inability or unwillingness of localities to fine trespassers are resulting in a collapse of the system. Conflicts over *olokeri* trespass have been on the rise in Loita, especially in the populated *olaiparak* area. The consequences for small herd-owners are in most cases worse than for large herd-owners, who usually have second homesteads in *osupuko* where they can move their herds when the grass of the *olokeri* is finished. The predicament of the small herd-owners can be illustrated with the following example: in another locality one of the largest herd-owners, whose herd is at least ten times larger than those of the small herd-owners, entered the closed *olokeri* with his whole herd, unannounced. By the time the other locality inhabitants had realised this he had practically 'finished the grass' so they quickly rushed to the *olokeri* to profit from the remaining grass before it got finished completely. In short, the restrictions to graze in a closed *olokeri* are being ignored more and more, affecting small herd-owners in particular. The development of the field-cum-*olokeri*, introduced by small herd-owners, responds to these concerns over a failing common *olokeri* system.

The locality where ole Keko lives has also been plagued by encroachment on the common *olokeri*. As a response, ole Keko only ploughed part of the area he had officially demarcated as his field after he had won the case from his uncle. On the other larger part he let the grass grow, creating in effect his own *olokeri*. This move did not go unopposed in the locality and resulted in a new series of dispute meetings. Not only was an individual *olokeri* unheard of, but also had he been granted the land for a field and not for an individual *olokeri*. Neighbours of the locality felt misled by ole Keko. During meetings ole Keko never acknowledged it was an individual *olokeri*, he simply said he had not been able to plough the whole field. But, as he confided to me, this was only a trick; if he had acknowledged in public that the purpose of extending and fencing the land was having an individual *olokeri*, he would never had won the case. And in fact, in the next ploughing season he just ploughed an extra 'symbolic' piece and left enough space to grow grass again.

Some individual *ilookeri* (plural of *olokeri*) had been created when pioneers settled beyond *olaiparak*. However, along *olaiparak* where common *ilookeri* are until now still the norm, the demarcation of an individual *olokeri* would not be accepted if somebody openly acknowledged it or requested it. Claiming land for an individual *olokeri* is not yet socially acknowledged and a 'hidden' way to attain this is to demarcate a large field and then use it as a field-cum-*olokeri*, until having an individual *olokeri* becomes an accepted practice. In the 18 months I stayed in Loita, this new system could be seen to spread from locality to locality. The pieces of land demarcated for this purpose were becoming bigger and bigger, pushing the limits of the accepted size of 'fields'. And as more and more people are doing so, or plan to do so, opposition during meetings is disappearing, because it is becoming a question of going with the flow or losing out. It follows that now the first large herd-owners have joined the small herd-owners in this new trend of 'booking' large areas and turning them into a field-cum-*olokeri*.

GROUNDING CLAIMS

The strategies of appropriation discussed in the former section take the form of visible landmarks that convey socially understood claims of individual property over that piece of land. I call the process of inscribing the landscape with these visible markers 'grounding claims'. The visibility of grounded claims creates a powerful and convincing justification to be used when others dispute these claims or to secure legal title when formal demarcation starts. We have seen in this paper various ways in which Loita Maasai ground claims. The first step in this process is when people stake out claims to land, an activity people in Loita aptly call 'booking land'.

Booking Land

I introduced this paper with a case where booking occurred by laying out cut branches on the land in more or less straight lines to demarcate a piece of land or to draw a rough boundary. Demarcating a piece of land for cultivation generally follows the same procedure: one first starts by demarcating the perimeter boundary with cut branches before proceeding to clear, plough and sow the land. An intention to build a new homestead is communicated by erecting the cattle enclosure first. Taking one's herd to a stock-friend can also be a form of booking for future settlement, the presence of the herd functioning as a marker, albeit a very mobile one. Booking land is thus like making reservations on land for future use. An intention to use the land in future needs to be communicated to others so that nobody can spoil the plan. This is where visible markers come into play (the cut branches that denote a boundary for example), to tell others that the land has already been booked by someone for a particular use. At this stage, grounded claims are still tenuous and can be undone under pressure if counter-claims lead to conflict and dispute meetings, or when the claimant simply changes his mind and time makes the markers invisible. To strengthen the claim they need to be followed up with more permanent visible markers.

Beacons of Permanency

Permanent settlement is a must for a herd-owner to have a socially recognised claim on land. When a herd and its caretakers leave an area after staying there for weeks or months in the temporary cattle camp (*ronjo*) set up to profit from the seasonally available resources of an area, the herd-owner loses his claim on the land occupied and used during that period. The only land that he might claim when coming back is the land where the visible remains of the constructed structures are located, like the cattle enclosure and adjacent shelters, but *not* the land beyond that. This means that, in theory, if another herd-owner wants to settle in the same area of a deserted cattle camp, no matter how many consecutive years that specific area has been used by a certain herd-owner for temporary grazing, he is within his rights as long as he leaves the structures intact, even if he completely surrounds it with for example a field, houses and a cattle enclosure. A claim on the land where the structures are built is thus practically useless without a claim on the surrounding land that is necessary for (agro-)pastoral use. To have a right on the latter a herd-owner needs to live there permanently.

The key factor that determines the difference between a temporary homestead (*ronjo*) and a permanent homestead (*emparnat*) is when the herd-owner brings in a wife who builds a house and comes to live permanently at that homestead. The house she comes to build should be her principal house, because occasionally a wife is taken to a cattle camp but then builds a smaller temporary house, while her main house at the permanent homestead remains locked until she returns. In case of a permanent move the wife's house at the old homestead is burnt down. Having a wife residing in a homestead gives settlement there a substantial degree of permanency because she will be there during wet and dry season. Even if the herd-owner migrates away with the animals, there will still be visible presence on and continuous use of the land, which in turn are important justifications for land claims. Wives, then, in a way, have become important assets for claiming land, as we have seen in the strategies of appropriation discussed in the previous section.

In addition to having a wife residing at the homestead, other factors add weight to a claim on land. One is the material with which the wife's house is built. Ole Reson's wife at *olpurkel* lives in a traditional Maasai house, made out of branches and plastered with a mixture of soil and cow-dung, that she built herself. His wives at *osupuko* and *olaiparak*, on the other hand, live in the more durable corrugated-iron and timber roofed houses constructed by hired labourers, which with time have replaced traditionally built Maasai houses. Ole Reson further plans to build a cement-walled and corrugated-iron roofed house for his wife at *olaiparak*. The investments made in the houses of his wives at *osupuko* and *olaiparak* reflect ole Reson's intention of permanency there. And indeed, why he hasn't replaced his wife's house at *olpurkel* with a 'nice' house yet, is because he is not sure yet about staying in *olpurkel* forever, the reason being the unreliable water supply at the borehole due to a defective machine that, when it breaks down, makes life in *olpurkel* impossible for both animals and people during the dry season.

By replacing traditional Maasai houses, suitable for a mobile livelihood, with corrugated-iron roofed houses and, even more, cemented or stone houses, Loita Maasai are progressively 'grounding' their homesteads in specific locales in accordance with a more sedentary lifestyle. A cement-walled or stonewalled house is the ultimate sign to others of a herd-owner's plan to stay there forever.[23] This change in house styles is widespread in Loita and reflects a process of sedentarisation that is closely related to the adoption of agriculture (see Maundu *et al.* 2001, 27). This is, again, reflected in the case of ole Reson who has fields in *osupuko* and *olaiparak* but not in *olpurkel*. Working the land for cultivation is another very visible way of 'grounding' a homestead to a locality. Having a field in the homestead is thus another beacon of permanency, which, like the construction of new-style houses, attests to the labour and money invested in a homestead and thus one's reluctance to move from there. In the process of 'grounding' a homestead (by building new-style houses and clearing a field) one is in fact simultaneously and firmly 'grounding' a claim on a specific locale that is visually very powerful. In other words, the more 'grounded' a homestead is, the more permanent, and the stronger a herd-owner's claim on the land occupied and used.

In sum, the residency of a wife with a (durable) house and a field that is being worked visibly mark a permanent settlement. They embody an advanced process of 'grounding' in the landscape, the visibility of which is instrumental for claims of occupancy and use on land. These claims will be most probably used to achieve legal ownership when formal land demarcation occurs.

Claiming Individual Property in Land

The rights that a herd-owner derives from permanent residency in a particular locality involve rights of use of areas that are used by all inhabitants of a locality, such as grazing areas and watering places. Apart from these communally used areas, there are also portions of land within the locality which a herd-owner refers to as 'mine' (*enaai*), implying his exclusive use of it. The size of the piece of land that can be claimed as individual property depends on the purported use of the land. This is important because land as such cannot just be divided. Social convention has it that only pieces of land that serve a particular purpose can be appropriated. The land where the buildings are located like the houses, the animal enclosures and the maize store can be claimed as the homestead (*enkang*). The area next to the homestead where the animals gather when moving in or out of their enclosures, where the saltlick trough is located and where the young and sick animals stay during daytime can be claimed as *auluo*. Likewise, the piece of land in cultivation can be claimed as the field (*enkurma* or *olchamba*). The expanse of land that can be claimed as 'homestead' and '*auluo*' depends on the size of the resident family and the size of the herd owned. The social norm dictates that the land should be large enough to serve its purpose, i.e. to accommodate the number of houses and to accommodate the size of the herd. Criteria for the size of the field, on the other hand, are unclear but its socially accepted limits are usually attained through trial and error – that is, until a new clearing or new extension meets a counterclaim

---

23. To move a corrugated-iron roofed house is still possible because the materials which were paid for (like timbers and the corrugated-iron sheet) can be dismantled and re-used, but with a cement or stone house one loses.

by the locality or another herd-owner. Issues like these are resolved during meetings open to all circumcised men of a locality. The arguments of the claimants are weighed in accordance with the social norms, past experiences but also new realities. However, experience shows that outcomes often benefit those claimants who are eloquent and persuasive speakers and/or have social standing in the community or whose supporters enjoy that ability and status. It is through this negotiation process that starts with the physical appropriation of more land that claims of individual property over land are rejected, adjusted or validated by the larger community and become ultimately socially accepted.

Another portion of land that is sometimes claimed as individual property is the area set aside for dry season grazing called *olokeri*. In the localities along the *olaiparak* area, which was the only settled area until the 1970s, the *olokeri* always was and still is a communally used and managed piece of land, although, of late, the system's survival is under pressure, as discussed earlier. Although people effectively hold individual *ilookeri* in the form of a field-cum-*olokeri*, publicly announcing or requesting a piece of land for an individual *olokeri* is still out of the question. In the areas of *osupuko* and *olpurkel,* where settlement was pioneered comparatively recently, one finds both common and individual dry season grazing areas. In these areas individual *ilookeri* are reluctantly accepted. For example, a pioneer to *osupuko* carved out his individual *olokeri* when newcomers settled in the area. These newcomers settled there through his patronage, which placed him in an advantageous bargaining position *vis-à-vis* the newcomers, who preferred to agree rather than challenge his individual *olokeri* to secure their own smooth settlement there. However, although officially accepted, he has encountered subtle and repeated opposition in the form of destruction of boundary markers and trespass in his absence.

Grabbing Land: Manipulating Land-Based Categories

In Loita, claims on land as 'mine' are endowed with social meaning when expressed in the language of agro-pastoralism. Every herd-owner has a right to claim a homestead, an *auluo*, and a field. These are acceptable reasons for the appropriation of land. However, in view of a perceived diminishing land base and imminent formal land demarcation, herd-owners have been seeking ways to manipulate these categories in order to grab as much land as possible. One way is to alter an existing category in content to suit private needs. This is clear in the category of *olokeri,* which is transforming from a communal dry season grazing area to an individual dry season grazing area. In other cases, herd-owners test the limits of land-based categories by appropriating more and more land in their name. For example, the word '*olale*' refers to the compartments inside a house for keeping calves (*olale loo lasho*) and kids and lambs (*olale loo lkuoo*) during the night. At times when space inside the house is limited, a small enclosure outside the house but within the homestead would function as *olale*. Ole Kipinat fenced a small area at some distance from his homestead at a place where during former land dispute meetings he had been prohibited from clearing a field, and claimed it was his *olale*. This claim was fiercely contested by the locality that disputed his interpretation of *olale* and saw this as an alternative tactic for him to appropriate that land anyway. Due to a number of circumstances, the discussion of which is beyond the scope of this paper, ole Kipinat eventually 'won the case' and since then has been extending his '*olale*' over the years, metre by metre, and has now even cultivated a piece of it. What ole Kipinat did was to 'take out' the category of *olale* from the realm of the homestead and use it to appropriate land outside the homestead when he did not succeed in doing this by using the category of 'field'. The same tactic is used when a demarcated piece of land is claimed as a field while in reality it is meant to create an individual *olokeri*, in what I call the field-cum-*olokeri* strategy. Whether a herd-owner stretches the meaning of such categories or alters their content the aim is, either way, to 'grab' as much land as is possible and subsequently to ensure that the appropriated land becomes recognised by the community as individual property, by either enforcing acquiescence or by confronting counterclaims during land dispute meetings.

CONCLUSION

I have described how translocal developments that led to land loss and threaten further land loss in Loita encouraged the Loita Maasai to push for formal land demarcation as a way to stop this process and secure land for themselves. I also showed how local processes of change in land use stimulate individualised appropriation of land that had been formerly used collectively for pastoral purposes. The combination of translocal and local developments created a situation of diminishing land availability and an expectation of imminent formal land demarcation that set the conditions for the current rush to book and grab as much land as possible. The strategies of appropriation that typified this land rush take the form of grounding claims. Grounding claims involves inscribing the land with visible markers that are socially understood and as such convey claims on land as individual property. Grounded claims are used as justifications when they are challenged by others. In anticipation of formal land demarcation, it is expected that these visible markers will also aid to obtain legal title over the claimed land.

Sikor and Lund made a call to study what they call the 'grey zone' between access and property (2009, 6). In this paper, I tried to address this grey zone by clarifying the process whereby Loita Maasai gain access to land for settlement and cultivation and subsequently seek to have their access claims recognised as individual property. Appropriation in Loita takes the form of grounding claims. Grounded claims are subsequently instrumental for social legitimisation of individual property claims and for legal sanction, both according to Loita Maasai law and, the expectation is, according to Kenya state law.

BIBLIOGRAPHY

Berman, B. 1990. *Control and Crisis in Colonial Kenya: The Dialectic of Domination.* Nairobi: East African Educational Publishers.

Berry, S. 1989. 'Access, Control and Use of Resources in African Agriculture: An Introduction', *Africa* **59**,1: 1–5.

Compagnon, D. and Constantin, F. (eds.) 2000. *Administrer l'environnement en Afrique: Gestion Communautaire, Conservation et Développement Durable.* Paris, Nairobi: Éditions Karthala, IFRA.

Galaty, J. 1992. '"The Land is Yours": Social and Economic Factors in the Privatization, Subdivision and Sale of Maasai Ranches', *Nomadic Peoples* **30**: 26–40.

Galaty, J. 1994. 'Ha(l)ving Land in Common: The Subdivision of Maasai Group Ranches in Kenya', *Nomadic Peoples* **34/35**: 109–22.

Hughes, L. 2006. *Moving the Maasai: A Colonial Misadventure.* New York: Palgrave Macmillan.

Kantai, P. 2001. 'In the Balance: The Loita Maasai Confront the Future of the Forest', *Ecoforum*, long rains: 39–42.

Karanja, F., Tessema, Y. and Barrow, E. 2002. *Equity in the Loita/Purko Naimina Enkiyio Forest in Kenya: Securing Maasai Rights to and Responsibilities for the Forest.* Series: Forest and Social Perspectives in Conservation. Nairobi: IUCN Eastern Africa Regional Office.

Kenya National Bureau of Statistics [KNBS]. 2010. *2009 Kenya Population and Housing Census Volume I A: Population Distribution by Administrative Units.*

Kimani, K. and Pickard, J. 1998. 'Recent Trends and Implications of Group Ranch Sub-division and Fragmentation in Kajiado District, Kenya', *The Geographical Journal* **162**, 2: 202–13.

Kronenburg, J. 1986. *Empowerment of the Poor: A Comparative Analysis of Two Development Endeavours in Kenya.* Ph.D. dissertation, Derde Wereld Centrum, Catholic University of Nijmegen.

Kronenburg García, A. 2003. *Ritual in Forest and Forest in Ritual: Relationships between the Naimina Enkiyio Forest and Ritual Practices among the Loita Maasai in Kenya.* Unpublished MA thesis, Department of Cultural Anthropology, University of Leiden.

Lamprey, R. and Waller, R. 1990. 'The Loita–Mara Area in Historical Times: Patterns of Subsistence, Settlement and Ecological Change', in P. Robertshaw (ed.) *Early Pastoralists of Southwestern Kenya.* Nairobi: British Institute in Eastern Africa. pp. 16–34.

Legilisho-Kiyiapi, J. 1999. *Preliminary Biodiversity Assessment of the Loita Naimina-Enkiyio Forest.* Nairobi: Loita Forest Integrated Conservation and Management Project, Preparatory Phase, Technical Report (3), IUCN.

Loita Naimina Enkiyio Conservation Trust Company [LNECTC]. 1994. *Forest of the Lost Child (Entim e Naimina Enkiyio): A Maasai Conservation Success Threatened by Greed.* Pamphlet by the LNECTC, Narok.

Maundu, P., Berger, D., ole Saitabau, C., Nasieku, J., Kipelian, M., Mathenge, S., Morimoto, Y. and Höft, R. 2001. *Ethnobotany of the Loita Maasai: Towards Community Management of the Forest of the Lost Child, Experiences from the Loita Ethnobotany Project.* People and Plants Working Paper, UNESCO, Paris.

120

Angela Kronenburg García

McCabe, J. 1997. 'Risk and Uncertainty among the Maasai of the Ngorongoro Conservation Area in Tanzania: A Case Study in Economic Change'. *Nomadic Peoples* **1**,1: 54–65.

McCabe, J. 2003. 'Sustainability and Livelihood Diversification among the Maasai of Northern Tanzania', *Human Organization* **62**, 2: 100–11.

McCabe, J., Perkin, S. and Schofield, C. 1992. 'Can Conservation and Development be Coupled among Pastoral People? An Examination of the Maasai of the Ngorongoro Conservation Area, Tanzania', *Human Organization* **51**, 4: 353–66.

Mwangi, E. 2007a. 'Subdividing the Commons: Distributional Conflict in the Transition from Collective to Individual Property Rights in Kenya's Maasailand', *World Development* **35**, 5: 815–34.

Mwangi, E. 2007b. 'The Puzzle of Group Ranch Subdivision in Kenya's Maasailand', *Development and Change* **38**, 5: 889–910.

Ngece, N., Kakuru, W. and Kimani, K. 2007. *Conflict Management and Community Development, Projects as Incentives for Partners to Participate in Participatory Forest Management (PFM): The Case of Loita and Lembus Communities in Kenya*. Conference proceedings: Participatory Forest Management, Biodiversity and Livelihoods in Africa, 19–21 March, Addis Ababa.

Peluso, N. 1992. *Rich Forests, Poor People: Resource Control and Resistance in Java*. Berkeley, Los Angeles: University of California.

Peron, X. 2000. 'Question de Pouvoir: Communauté Locale Contre Collectivité Locale (Maasaï-Loïta)', in D. Compagnon and F. Constantin (eds.) *Administrer l'environnement en Afrique: Gestion Communautaire, Conservation et Développement Durable*. Paris, Nairobi: Éditions Karthala, IFRA. pp. 383–404.

Ribot, J. 1998. 'Theorizing Access: Forest Profits Along Senegal's Charcoal Commodity Chain', *Development and Change* **29**, 2: 307–41.

Ribot, J. and Peluso, N. 2003. 'A Theory of Access', *Rural Sociology* **68**, 2: 153–81.

Robertshaw, P. (ed.) 1990. *Early Pastoralists of Southwestern Kenya*. Nairobi: British Institute in Eastern Africa.

Ros-Tonen, M. and T. Dietz (eds.) 2005. *African Forests between Nature and Livelihood Resource: Interdisciplinary Studies in Conservation and Forest Management*. Lewiston: The Edwin Mellen Press.

Rutten, M. 1992. *Selling Wealth to Buy Poverty: The Process of the Individualization of Landownership Among the Maasai Pastoralists of Kajiado District, Kenya, 1890–1990*. Saarbrücken: Breitenbach.

Schegget, R. ter and Schoenmakers, J. 1988. *Survey Results: Historical Analyses, Data-tables and Preliminary Results of a Survey on the Impact of the Ilkerin Loita Integral Dvelopment Project in Kenya*. Study commissioned by Ilkerin Loita Integral Development Project.

Shelley, S. and I. Lempaka. 1999. *Survey of Tourism Activities in the Loita Forest and Environs*. Nairobi: Loita Forest Conservation and Management Project, Preparatory Phase, Technical Report (2) IUCN.

Siloma, M. ole and Zaal, F. 2005. 'Neo-African Governance: Old and New Institutions for Resource Conflict Resolution', in M. Ros-Tonen and T. Dietz (eds.) *African Forests between Nature and Livelihood Resource: Interdisciplinary Studies in Conservation and Forest Management.* Lewiston: The Edwin Mellen Press. pp. 255–83.

Sikor, T. and Lund, C. 2009. 'Access and Property: a Question of Power and Authority', *Development and Change* **40**, 1: 1–22.

Spear, T, and Waller, R. (eds.) 1993. *Being Maasai: Ethnicity and Identity in East Africa.* London: James Currey.

Voshaar, J. 1998. *Maasai: Between the Oreteti-tree and the Tree of the Cross.* Kampen: Kok.

Waller, R. 1990. 'Tsetse Fly in Western Narok, Kenya', *Journal of African History* **31**: 81–101.

Waller, R. 1993. 'Acceptees and Aliens: Kikuyu Settlement in Maasailand', in T. Spear and R. Waller (eds.) *Being Maasai: Ethnicity and Identity in East Africa.* London: James Currey. pp. 226–57.

Zaal, F. and ole Siloma, M. 2006. *Contextualising Conflict: Introduced Institutions and Political Networks Combating Pastoral Poverty.* Conference paper: Pastoralism and Poverty Reduction in East Africa, June 27–28, Nairobi.

~ 6 ~

ADAPTING TO BIODIVERSITY CONSERVATION: THE MOBILE PASTORAL HARASIIS TRIBE OF OMAN[1]

Dawn Chatty

University of Oxford

Throughout most of the twentieth century, pastoral peoples in the Middle East have faced enormous pressure to change their way of life and adapt to a more settled and hence modern existence. During the first half of the twentieth century, an ambivalent attitude towards nomadic or mobile pastoralists prevailed, with various efforts at private land registration and large-scale settlement schemes being set up with varying degrees of failure. With the consolidation of state power and authority after the Second World War, however, most of the nations of the Middle East and North Africa turned to their pastoral peoples with a determined view to making them stay put in one place. People who moved were regarded as a threat to the security of the settled. Settlement schemes, it was assumed, would assure control over these far-flung peoples. Jordan, Iraq, Syria, Saudi Arabia and Egypt all attempted the sedentarisation of these communities (Sammane 1990). Indeed the resulting disintegration of the pastoral community frequently created new problems for the nation-state. The international development efforts of this era designed to make nomadic peoples 'modern' also largely failed, resulting in a stalemate and often a national policy of benign neglect.

One significant new element in this universe is the budding international pressure for accountability, transparency and respect for human rights among conservation NGOs (Moser and Miller 1999). This pressure is resulting in some corners in greater focus on sound social policy and respect for the human rights of indigenous peoples through greater efforts at participation or partnerships (see, for example, May *et al.* 1999; Pimbert and Pretty 1995; IIED 1994). This move has given some pastoral communities in the deserts of the Middle East a new voice and leverage in demanding sound social policy from conservation bodies as well as from national government (see, for example, Irani and Johnson 1998; Chatty 2003; Chatty and Colchester 2002). In

---

1. An earlier version of this paper was published in Andrzej Kapiszewski, Abdulrahman Al-Salimi and Andrzej Pikulski (eds.) *Modern Oman: Studies on Politics, Economy, Environment and Culture of the Sultanate*, Krakow-Muscat: Ksiegarnia Akademicka Press, 2006. The present version appears here with the kind permission of the editors.

Oman, however, such moves have lagged behind and recent experiences suggest that moves to integrate a better understanding of indigenous or local and traditional mobile pastoral societies into the largely natural science focus of its biodiversity conservation effort would now be timely and constructive.

THE NATURE OF MOBILE PASTORAL SOCIETIES

Mobile or nomadic pastoral societies in the Middle East have a number of features in common, and it is possible to formulate some generalisations about them. The definition of pastoralism that is used here is *animal husbandry by natural graze and browse with some access to crop cultivation*. As no pastoral group is ever entirely self-sufficient, it must maintain reciprocal and interdependent relations with sedentary communities on the margins of its grazing areas. The pastoral adaptation to the ecological environment has always presupposed the presence of sedentary communities and access to their products. Today, with ever more sophisticated technology in the form of trucks, water bowsers, metal utensils and shelter frames, bottled gas, mobile phones and other trappings of the twentieth and twenty-first century, the dependence on people outside the pastoral group is particularly apparent.

The pastoral way of life is shaped by movement – a mobility that is both philosophical and physical. The combination of seasonal and regional variability in the location of pasture and water makes movement of herds from deficit to surplus areas both logical and necessary. Pastoralists have a double reliance on land in the form of pasture for graze and browse and in the form of access to water resources for themselves and their herds. Each discrete unit or tribe seeks to control sufficient land and water for the livestock holdings of the group. The borders between tribes have always been fluid and subject to constant reinterpretation as the relative political and physical strength of one group *vis-à-vis* another fluctuated or as pasture conditions became desiccated. Up until the mid-twentieth century, tribes were in constant competition with each other for the use of these precious resources, and the weaker units, or less ably represented ones, were often forced to give up their rights to use certain areas. In some cases this meant only minor readjustments in the allocation of resources within the tribe. In other cases it meant wholesale tribal displacement.

The pastoral tribes of the Arabian Peninsula are often referred to as Bedouin, a term derived from the Arabic word, *bedu*, meaning an inhabitant of the *Badia* – the large stretch of semiarid land or desert that comprises nearly 80 per cent of the Arabian landmass (Map 1). They have, for centuries, pushed their frontier regions into border areas of agricultural settlement and have as often been repulsed when central governments have had the strength to do so. This tug-of-war between agricultural and pastoral-based modes of existence often encompassed peoples that moved between both types of economic orders. When central authority was weak, the pastoral tribes conquered the land and associated agricultural villages and oases by *ghazu* (raiding)

Dawn Chatty

Figure 1. Map of Arabia.

or by collecting tribute (*khuwa*).[2] When central authority was strong, however, the tribes were forced to make payments to the government or retreat into the *Badia*. These expansions and retreats have been documented in the works of Ibn Khaldun (1958), Volney (1787), Oppenheim (1939), and Rafiq (1966) to mention a few. Throughout the nineteenth and twentieth centuries, these tribes continued to jostle and fight for control over large stretches of pastureland and associated agricultural villages.

---

2. At one time, tribute (*khuwa*) was exacted from sedentary farmers, generally in the form of crops in return for protection from raids (*ghazu*) by their tribe or others in the surrounding areas. This tribute–raid relationship was a simple business proposition whereby the pastoralist received a needed produce (grain) and the farmers gained a scarce service (security). In principle, it was not very different from a more widespread relationship whereby animal products were exchanged for dates or grain.

At the close of the First World War, Northern Arabia, nominally an Ottoman province, was partitioned by the League of Nations. The semi-arid lands of the *Badia* were divided up and distributed, under 'mandate status', to France and Great Britain. The southern wedge alone remained in the hands of Abdul Aziz Al-Saud, the founding father of Saudi Arabia. This step, along with the subsequent establishment of British and French administrations in their respective regions, telegraph and road infrastructure, and the introduction of mechanised transport, had a tremendous impact on the pastoral tribes of the region. Many were to prophesy that these developments spelled out the death of their way of life. Most of these changes, however, were quickly absorbed by the Bedouin and altered to meet their own highly adaptive system.

In the second half of the twentieth century, Western development aid became the single greatest export from Europe and the United States to the 'Third World'. Development experts came to regard pastoral peoples with disdain, if not scorn (Bocco 1990). Pastoral systems of livestock management came to be regarded as minimal – if not controversial – by national and international experts (Dyson-Hudson 1991). In addition, many 'development' experts assumed that the pastoral peoples were ruining their physical environment (Dyson-Hudson 1991, 219).

Unlike sub-Saharan Africa, the Middle East and North Africa have never been the focus of mass international pastoral development assistance (Dyson-Hudson 1991, 220). Governments of the Middle East, perhaps because they regarded their pastoral populations as signifiers of internal political problems, sought local rather than international solutions. Accordingly, government policy in the Middle East has been directed at settling these peoples either by physical force or by economic entice-ment. Settlement of mobile pastoralists has been seen as the only way to control and integrate marginal and problematic populations that did not conform to the modern nation-state aspirations of the newly created republics and kingdoms of the regions.

SETTLEMENT EFFORTS IN THE MIDDLE EAST

In the northern part of the Arabian Peninsula and in parts of North Africa, governments have attempted to lure the mobile pastoralists out of the deserts and arid rangelands to settlement schemes and agricultural pilot projects. These, in large measure, have failed. More forceful approaches have included revoking the traditional communal land holdings of these people. Modern private registration of land has been encouraged, particularly in the marginal areas of the desert that border the agricultural belt, the Fertile Crescent, where dry farming of cereals can be supported in years of good rain. This last approach has had some success from the government point of view. At the time of the various cadastral surveys in the nineteenth and early twentieth centuries, many tribal and sub-tribal representatives were able to register themselves as private owners of land that tribesmen previously had considered to be held in common. Impoverished families who were forced to leave the pastoral way of life through loss of herds or manpower – or both – often found themselves transformed into hired shepherds or, worse, agricultural labourers for their landowning tribal leaders. Even after several generations of uneasy compromise, these families have continued to keep some livestock – generally goat and sheep – and many maintained that they would return to their former way of life if circumstances made it possible (Chatty 1995).

In Saudi Arabia and the southern region of the Arabian Peninsula, the situation of mobile pastoral peoples has been complicated first by the discovery of oil, and more recently, the tremendous wealth that has come into the hands of these governments. Saudi Arabia has for decades tried to settle its large mobile pastoral peoples. Beginning as early as the 1920s, settlement schemes were built to house these people. Initially the urgency of the projects reflected the government's need to consolidate their hold over the country by controlling their far-flung and highly mobile peoples. The association of this way of life with a backward, less evolved human state, also contributed to government efforts to suppress it. In later decades settlement projects built at tremendous expense were financed locally from oil revenues. Predictably, the schemes failed (for example, the Wadi al-Sarhan Project, the King Faysal Settlement Project). The mobile pastoralists, discouraged by attempts to turn them into settled tillers of the soil, flitted away. Some returned to their old way of life; others turned to new endeavours more compatible with pastoralism, such as in the transport industry or in trade.

With the huge increase in the profit from petroleum extraction which the Arabian Gulf States, Saudi Arabia, and the Sultanate of Oman experienced in the early 1970s, came a new approach to the 'problem of nomadic pastoralists' (Chatty 1996). Mass settlement schemes were abandoned in favour of enticements to individual citizens. Control, in a political sense, was attempted by encouraging the individual tribesman to come forward and register himself as a citizen. In return, these governments granted various privileges. In the wealthier states, with very small settled populations, registration carried with it an entitlement to a plot of land, a house, an automobile and a subsidy for each head of livestock. In other states, registration meant a monthly stipend – generally in the region of the local equivalent of several hundred US dollars – often disguised as a salary for some form of national paramilitary service. As a general rule, two approaches to the problem of mobile or nomadic pastoralists have operated in the Middle East since the second half of the twentieth century: one of disdain and the other of enlightenment shadowed by neglect.

ENLIGHTENED VIEW OF PASTORAL ADAPTATION SHADOWED BY NEGLECT: THE CASE OF OMAN

The six largest pastoral tribes of Oman divide themselves into two groups: those descended from Qahtan and those whose origins go back to Nizar (or some use the name Adnan). The main Qahtani tribes are the Mahra, the Jeneba, the Beit Kaythir and the Harasiis (Chatty 1984, 6). These tribes gradually moved north into Oman from Yemen and the Hadramaut beginning two or three millennia ago. The Nizari or Adnani tribes include the Duru' and the Wahiba. These tribes as well as other sedentary groups are said to have come to Oman from the north or through the Buraimi pass some time between the second and third century AD. There are other categories by which these largely pastoral peoples identify themselves. These include the differentiation between Hinawi and Ghafiri supporters – the opponents in the early eighteenth-century civil war in Oman. In many cases, the Ghafiri supporters tend to believe in their Nizari or Adnani origins and the Hinawi supporters tend to hold to Qahtani myths of origin. Increasingly, members of these pastoral tribes have also self-identified themselves as Bedouin. Sustainable livelihoods of all these groups are based on domesticated livestock that can exist and sometimes thrive on the natural graze and browse of the desert. The wellbeing of these herds, and by association, these peoples, depends upon their continued access to the widely scattered grass, tree and shrub cover throughout the desert regions they regard as their homeland. Livestock is the key to this way of life and mobility a basic feature in herd management and cultural identity.

For all the pastoral tribes of Oman, the organising principle of social life is the herd. The wellbeing of the family depends upon the careful manipulation of the breeding cycle of the herds of camels, sheep and goats in order to have milk available to drink all year round. The daily routine, the seasonal routine and any migrations are determined by the needs of the herds. Whether living in a cement house, a house of plywood, or one made up of dead tree branches and tarpaulin, the organising principle of their daily life is still livestock and access to natural graze and browse.

Throughout all the desert regions of Oman, life depends upon access to water. In the past, survival depended upon moving herds and households to water sources. Today, however, in most of Oman, water is moved to the herds and the households by truck or water bowser. The Harasiis tribe, which is the focus of this chapter (Map 2), represents perhaps the most distant community from urban centres and hence the most extreme case. Up until the late 1950s, the rock and gravel desert plain (Jiddat-il-Harasiis) which composed most of their traditional territory of about 40,000 square kilometres contained no water whatsoever. The only source of water available to them was found along the Awta – the lowlands of the Huqf escarpment lying just along the coast of Oman from Duqm north towards Al-Hajj. During the winter months, the Harasiis moved along the Jiddat-il-Harasiis searching for pasture and browse for their herds of camels and goats. In the event of heavy condensation, water would be collected by spreading blankets out and later wringing the water from them into drinking vessels. Their water consumption, however, was kept to a minimum with the family relying on their herds to provide them with enough milk for their nutritional and physiological requirements. During the summer the Harasiis abandoned the extremely hot Jiddat plateau altogether and moved down into the Awta where their herds had access to the brackish springs of the region.

In the late 1950s the national oil company that had been exploring for oil in the northern desert of Oman, moved into the Jiddat-il-Harasiis and drilled two water wells, one at Al-Ajaiz and the other at Haima. Within a few years, several families began to remain on the Jiddat during the hot summer months, relying on their access to the

Dawn Chatty

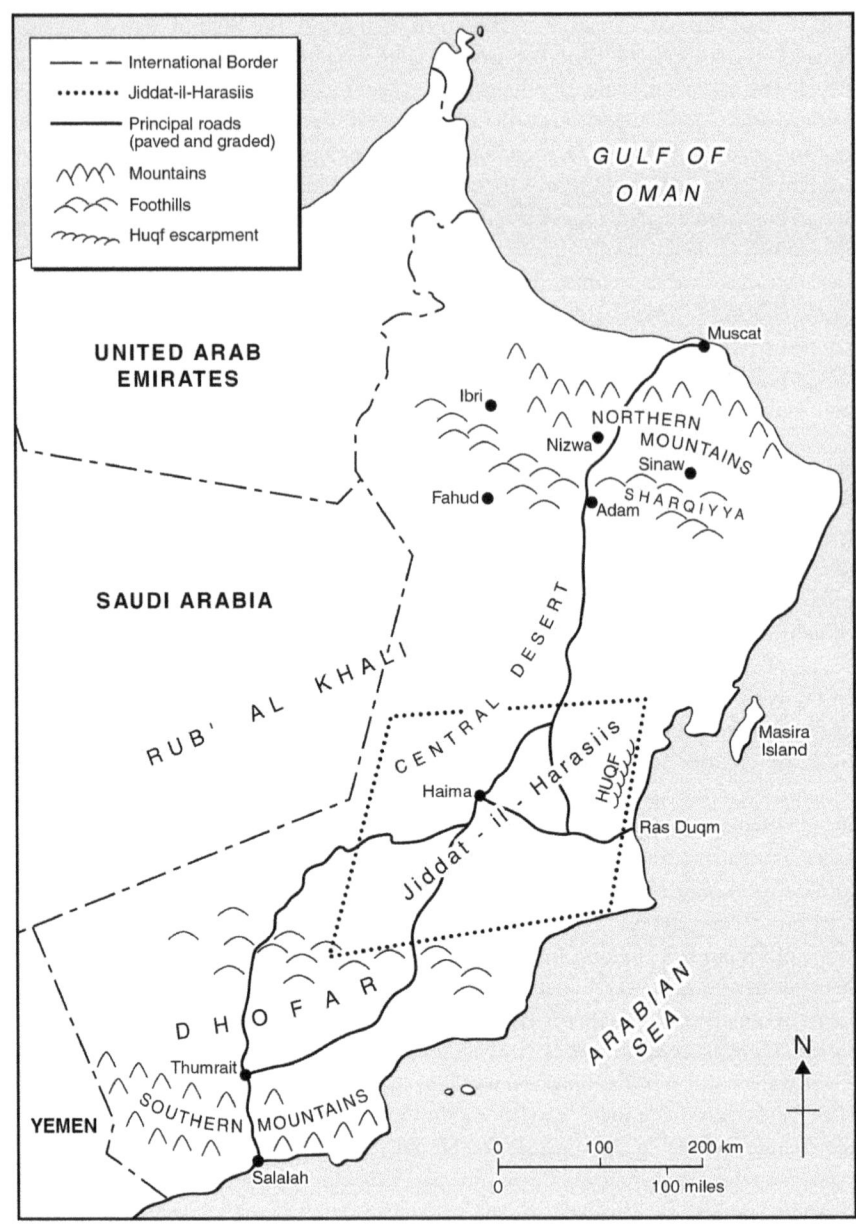

Figure 2. Map of the Sultanate of Oman.

water well and some sporadic delivery of water by tankers under the direction of the oil company. For the Harasiis tribe a revolution was in the making – as had happened earlier in other tribal areas, like that of the Duru' near Ibri. Wells for water were being sunk, animal troughs built and oil company bowsers were occasionally delivering water to key households.

The 1970s was a period of tremendous transformation for Oman as a whole. Disillusionment with the enforced backwardness of the state and medieval nature of the government of Sultan Said had reached such alarming proportions that rebellion was inevitable. In July of 1970, the 38-year reign of Sultan Said ended, when he signed a formal abdication document in favour of his son, Qaboos bin Said. Oman was propelled into the twentieth century with significant road building and other infrastructural development. The country's development budget in 1971 for example, during Sultan Qaboos bin Said's first year as ruler, was $60 million. By 1975 it had grown to $1,000 million. By the mid-1970s, the country had established modern road, sea and air communications with the rest of the world. Telegraph and telephones were becoming widespread, as were schools, health clinics and hospitals. Social welfare services and the extension of water and electricity were also rapidly expanding in ever growing circles from Muscat and Salalah.

In the early 1980s, with basic social services rapidly and methodically extended into the rural countryside of Oman, Sultan Qaboos issued a number of decrees of vital interest to the remote mobile pastoral communities. These peoples were to be targeted for development. The Sultan's wishes, reiterated in a number of speeches, were that the desert regions of Oman were to receive the same care and attention as the villages and towns of the rest of the country. This mandate was interpreted by the leading government ministers to mean that a way was to be found to extend the same social services to pastoral nomads without forcing them to give up their traditional way of life. Plans were drawn up to create a number of tribal administrative centres throughout the desert where the basic social functions comprising health care, education facilities and welfare services would be available.

In 1981, the first UN project aimed at the development needs of a pastoral population in the Arabian Peninsula was initiated at Haima in the central desert area of Oman (Map 3). The first year of the project was devoted to conducting an anthropological study of the indigenous population and identifying their felt needs and problems. The second and further years were focused on recommending and implementing practical programmes that would extend basic social services to this remote and marginal mobile pastoral community. The pastoral tribe associated with this region was the Harasiis, a South Arabian speaking people numbering 3,000 occupying a large, nearly waterless gravel and rock plain – the Jiddat-il-Harasiis – about the size of Scotland (Chatty 1996). Raising herds of camel and goat, mainly for the production of milk, these communities migrated across the vast arid expanse of the Jiddat. By the mid-1970s, the Harasiis had engaged in a major technological change shifting from camels to trucks for transport. By the early 1980s every household of the

Dawn Chatty

17 sampled in the UN study had a four-wheel-drive vehicle. Such a transformation required a fundamental shift in household economic organisation. Each household had to find means of keeping these vehicles running and 'local' employment for one member of each family became a significant survival strategy.

The Harasiis had first become exposed to opportunities for wage labour as early as the late 1950s, when the oil company was exploring for oil in their territory. After two decades of unskilled and poorly paid work in this sector, the Harasiis were eager

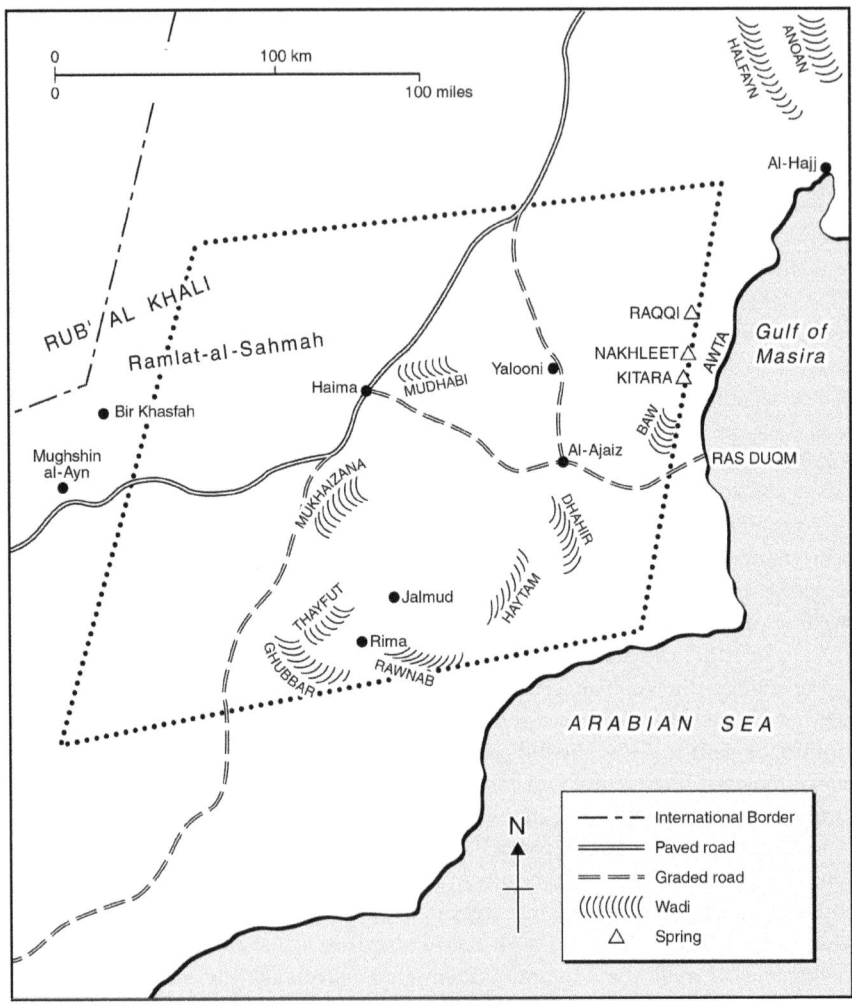

Figure 3. Map of Jiddat-il-Harasiis.

to improve their opportunities. When the joint United Nations–Omani Government effort to extend permanent and outreach (mobile) social services to these people commenced its work, it was met with great support and enthusiasm by the community. Their logic was that this project would be able to offer schools, which would transform their youth from potentially unskilled labourers into skilled, well-paid professionals. They saw this institution as a way out of the 'non-jobs' that were currently available to them as well-guards and installation watchmen. Instead they looked to future employment with the oil company, the border police and the army. But these forms of employment required literacy in Arabic, high school diplomas and, in some cases, English fluency.

Within two years and with the full support of the community, the joint UN–government project was able to set up a boarding school for boys (girls were admitted on a day basis), two mobile primary health care units, a welfare office for social affairs and a veterinary clinic with an outreach programme. School enrolment, which began with 42 boys and three girls in 1982, climbed yearly. By the mid-1990s the boarding school, which included a primary and a secondary school, had over 150 boys and girls in attendance. Some of the graduating boys had succeeded in getting jobs with the police, the army and in the government civil service.

Efforts to develop their economic base, to improve their animal husbandry practices or help develop their marketing and trade interests did not attract government interest. Instead, what government administrators did notice was the increasing number of pastoral people coming forward to request monthly welfare assistance from the government. These officials could respond to it as it fitted in with patterns of engagement already established with sedentary communities in the towns and villages of Oman. However, these same officials came to regard such requests as proof of increased poverty among the pastoral sector of the country's population, evidence which required solutions in order to make these people 'economically productive'.

The pastoral tribes of Oman came to be increasingly classified by government administrators as a 'poor' people who were making no productive contribution to the national economy. They were seen as a drain on the country rather than as an asset. This assessment was not derived from any particular facts of empirical study, but rather from the long-standing ambiguous nature of the relations between the urban, settled societies of the towns and cities and the mobile, remote, pastoral peoples of the desert interiors. Hence government 'income-generating' schemes were put forward which ignored the livestock livelihood base of these communities. Instead, government focused on developing or teaching regionally acceptable craft skills (sewing, weaving, and spinning) which might result in goods for sale at annual government-sponsored cultural events. Government schemes for pastoralists, generally an imitation of 'community development programmes' for oasis farmers, were regarded as a way to turn these 'poor' debt-ridden communities into productive contributors to the country's gross national product.

The Harasiis initiatives to persuade government – and its most visible associate, the oil company – to 'develop' their traditional homeland have been met with resistance or rejected outright. Tribal requests for government support of a system of water distribution which would rotate and change as households shifted their camp-sites around the desert were denied in favour of creating a system of 'fixed' facilities around brackish water wells where permanent water purification plants would be set up. Local efforts by the Harasiis to grow fodder in the desert and to introduce salt resistant plants were met with no interest by Ministry of Agriculture personnel, who continued to subsidise fodder farming and improved water spreading systems in the agricultural regions of the country.

The Harasiis have been changed by these experiences. Their expectations of government support and assistance have grown and their political consciousness has also been raised as they compare their lot to that of their settled neighbours in the north and the south. They have taken, and perhaps will always take, every opportunity to plead their case, to ask for assistance, to request help from the large society on the fringe of their universe. Their pragmatic position has been that sometimes they suc-ceed and sometimes they don't. Although some of their material expectations – mainly centred on their acceptance of the motor vehicle and the way it has transformed daily life – have grown, their cultural integrity remains.

For the Harasiis, subsistence animal husbandry remains the central focus of their lives. A short study completed in 2001 revealed that over the past two decades household herds have remained remarkably stable with 100 head of goats and 25 head of camel remaining an average figure.[3] Employment of at least one male member of each household remains crucial for the wellbeing of the group. What has changed is the development of a growing sense of frustration at the kinds of employment avail-able. Having engaged wholeheartedly with the government effort to provide them with education, the Harasiis now ask why they see so little return. They question why the oil company and its sub-contractors still employ so many unskilled labourers from abroad when they themselves seek employment and they are puzzled as to why so few of their educated youth seem to be able to gain training and employment in the oil sector, or in government. There is a perceptible sense of being 'left behind', of not benefiting from the wealth which oil – extracted from their own tribal land – has generated for the rest of the country's citizens.

How the individual tribespeople will adapt to the recent developments in the middle of the Jiddat-il-Harasiis is problematic. Here are a people caught in the mod-ern post-colonial world of development and planning. In spite of the remoteness, the marginality and the isolation that characterise the Harasiis and their tribal lands, they are now beginning to face problems similar to the nomadic pastoral tribes of the rest of Arabia. Their lands have been, in a sense, confiscated and are controlled *de facto*

---

3.   Household figures for livestock numbers derived from 1981–82 and 1991–92 (Chatty 1996, 94–100) are generally comparable with figures derived from a social impact assessment which was carried out for the national oil company in the region in August 2001 (see Rae and Chatty 2001). These figures show that although human numbers are rising, livestock numbers have been maintained at reasonably steady levels, in keeping with the Harasiis assessments of what is a sustainable size of animal herd in the Jiddat.

and *de jure* by the nation-state. Recent infrastructural growth has meant that they have access to and are affected by development hundreds of kilometres away. Motor transport and motorised water pumping facilities have revolutionised their lives, as have telecommunications. Some have had the opportunity to leave and take up new lives. But many have chosen to remain.

BIODIVERSITY CONSERVATION IN THE JIDDAT-IL-HARASIIS

Unlike Africa, the Arabian Peninsula does not have a long history of interest in conservation. Its neo-colonial period was very short and only lasted a few decades in the middle of the last century. Its land mass is, in the main, arid and not suitable as a wooded reserve. It has limited large mammal species, making it unattractive for wildlife or tourist reserves. The earliest expression of interest in conservation in Arabia came about a decade or so after the Second World War, as the alarming rate at which gazelle, oryx and other 'sporting' animals were being caught or killed became clear. In the south-east corner of Arabia, the Sultan of Oman issued a decree in 1964 banning the use of vehicles for hunting gazelles and oryx.[4] He also commanded the setting up of a 'gazelle patrol' to protect these graceful mammals in the central Omani desert which borders Saudi Arabia and the Trucial States. Hunting parties from outside Oman were most probably taking advantage of its open and indefensible borders to enter the country for sport. Despite the Sultan's ban, the oryx was declared extinct in Oman and the rest of Arabia in 1972. The loss was lamented by the Harasiis tribe. Nearly two hundred years earlier, the Harasiis tribe had been pushed into the remote and desolate region which came to be known early in the twentieth century as the Jiddat-il-Harasiis. There they found few large mammals other than the oryx and the gazelle, which they occasionally hunted for food. As Stanley Price makes clear, it was unlikely that sporadic Harasiis hunting pressure – in open country with only ancient rifles and camels to hide behind – could ever have eliminated the population (Stanley Price 1989, 42). It was the motorised hunting parties with automatic weapons from outside the area that succeeded in doing so, despite the indigenous tribe's wishes to preserve the animal in its vast arid environment which they shared. In 1976 Sultan Qaboos put into effect a ban on the hunting or capture of all large mammals – specifically oryx and gazelle. The following year a second decree was issued clarifying this ban. It unequivocally stated that no permission would be given to foreign hunting parties to enter and operate in Oman.

For several decades before the extermination of the world's last herd of wild oryx in 1972, plans had been implemented to create a World Herd in captivity, at a number of zoos around the world, for eventual reintroduction into the wild. In 1974 Sultan Qaboos gave the green light to his expatriate advisor on the conservation of

---

4.   There are only three species allocated to the genus Oryx in contemporary taxonomy although there are commonly believed to be five forms: *Oryx gazella gazella* (gemsbok); *O.g. beisa*; *O.g. callotis*; *O. dammah*; and *O. leucoryx* (Arabian oryx or white oryx).

the environment to explore the potential for restoring the oryx to Oman as part of its natural heritage. In 1977 and 1978 a consultant attached to the International Union for the Conservation of Nature (IUCN) toured extensively throughout the interior of Oman, with a Harasiis guide, searching for the best location to set up the reintroduction effort. Two unpublished reports were produced for the IUCN (Jungius 1985), both concluding that the ideal habitat for the oryx reintroduction project should be in the Jiddat-il-Harasiis, and concentrated in an area known as Yalooni, as it had 'the best vegetated pan on the Jiddat, with resources of grazing, shrub and tree browse' (Stanley Price 1989, 60). The reports also recommended that the whole of the Jiddat-il-Harasiis should be proclaimed a wildlife reserve or sanctuary. These recommendations were accepted and, in 1980, the first oryx from the World Herd were flown back into the country and released into the main oryx enclosure at Yalooni. Ten Harasiis tribesmen were hired to serve as oryx rangers, tracking these animals and generally keeping accurate daily records of their movements.

The project experienced a prolonged 'honeymoon' period and for the first three years there were no conflicts between the indigenous Harasiis population, the growing expatriate conservation management team and other Omani employees. Gradually, however, difficulties began to appear. The first of these difficulties manifested themselves in terms of competition over grazing between the herds of domestic goat and camel and the reintroduced oryx during prolonged drought (Stanley Price 1989, 212–13). That was followed by conflict between the lineages of the Harasiis tribe over access to employment and special benefits and later between the Harasiis and their neighbouring tribes (Duru and Wahiba to the north, Mahra to the south and Jeneba to the east) who had been ignored in this conservation effort. Although the goodwill with which the project was initially accepted remained evident among the older generation who had grown up with the oryx, others began to express their lack of commitment. The appearance of poaching (first reported for gazelle in 1986) and its yearly increasing level by rival tribesmen pointed to the flaws in planning, design and implementation which top-down conservation projects all too often make.

The Harasiis were greatly saddened by the extermination of the oryx. They had shared the same ecological niche with the oryx for centuries. The tribe had been pushed into the remote, waterless plain of the Jiddat nearly 200 years earlier by stronger pastoral tribes (Chatty 1986, 81); the oryx, which had once graced the whole of the arid desert regions of south Arabia, had been pursued and hunted until, by the middle of the twentieth century, it too was found only in the Jiddat (Stanley Price 1989, 37). The Harasiis had seen the progressive decline in numbers take place and had recognised the looming tragedy. Their stories and campfire tales spoke about this decline. But they had been unable to stop the motorised hunting parties that descended upon them from the Emirates and elsewhere in their search for oryx. The idea of setting up an oryx sanctuary in their traditional territory had never been discussed with them, nor had they been consulted on the most suitable area to place such a sanctuary (Chatty 1996, 136). The aims of the project, its goals, the implied restrictions on infrastructural development and even the importance of their cooperation were never put forward to the tribal community. Once this internationally supported project had actually commenced, however, the Harasiis went along with the spirit of the enterprise; they were sincerely pleased to see the oryx returned to the Jiddat-il-Harasiis. And for a limited number of men there was the opportunity of paid employment as 'oryx rangers' tracking and generally keeping an eye on the reintroduced animals.[5]

As long as the Harasiis were perceived to have no aspirations of their own, no desire to see an improvement in their access to water, no desire to have regular road grading or infrastructural development in their traditional homeland, relations with the oryx reintroduction project remained untroubled. But the Harasiis, like people everywhere, are opportunistic. They wished to improve their lives and had no special desire to remain in some sort of pristine traditional state just for the sake of not changing. Slowly at first, and later with greater speed, the Harasiis came to realise what was being expected of them and what constraints they were under. They came to understand that, in drought conditions, they were expected not to camp within the vicinity of an oryx herd, even when all other grazing areas were depleted.[6] At about the same time, the tribe's long-standing campaign to have a water well dug by the Ministry of Water and Electricity in a promising area north of Yalooni, appeared to be blocked by the staff at the oryx reintroduction project. Furthermore, the Harasiis felt that efforts to get the national petroleum company to regularly grade roads in the vicinity were also being thwarted. At the same time, the long-standing rivalry between the Harasiis and their neighbours, the Jeneba, found new expression. An old blood feud between the two tribes had been settled by the Sultan's representative in 1968, and relations between them cooled down. More numerous and better educated, having had longer exposure to schooling, Jeneba tribesmen managed to get most of the skilled jobs available in the tribal centre of Haima, the administrative capital of the Jiddat-il-Harasiis. Some wanted the better-paying jobs at the oryx project but discovered that these positions were restricted to Harasiis tribesmen. Although the relationship cannot be proved, the fact that there has been a tremendous rise in the rate of poaching (by 1998 only 130 animals remained of a herd estimated at around 400 in 1996) and that those poachers caught have all been Jeneba tribesmen, suggests that intertribal rivalry is on the rise.[7]

---

5.   Ten Harasiis men were given jobs as rangers in 1980 and the number grew to 17 by 1986 (Stanley Price 1989, 203). These jobs were well paid by local standards. But more significantly they were meaningful and involved using skills already honed after a lifetime in the desert tracking animals, cars, and people.

6.   A confrontation over grazing competition in the mid-1980s should have raised the alarm with conservationists. Several oryx calves had been frightened either by the Harasiis camps or the presence of their goats and the oryx reintroduction manager requested that the Harasiis move away. Some refused. They simply could not understand that the survival of their herds of goats was less important than a few wild oryx.

7.   The estimated number of oryx poached in 1996 is drawn from several informants both on the Jiddat itself and in the capital, Muscat. In 1997 poaching of mainly female oryx increased dramatically and in 1998 only 30 female oryx were reported to remain in the wild. In 1999 the project management team brought all the 30 female oryx back into the camp enclosure at Yalouni while it reconsidered

Furthermore, to many disaffected, largely unemployed men and rival tribesmen, the oryx sanctuary makes no sense other than to put wild animals first, before people and domesticated herds. They see no benefit to themselves, their families or their community. The opportunity to make some money by illegal capture thus becomes a temptation difficult to resist, especially as they have no sense of ownership or participation in the animal sanctuary or the larger, national biodiversity conservation effort in general.

Nearly a third of the Jiddat-il-Harasiis was identified for a national nature reserve in 1986 as a preliminary step in turning the area into a UNESCO World Natural Heritage Site. In 1994 the northern and eastern section of the Jiddat-il-Harasiis, an area of 27,500 square km, was established by royal decree as the Arabian Oryx Sanctuary. The Harasiis tribe was not consulted or educated as to the significance of this decree. Few, if any, Harasiis understood that the decree was the first step towards dividing the Jiddat into three land use zones: a core area with the strictest environmental protection; a buffer zone, with fairly strict protection, in which a limited number of activities would be permitted if they were compatible with conservation objectives; and a transition zone where most activities would be permitted unless clearly damaging to conservation objectives. Nor did they know that a land use and management plan was being prepared for the entire area (Ministry of Regional Municipalities and Environment 1995). A cursory examination of the preliminary report clearly revealed that the Harasiis were still not being consulted or integrated into the conservation scheme in any way other than as passive participants. This lack of consultation with the indigenous population was defended by some of the conservation advisors in the country with the claim that the tribe would not have understood the 'sophisticated' issues involved.

Working quietly and consistently for the past ten years, the Harasiis tribe have begun to challenged this conservation zoning system. They have succeeded in overcoming strong resistance to having a reverse osmosis water plant built by the government in an area that is considered a buffer zone of the sanctuary. This has created some difficulties for the oryx sanctuary management team. A similar situation is likely to occur in respect to local roads. The management plan intends that a careful network of local roads be established 'in consultation with the stakeholders' requirements in the area'. These are listed in the following order as: wildlife conservation, tourist access, mobility of government staff and finally the '*legitimate movements* of the indigenous pastoralists' (emphasis mine). The Harasiis and Jeneba tribes are unlikely to allow themselves to be considered last and they are likely to challenge who has the right to determine the 'legitimacy' of their own movements. Quietly and persistently, as in the past, they will work to achieve what they feel is necessary for the needs of their communities.

---

how to keep the project alive. Omani solders were then posted at the oryx sanctuary in order to protect the female oryx and also to discourage any further illegal capture.

Poaching for live oryx has been spurred by the large purses (sometimes in excess of $30,000) which the wealthy elite in neighbouring countries are offering for wild oryx to add to their private zoos. The pattern of poaching in the Jiddat is suggestive of traditional tribal raiding. The Jeneba obviously see the oryx as 'belonging' to the Harasiis. So the act of poaching can be regarded as an expression of economic and political rivalry.

Fortunately, the goodwill of the Harasiis tribe remains largely intact. Being a small, marginal tribe, and for decades far removed from the seat of government, they are used to protracted battles until their points of view are recognised. However, for the long-term sustainability of biodiversity conservation development, it is in the interest of the state and the conservation authorities to try to bring the Harasiis population and neighbouring tribes into a truly participatory relationship with the project. Otherwise, the project has no long-term future. With ever-increasing numbers of Harasiis youths attending the high school at Haima (the first class graduated in 1993) there is still the possibility that the local population could be drawn gradually into the conservation project – through concerted education, curriculum development, and skilled employment – in a more significant capacity than the 'passive participation' (Pretty *et al.* 1994) of the past. Truly interactive participation may prove to be the solution to the current malaise.

Sustainable conservation requires, above all else, the goodwill of indigenous populations. As McCabe *et al.* (1992) and others have demonstrated, linking conservation with human development offers the most promising course of action for long-term sustainability of nature and human life. McCabe *et al.* argue that nature reserves and other protected areas must be placed in a regional context. If the economy of the human population is in a serious state of decline, the establishment of a wildlife reserve in their midst does not augur well for long-term sustainability. On the other hand, if the problems of the human population are addressed and the community envisages benefit from a combined conservation / development scheme, then cooperation and long-term sustainability is possible. It is this lesson which the Oryx Sanctuary management team now seems to be heeding with its newfound interest in bringing a social scientist on board to work with its largely natural science oriented staff.[8]

CONCLUSION

Although each country in the Arabian Peninsula has to face different sets of economic, political and social factors, a feature that is found in common throughout is the plight of the subsistence mobile pastoralist. Without exception, their territorial usufruct is no longer recognised by the central government; their struggle to subsist has required that they acquire modern forms of transport that can only be supported by some form of wage labour. By accident, mismanagement, and force of circumstances, these pastoral peoples have been left to find their own solutions. Their dependence upon government has remained superficial and these communities continue to adapt to changes in their environment; ever searching for a meaningful and viable existence for themselves and their herds. What remains to be seen is whether international pressure for accountability,

---

8. Although the Oryx Sanctuary website still maintains very little focus on the indigenous mobile pastoral peoples in their midst, information from recent Omani graduates studying in the UK indicates that the Oryx management staff are concerned to better understand pastoral tribal systems and are considering hiring a social scientist to join their team.

transparency and respect for human rights among international conservation agencies will continue to hold weight (Kimmerling 2001). Within the global conservation movement, concern for the human rights of indigenous peoples has been translated into a local search for more participatory forms of natural resource management so as to exhibit greater respect for indigenous livelihoods. How effective that recognition becomes depends on the continuing demand internationally for accountability and transparency. All indications are that the global environmental movement is making strides in that direction, most notably with articles 8j and 10c of the Convention on Biological Diversity (CBD 1992), the Statement of Principles on Indigenous Peoples and Conservation (WorldWide Fund for Nature 1996), the World Conservation Congress Resolutions on Indigenous Peoples (IUCN 1996) and most recently the Dana Declaration on Conservation and Mobile Peoples (2002), which fed into the World Parks Congress Recommendation on Conservation and Mobile Indigenous Peoples in Durban, South Africa in 2003, and finally in 2008 was endorsed by the World Conservation Congress in Barcelona.

In the remote and largely arid lands inhabited by mobile pastoralists in the Middle East, indigenous human rights movements are non-existent. Good social policy recommendations by international conservationists and pressure on national governments to respond will depend upon continuing global efforts to promote sound social policy and prioritised local partnerships. Without such external efforts, it is unlikely that the mobile pastoral communities of the Middle East alone would be able to leverage support for their rights, interest, and desire to see investment in their traditional territory take on the shape which they, themselves, feel would benefit them.

BIBLIOGRAPHY

Anderson, D. and Berglund, E. (eds.) 2003. *Ethnographies of Conservation: Environmentalism and the Distribution of Privilege*. Oxford and New York: Berghahn Books.

Bocco, R. 1990. 'La Sédentarisation des Pasteurs Nomades: Les Experts Internationaux Face à la Question Bédouine au Moyen-Oriente Arabe (1950–1970)', in Pouillon and Bernus (eds.) *Les sociétés pastorales: analyse critique et histoire des doctrines*. Paris: ORSTOM, Cahiers des Sciences Humaines.

Cernea, M. (ed.) 1991. *Putting People First: Sociological Variables in Rural Development*. 2nd edn. New York: Oxford University Press.

Chatty, D. 1984. 'The Bedouin of Central Oman', *Journal of Oman Studies* 1: 149–63.

Chatty, D. 1986. *From Camel to Truck*. New York: Vantage Press.

Chatty, D. 1995. *Hired Shepherds: Impoverization and Marginalization of Bedouin in Jordan and Syria*. Amman: Centre for Agricultural Reform and Development in the Near East.

Chatty, D. 1996. *Mobile Pastoralists: Development Planning and Social Change in Oman*. New York: Columbia University Press.

Adapting to Biodiversity Conservation

Chatty, D. 2003. 'Environmentalism in the Syrian Badia: The Assumptions of Degradation, Protection and Bedouin Misuse', in Anderson and Berglund (eds.) *Ethnographies of Conservation: Environmentalism and the Distribution of Privilege.* Oxford and New York: Berghahn Books.

Chatty, D. and Colchester, M. (eds.) 2002. *Conservation and Mobile Indigenous Peoples: Forced Settlement, Displacement and Sustainable Development.* Oxford: Berghahn Books.

Dana Declaration on Mobile Peoples and Conservation. 2002. Accessed at www.danadeclaration.org.

Dyson-Hudson, N. 1991. 'Pastoral Production Systems and Livestock Development Projects: An East African Perspective', in Cernea (ed.) *Putting People First: Sociological Variables in Rural Development.* 2nd edn. New York: Oxford University Press.

Ibn Khaldun, translated by F. Rosenthal. 1958. *The Muqqadimah.* New York: Pantheon.

International Institute for Environment and Development (IIED). 1994. *Whose Eden? An Overview of Community Approaches to Wildlife Management.* London: IIED.

Irani, K. and Johnson, C. (eds.) 1998. 'Making it Pay: Can Community Based Biodiversity Conservation Programmes be Sustained through Market-driven Income Generating Schemes?' Paper presented at the International Workshop on Community-Based Natural Resource Management, Economic Development Institute of the World Bank, Washington, DC.

Jungius, H. 1985. 'Prospects for Reintroduction', *Symposium of the Zoological Society of London* **54**: 47–55.

Kimmerling, J. 2001. 'Uncommon Grounds: Occidental's Land Access and Community Relations Standards and Practices in Quichua Communities in the Ecuadorian Amazon', *Law and Anthropology* **11**: 179–247.

McCabe, J.T., Perkin, S. and Schofield, C. 1992. 'Can Conservation and Development be Coupled among Pastoral People? An Examination of the Maasai of the Ngorongoro Conservation Area, Tanzania', *Human Organization* **51**, 4: 353–66.

May, P., Dabbs, A., Fernandez-Davila, P., Goncalves da Vinha, V. and Zaidenweber, N. 1999. *Corporate Roles and Rewards in Promoting Sustainable Development: Lessons Learned Form Camisea.* Berkeley: Energy and Resource Group, University of California.

Ministry of Regional Municipalities and Environment. 1995. *Preliminary Land Use and Management Plan: The Arabian Oryx Sanctuary.* Muscat: Ministry of Regional Municipalities and Environment.

Moser, T. and Miller, D. 1999. 'Multinational Corporations' Impacts on the Environment and Communities in the Developing World: a Synthesis of the Contemporary Debate', in Wehrmeyer and Milugetta (eds.) *Growing Pains: Environmental Management in Developing Countries.* Sheffield: Greenleaf Publishing.

Oppenheim, M. 1939. *Die Beduinen*, 4 vols. Leipzig: Otto Harrassowitz.

Pimbert, M. and Pretty, J. 1995. *Parks, People and Professionals: Putting Participation into Protected Area Management.* Geneva: United Nations Research Institute for Social Development (UNRISD). Discussion Paper 57.

Pouillon, F. and Bernus, E. (eds.) 1990. *Les sociétés pastorales: analyse critique et histoire des doctrines.* Paris: ORSTOM, Cahiers des Sciences Humaines.

Pretty, J. *et. al.* 1994. *A Trainer's Guide to Participatory Learning and Interaction.* IIED Training Series no. 2. London: IIED.

140

Dawn Chatty

Rae, J. and Chatty, D. 2001. 'Participatory Project Appraisal for the Mukhaizana Field Development: A Social Impact Study' for Petroleum Development Oman. Oxford: Oxford University Consulting.

Rafiq, A. 1966. *The Province of Damascus: 1723–1783*. Beirut: Khayat.

Sammane, M. 1990. *Bedouin Population Development: Findings and Recommendation*. New York: United Nations.

Stanley Price, M. 1989. *Animal Re-introductions: the Arabian Oryx in Oman*. Cambridge Studies in Applied Ecology and Resource Management. Cambridge: Cambridge University Press.

Volney, C.-F. 1787. *Voyage en Egypte et en Syrie*. La Haye: Mouton.

Wehrmeyer, W. and Milugetta, Y. (eds.) 1999. *Growing Pains: Environmental Management in Developing Countries* (Sheffield: Greenleaf Publishing).

TRADITION AND TRANSITION IN THE MONGOLIAN PASTORAL ENVIRONMENT

Troy Sternberg

School of Geography, Oxford University

INTRODUCTION

Pastoralism has been an integral part of the Asian steppe environment for millennia. Recent changes significantly impact on livelihoods across the region; these include rapid socio-economic and political transition, evolving land use practices, changing climates and increasing aridification affecting the steppe grasslands (Lioubimtseva *et al.* 2005; Yang *et al.* 2005; Geist 2005; Rossabi 2005; Zhang *et al.* 2007). In fact, Asia now has the world's 'greatest concentration of areas of rapid land-cover changes, and in particular dryland degradation' (Lepers *et al.* 2005, 122). Asia's pastoral dynamics and geographical conditions represent localised physical and human influences that make a regional perspective key to understanding the pastoral environment. Research embedded in Asia is critical to assess dominant ecological and human concerns on the steppe, yet previous environmental and livelihood studies and discourse has centred on African environments (Sporton and Thomas 2002; Sallu 2008). Knowledge of factors affecting herding viability is critical to the future of Mongolian pastoralism.

Inner Asia has undergone major political and social transition from communism to a market-oriented development model. Within the region, Mongolia is a country where pastoralism evolved in a harsh landscape and now adapts to modern livelihood challenges. The environment is experiencing a warming climate, increased precipitation volatility, land cover change and natural phenomena such as drought and *dzud* (extreme cold winter weather) that have been little studied (Batima *et al.* 2005). Concurrently, socio-economic factors, changing herder perceptions and practices and modernising processes affect pastoralism.

Serious climatic events occur with increasing frequency on grasslands identified as highly degraded, with this resulting in an intensification of natural hazards (Fernandez-Gimenez 1999; Bold 2001; UNEP 2002; Yang *et al.* 2004). Traditional, ecologically-based practices continue to evolve as herders concentrate on income generation while government support and development efforts decrease. Pastoral livelihoods, practised in open-range grasslands, adjust to changing conditions in a harsh landscape. The dryland setting exemplifies how physical and human modifications affect desert and steppe grasslands (Lioubimtseva *et al.* 2005; Nandintsetseg *et al.* 2007; Normile 2007).

Expanding the existing dryland focus beyond Africa and the Middle East broadens knowledge and provides an understanding of Inner Asian pastoral environments. Regional landscape dynamics and herders' ecological interactions and perceptions can be examined to determine environmental parameters and steppe-ecological processes in Mongolia. This enables comparison with land use and herding practices, both within the wider region and globally, and can convey steppe environmental dynamics to the international scientific community (Li *et al.* 2006). Critical pastoral elements focus on drought, *dzud*, degradation, and human interactions within the natural landscape as herding takes place in an ecosystem confronting changing global processes and socio-economic influences (Sternberg *et al.* 2009). This paper synthesises local geography, evolving environmental forces and herder transformation on the Mongolian steppe.

BACKGROUND

Drylands cover a third of the world's land mass and are inhabited by a billion people (Veron et al. 2006; Washington-Allen *et al.* 2008). In these landscapes pastoralists engaged in mobile livestock-raising are a subset concentrated in Africa and the Middle East (Thomas *et al.* 2000; Evans and Geerken 2004; Herrmann and Hutchinson 2005; Hein 2006); pastoral research has traditionally focused on these regions. Past geopolitical constraints have led to under-representation in the academic literature of pastoral environments in the arid and semi-arid zones of Central and East Asia (Fernandez-Gimenez 1999; Li *et al.* 2006). The steppe landscape is characterised by extensive dry plains, great seasonal temperature variability and extreme cold, in an inland continental location where rangelands provide 80 per cent of livestock feed (Sugita *et al.* 2007). Mongolian pastoralism has not faced the common pastoral pressures of expanding population and agricultural and, until recently, economic forces. Remote from developed-world paradigms, alternative government interaction models have created a landscape that offers both divergent physicalities and perspectives that differ from conventional pastoral environments. Previous disengagement from western development approaches provides the opportunity to expand dryland understanding. This work broadens knowledge and definition of pastoral environments in the Gobi Desert, an area of 1,295,000 km² in Inner Asia, expanding existing dryland focus beyond Africa and the Middle East (Figure 1) (Allen and Warren 1993).

Nomadic pastoralism, the movement of livestock and herders according to seasonal and ecological conditions (Bazargur 2002), is practised on the Mongolian steppe with this customary activity continuing to provide a livelihood for 40–50 per cent of the national population (Fernandez-Gimenez 2006; Chuluundorj 2006; Johnson *et al.* 2006). Historically, limited ecological resources and restricted livestock numbers encouraged mobility as a means to use grasslands productively. Today pastoral inputs

Tradition and Transition in Mongolia

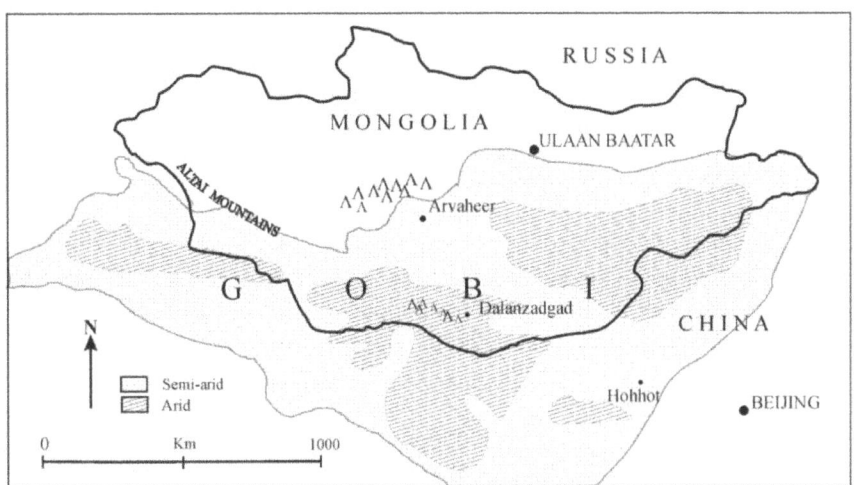

Figure 1. Map of Mongolia featuring the Gobi Desert.

function within a complex system balancing physical and anthropogenic change with environmental and socio-economic limitations. Sustainable land use, income, modernisation and climate variability are pastoral concerns in an era of social transition. In the steppe landscape bio-physical and human determinants shape pastoral viability and the environment in the Gobi Desert, Mongolia.

Water, land cover and the human impact on drylands are well studied; these factors can segue into degradation, sustainability and development. In desert landscapes these issues combine to shape both physical and human pastoral environments. In Mongolia, water exemplifies this interaction; its availability determines pasture resources and grazing patterns whilst its scarcity affects land use and cover and engenders degradation, particularly where livestock intensification has taken place. Water resources are dependent on climate and human action – the former affects surface sources, underground recharge and grassland growth; the latter controls water infrastructure (wells), use patterns and development. Both the environment and pastoralists react to changing pastoral parameters (e.g. livestock, mobility, economic forces) that impact on land cover, degradation and livelihood practices. On the steppe there are multiple inter-related factors; these require geographical description, environmental definition and an understanding of the composite layers of pastoralism.

Setting

Knowledge of the physical and historical setting is essential for defining the parameters of the pastoral environment. The Gobi Desert of Mongolia encompasses desert, desert steppe and steppe landscapes that represent the majority of the country's terrain (Geographical Atlas of Mongolia 2004). Factors that once ensured seclusion – isolation, distance, limited opportunity – now constrain development. Societal transition from Soviet communism to democratic capitalism since 1990 has reconfigured pastoralism. The customary subsistence approach to livestock-raising has given way to market-oriented demands and intensification around limited water points. Natural hazards, once mitigated by a strong state, are now more likely to become disasters. As pastoral needs and motivations evolve within a modernising society the key to understanding past and present processes on the steppe is awareness of the physical–human nexus framing the environment. Historically transhumanance has been an effective adaptation to natural limitations; today's challenges offer perhaps the greatest test to pastoralism's continued existence.

Physical

Mongolia, located in Inner Asia, is bordered by Russia to the north and China to the south. Grasslands comprise 80 per cent of the country's 1.56 million km^2, an area that supported 34 million livestock (sheep, goat, horses, camels, cattle/yak) in 2006 (Mongolian Statistical Yearbook 2006). An upland country, 85 per cent of the land is above 1000 m asl with most grassland between 1000 m to 2500 m asl. Bio-climatic zones include montane (8 per cent), forest steppe (15 per cent), steppe (34 per cent), desert steppe (23 per cent) and desert (19 per cent) (Geographical Atlas of Mongolia 2004). The continental climate, extreme temperature variation (40°C to -40°C annually, diurnal ranges of up to 30°C), short growing season and poor soils limit crop agriculture to <1 per cent of the surface area (Batima and Dagvadorj 2000). Annual precipitation ranges from <50 mm in the southern Gobi region to >400 mm in mountain areas; the national average is 224 mm (Batjargal 1997). Two thirds of Mongolia has no open water sources and is dependent on wells to water livestock and 70 per cent of the country's potential underground water resources are located in the Gobi Desert and steppe regions (Johnson *et al.* 2006). Recent out-migration from rural areas has increased the population of the capital Ulaan Baatar to 1 million inhabitants. As a result, the country's urban centre determines the national agenda, leaving herders with minimal input into politics and policy. The low population density (1.7 people per km^2) accentuates the livelihood challenges extant in Mongolia's harsh landscape.

Historical and Political

Recent luminescence dating applications to sediments suggest a 6,500 year history of grazing on the Inner Asian steppe (Mandzy-Herring 2008); conventional sources trace pastoralism on the Mongolian plateau over more than 4000 years (Fernandez-Gimenez, 1999; Landsberg *et al.* 2003; Sasaki *et al.* 2008). The inhabitants, identified variously as Turkic or Proto-Mongol, were pastoral nomads later supplanted by Mongols. Chinese sources from the eighth century BC identify nomadic people whose 'power rested in their supremacy as horsemen and warriors, living a nomadic existence based on sheep and goats, with oxen and camels as draft animals' (Moses and Halkovic 1985, 17). The loosely-organised tribes that dominated the central steppe were unified in 1206 by Genghis Khan.

Initial western contact with and commentary on Mongolia came from the Italian John of Plano Carpini and the Frenchman William of Rubruck in the thirteenth century. Writings in the eighteenth century by Ides (in 1705) and Bell (in 1763) provided additional description of the country. Geographical knowledge of the region was expanded in the later nineteenth century through the explorations of Przhevalsky, Elias (of the Royal Geographical Society) and Gilmour and by Hedin and Verbrugge at the start of the twentieth century (Hedin 1925; Miller 1952; Bold 2001). This work was descriptive; over the last hundred years the physical landscape and pastoral practices have been documented by Russian scholars and western researchers. Early notable observations were made by the naturalist Roy Chapman Andrews on his paleontological expeditions in the 1920s in southern Mongolia. At the same time the Russian geographer Andrei Simukov undertook a systematic examination of Mongolian pastoralism.

Though historical pastoral practices are recognisable today, the political and economic structure within which pastoralism is now practised has evolved markedly over the last century. The current market-oriented, privatised livestock system contrasts with the feudal approach of one hundred years ago and seven decades of Soviet communism in the twentieth century. During the earlier era pastoral administration was exercised by secular princes or leaders of Buddhist monasteries through informal regulatory institutions that coordinated seasonal movements and controlled large numbers of livestock maintained by local herders ('serfs') following 'unwritten law' (Fernandez-Gimenez 1999; Bold 2001; Suttie 2005). In 1924 Mongolia became the first Soviet satellite nation to adopt a communist system of state-owned rangeland. Collectivisation was unsuccessfully attempted between 1929–1932 as Mongolians preferred to let animals perish rather than become state property. Nevertheless, by 1960 re-implementation led to 99 per cent of herders becoming collectivised (Moses and Halkovic 1985; Middleton 1992). From this time a government-directed, centrally-planned economy controlled herding, allocated rangeland, regulated migration and provided livelihood support. This was a period of infrastructure expansion, water development, veterinary services, subsidised transport, emergency fodder and relief. Herders received a salary and had limited livestock (75–150), though in the event of mortality they had to repay the government (Fernandez-Gimenez 2000; Ykhanbai *et al.* 2004). The era transformed pastoralism from its traditional subsistence basis to a production-oriented system. By maintaining highly mobile, low impact grazing patterns the environmental consequences during collectivisation were limited.

With Soviet rule the state favoured Russian researchers in the Mongolian territory. The difficulty with this is that much written in Russian has not been translated (Fernandez-Gimenez 1999) and that at times articles stress a 'Soviet man' angle, such as class formation in nomadic society, for political reasons that do not ensure objectivity.

Troy Sternberg

Works by Russian scholars such as Simukov, Vladimirtsov, Shul'zenko and Murzaev that address pastoralism are often inaccessible to western academics today. Similarly, access to later work by Mongolian researchers of the period including Natsagdorj, Batnasan, and Bazargur is limited. During the communist era, some information on the people and ecology of Mongolia that derived from original and secondary sources was provided by western researchers including Lattimore and Krader and, in the late 1970s, by Humphrey (Krader 1955; Fernandez-Gimenez 1999). However, as late as 1987, Middleton reported that, as the first British Council scholar to Mongolia, he was permitted no travel or fieldwork outside the capital.

Political upheaval in the Soviet Union coupled with a pro-democracy movement in Ulaan Baatar, Mongolia's capital, brought societal transformation in 1990 (Rossabi 2005). Events over a short period saw countrywide transition from state communism to a democratic market economy stressing private ownership and responsibility and a drastically reduced government role. Elections were held and in 1992 a new constitution was ratified that enshrined human rights, personal freedoms, communal land stewardship, and decollectivised livestock (Bilskie and Arnold 2002). After 15 years of reform Mongolia now follows into the more universal pastoral norms of maximised livestock production, reduced mobility, increased sedentarisation and concentration on income-producing animals, with herder motivation and options changing from meeting quotas to generating income similar to other pastoral regions in the world (Bedunah and Harris 2002; Sorbo 2003). Concurrently government levels of support and control have been slashed, land tenure has evolved towards private possession and poverty is widespread (Sneath 2003). The predictable results are the deterioration of the rural water infrastructure, intensified grazing patterns, increased land degradation and an end to cooperative herding decision-making and implementation (Batjargal 1997; Janzen and Bazargur 2003).

Climate

Inner Asian pastoralism encounters significant climate challenges. The region combines African summers with Siberian winters, Saharan levels of precipitation with alpine environments. *Dzud*, the primary natural hazard caused by extreme winter snow and ice conditions, prevents livestock from foraging and causes high mortality and human displacement (Suttie 2005).

Drought is a major concern throughout drylands, particularly its impact on land degradation (Herrmann and Hutchinson 2005) – yet in Mongolia it has received little attention. Fluctuating precipitation, warming temperature (1.8°C increase over 60 years), changes in seasonality, shifting frost-free days and high climate Coefficients of Variation make a chaotic weather background for pastoralism (Begzsuren *et al.* 2004; Batima *et al.* 2005; Munkhtsetseg *et al.* 2007). As elsewhere, climate defines pastoralism but with factors distinct from most other arid zones. Variable climate patterns and precipitation seasonality control pasture growth, limit agricultural opportunities and reduce alternatives to herding. The combination of climatic stress and land cover change can cause physical disturbance and social disruption (Williams and Balling 1996).

Climatic benchmarks are important in any ecological system. Several dryland regions have well-established climatic data records and numerous historical analyses of climatic patterns, their impacts and their implications have been carried out (Hayes *et al.* 1999; Lloyd-Hughes and Saunders 2002; Sonmez *et al.* 2005). During the communist era, meteorological capabilities were developed in Mongolia; data collection continues with the potential for analysis and interpretation that could be instructive for rural livelihoods and provide source material available for informing government action. Detailed knowledge, critical for rangeland planning in other countries, has yet to receive local scientific enquiry. Precipitation anomalies have growing importance for local herders and government pasture management as climate change increasingly affects regional weather patterns and temperature gradients (Wu *et al.* 2007; Nandintsetseg *et al.* 2007).

The Mongolian landscape presents atypical physical parameters for pastoralism, such as extreme cold. Whereas drought is common in arid regions, its coupling with severe winter conditions (*dzud*) causes a natural hazard of paramount concern to local pastoralists but unknown outside Inner Asia (Batima *et al.* 2005). The common perception is that the two hazards are related, with drought exacerbating the effects of *dzud* and leading to increased livestock mortality (UNCCD 2002; World Bank 2004; FAO 2006). However, recent investigation of the potential interaction between drought and *dzud* through analysis of meteorological records suggests these hazards may occur independently in Mongolia (Sternberg et al. 2009).

DEGRADATION AND RANGELAND DYNAMICS

Degradation

A primary concern across the world's rangelands is the effect of land cover change, desertification and degradation on grassland productivity and pastoral livelihoods (Veron *et al.* 2006).

While degradation may represent a loss of land productivity, desertification can signify a system crossing a negative threshold, resulting in permanent decline and an inability to return to its original state (Geist 2005; Sasaki *et al.* 2008). The concept of desertification, which remains somewhat controversial, originated to describe dryland changes in Africa. Reports of the southward expansion of the Sahara desert in the 1970s and the United Nations Conference on Desertification in 1977 created international awareness of the issue (Lamprey 1975; Sallu 2008). Though it is well known that landscapes are impacted upon by changing climatic and physical factors as well as human action, only recently have the previously remote regions of Inner Asia been assessed (UNEP 2002; Yang *et al.* 2004; Flores-Flores *et al.* 2008). Research into desertification and degradation on the Mongolian plateau has global implications

Troy Sternberg

due to the Pacific-wide effect of associated dust transport and its potential impact on populations (Chen and Tang 2005; Akata *et al.* 2007; Wang *et al.* 2008).

The United Nations (UNU 2007, 1) identifies desertification exacerbated by climate change as the 'greatest environmental challenge of our time' – yet there is a lack of consensus on how degradation is identified and measured. Goudie (1990) highlights several formative processes for desertification. These range from human or natural causes to climatic, temporal and spatial agents. Differing definitions reflect the variability and disorder surrounding the science of desertification that continues today (King *et al.* 2007; Stringer 2008). Although assessment of desertification is elusive, it has become an important part of the Mongolian national debate (Batjargal 1997; Rudaya *et al.* 2008). While some literature acknowledges data limitations and a shortage of field observations (Wang *et al.* 2005), claims for desertification in Mongolia vary greatly depending on the assessment method and location. Sasaki *et al.* (2005) draw their conclusions from one piosphere whereas Yang *et al.* (2005) suggest that 640,000 square kilometres of Mongolia are vulnerable to degradation.

Regional assessment methodologies vary widely, including measurement of biomass, soil, erosion and vegetation cover, lay and expert analysis, remote sensing, climate modelling and meta-data studies (Yang *et al.* 2005; Li *et al.* 2006; Huang and Siegert 2006; Bayarjargal *et al.* 2006; Sternberg *et al.* 2011). Consequently, the effectiveness of methods used in this vast region, the applicability of results from specific research sites and the limited numbers of surveys and validity of analyses remain uncertain.

The challenge in Mongolia is to evaluate degradation and, if relevant, identify whether it is influenced by anthropogenic pressure, natural processes or a combination of factors (Rudaya *et al.* 2008). Locally multiple causes of degradation are cited, ranging from a warming climate, extreme winter weather, drought, loss of land cover, biomass and rodent damage to overgrazing, lack of wells and transport and mining practices (Okayasu *et al.* 2007).

Mongolia's under-researched drylands (Sasaki *et al.* 2008) offer a prime example of how land cover change in arid and semi-arid environments continues to be poorly documented and its causes remain inadequately understood. The UNCCD (United Nations Commission to Combat Desertification) (2002) found a lack of information and monitoring of desertification in Mongolia. The country's pastoral dynamics, including extreme cold, limited agricultural viability, low population pressure and high percentage of the population dependent on pastoral livelihoods, create a pastoral system that does not fit well in established international categories (Johnson *et al.* 2006). Incorporating the diverse elements that shape pastoralism can determine if land cover change is part of ongoing resilient processes or represents a transition to irreversible ecological states, signifying desertification (Thomas and Middleton 1994; Veron *et al.* 2006).

Research on land degradation, desertification and human impact on the environment has taken place across the globe. Africa has traditionally been well-studied by western academia for historic, cultural and political reasons, with much critical thinking on pastoralism, degradation, sustainability and land cover change emerging from the region (Thomas *et al.* 2000; Hein 2006; Herrmann and Hutchinson 2005). The Mongolian landscape, due to its remote location and prior Russian orientation (Fernandez-Gimenez 1999), has received limited documentation and there have been few linkages between Inner Asia and a broader international context. Research methods and procedures for investigating herding and land cover change have been established globally that can be replicated and implemented through local fieldwork and remote sensing techniques.

Mongolian Rangelands

Unlike some rangelands (e.g. Australia or the United States) where there has not been long-term exposure to managed grazing, the Mongolian environment has evolved with domesticated livestock (Fernandez-Gimenez 1999; Landsberg *et al.* 2003). This posits that continual interaction between livestock and vegetation may have contributed to today's landscape where grazing, limited water supply, stable species richness and variable plant distribution patterns coexist. Sasaki *et al.* (2008) propose that, due to a long history of livestock use, Mongolia's vegetation is relatively resistant to grazing. Few places have had such longstanding human/nature interaction, with this making a distinction between the two either impossible or inappropriate (Dearing 2006). Over this long trajectory the fundamental strategies of pastoralism have been consistent: mobile and adaptive grazing to cope with variable precipitation and production conditions in a harsh environment (Fernandez-Gimenez 2006). With societal and systemic transformation it is essential to examine current pastoral practices, their impact on the land and how the human–physical interchange shapes grassland conditions and viability.

The Asian steppe ecosystem is sensitive to climate change and human disturbance across the Mongolian plateau that comprises Mongolia and Inner Mongolia, China (Shinoda *et al.* 2007; Jun Li *et al.* 2007). Two divergent governmental systems and policy frameworks further influence land cover dynamics in the greater Gobi environment. Differing livestock grazing, human population, agricultural pressures, land tenure systems, management decisions, production inputs and state support create disparate grassland conditions in Mongolia and China with both facing land degradation risks (Chen and Tang 2005; Kawamura *et al.* 2005). A decline in rangeland functionality and an increase in desertification in China and Central Asia makes understanding vegetation dynamics a prerequisite before addressing regional environmental conditions (Yang *et al.* 2005; Li *et al.* 2006). The United Nations Environment Programme (2002) cites high pasture vulnerability to desertification whilst across the border, field surveys and expert assessments identify China as one of the world's most desertified countries (Zhao *et al.* 2005; Yang *et al.* 2005). Studies show an increase in desertification from an annual rate of 1,100 km^2 in the 1960s, to 2,260 km^2 in the 1990s, to 3,600 km^2 today, with 861,000 km^2 now desertified (Li *et al.* 2006; Normile 2007). However, differing methodologies, approaches to analysis and levels of data accuracy make these claims of high desertification rates in the region difficult to assess.

150

Troy Sternberg

In arid and semi-arid environments like the Mongolian plateau, livestock grazing is often considered a major cause of land degradation (Zhao *et al.* 2005; Okayasu *et al.* 2007). Additional detrimental impacts in drylands centre on fragility vs. resilience in dryland ecosystems, persistence of 'irrational' traditional herding practices and whether human activity (stocking strategies) or natural conditions define grassland productivity (Perkins and Thomas 1993; Reynolds *et al.* 2007). In northern China degradation is driven by livestock grazing, agricultural practices, inappropriate land management decisions, population pressure, mining and erosional processes (Chen and Tang 2005; Kawamura *et al.* 2005). In Mongolia, low population density, negligible agriculture, a lack of private tenure as well as limited livestock production inputs, capital and state support create different grassland conditions (Johnson *et al.* 2006). Although these conditions remain largely unexamined, livestock grazing is thought to be the main cause of rural land degradation in Mongolia (UNCCD 2002).

The topicality of degradation in Asia stresses the need for understanding broader regional and global complexities. Not only is Mongolian pastoralism different from that in Africa and the Middle East, it is distinct from Chinese herding practices as open grazing, common land stewardship, a lack of fencing and low government support contrasts markedly with China's controlled and intensified livestock raising patterns. This is important as degradative processes on the Mongolian plateau now spread beyond national borders. International land cover change studies suggest that soil particles in southern Mongolia and northern China are the source of Asian dust, with this having a significant influence on the regional and global environment as it spreads to Japan, Korea and further afield (Akata *et al.* 2007; Normile 2007).

Although discussion of desertification rates in Mongolia cannot directly benefit from the application of African experiences, prior research has demonstrated the importance of underlying processes and examination of causal factors when assessing deteriorating physical conditions and increased human impact on land cover (Hein 2006). The strength of research efforts over time in Africa is that these have addressed the question of whether the causes and claims of degradation/desertification represent crossing an ecological threshold or a normal fluctuation in precipitation and grazing response (Thomas *et al.* 2000; Fernandez-Gimenez and Swift 2003). Lacking adequate study, the degradation debate in Mongolia has been defined by international organisations such as the World Bank and United Nations rather than academic investigation (UNEP 2002; World Bank 2004).

Though Mongolia covers a vast area, greater than Botswana and Namibia combined, negligible local funding and low global awareness have resulted in limited attention in the Gobi Desert region. While in Africa environmental research drawing together physical and human dimensions has a long history, in Mongolia there is a dearth of similar research. The lack of regional investigation provides a superb setting to research environmental processes and identify how indigenous land-use patterns impact land degradation in the Gobi Desert. Until this is empirically tested we cannot make claims for the universality of previous findings from other drylands.

HERDER DIMENSIONS

Physical parameters that determine the natural environment intersect with anthropogenic factors to shape the pastoral landscape (Middleton and Thomas 1997; Geist 2005; Sallu 2008). The nexus of these forces attracts much attention, highlighting intensified interest in dryland sustainability and degradation. Combined physical and social research can lead to understanding the dynamics and differences between the two realms shaping today's pastoralism. In drylands, where there is often a balance of limited resources in variable ecosystems, the setting provides determinants that human action can either engage with constructively or use detrimentally. This pattern of engagement and research is well established in Africa (Perkins and Thomas 1993; Sallu 2008) and is relevant to the Asian steppe.

Across drylands, pastoral communities have common concerns regarding environmental productivity, evolving landscapes, and livelihood viability (Zhang *et al.* 2007). Mongolian socio-economic issues focus on the efficacy of traditional pastoral patterns, market forces, water availability, mobility, pasture access, modernisation and out-migration. In the Gobi Desert these factors revolve around income sources, particularly goat-cashmere, access to transport for seasonal migration, adequate wells in suitable pasture and overgrazing/livestock concentration. An additional challenge is maintaining a modified herding lifestyle that incorporates traditional approaches, such as mobility and continued access to seasonal pasture, while accommodating new features including basic technologies (vehicles, solar power, mobile phones), economic forces and evolving forms of land tenure (Sternberg 2008).

Sustainability concerns incorporate the dryland dilemmas of climatic variability, temperature, limited resources and evolving herd composition with unusual social factors caused by transition from a Soviet to a market-oriented development model. Dependence of half the population on pastoral livelihoods, slashed government investment and, recently, competition for water and labour from small-scale mining further stress livelihoods. An understanding of herder motivations and desires, whether economic, social or ecological, shows how human actions impact the landscape and affect the resilience of both herding lifestyles and the natural environment. This allows the separation of physical and social factors, such as the effect of drought from the role of grazing practices on pasture productivity or the impact of livestock intensification on land degradation. Once roles are clarified, sustainability and degradation and their proximate causes, whether physical or social, can be discussed.

The importance of determining the physical landscape is that it will frame the coming decades of pastoralism on the steppe. The mechanisms that have maintained pastoralism – mobility, seasonal migration, moderate livestock numbers for a subsistence existence and some regulation of movement and location, are no longer institutionalised. Today's realities place pastoralism as an economic pursuit within a modernising society, with animals as a source of wealth to provide goods, from food to technology to education. Population, development and the role of herding in society will affect environmental productivity and thus livelihoods.

Troy Sternberg

Income decisions are weighed against expenses so that financial motivations can lead to behaviour that may stress limited pasture resources. Secondary to livelihood concerns are daily pressures in an uncertain environment, particularly declining water sources, marked by a 50 per cent reduction in the number of wells (Tanaka *et al.* 2005). These pressures shape the pastoral equation because they determine accessible pasture and thus feasibility of movement. The lack of water sources leads to stock intensification around a reduced number of sources. Inability of government or herders to develop new water points, due to financial or technical constraints, then accentuates and perpetuates the scarcity, resulting in increased pressure on the environment. This process resonates through multiple layers as it influences mobility, marginalisation and differentiation within the herding community, factors that are best evaluated in totality rather than isolation to explain the drivers creating the Gobi steppe environment.

PERSPECTIVES ON THE MONGOLIAN PASTORAL ENVIRONMENT

Because of relative isolation pastoral concepts and research parameters have been established in other dryland environments. Non-equilibrium dynamics, Social-Ecological System theory and the desertification debate are examples of discourse that originated globally and are now applied in Mongolia. Methods developed elsewhere, from vegetation box plots and soil sampling to socio-economic household surveys, are now undertaken in Mongolia. Greater *in situ* research, increased localised knowledge and interpretation and dissemination of findings will add a Mongolian dimension to global pastoralism.

Regional Setting

The Inner Asian pastoral region loosely comprises northern and western China, Mongolia and parts of Central Asia, particularly Kazakhstan and Kyrgyzstan. In the past the area was approached as a distinct whole, whereas now it is separated by national boundaries (Miller 1952; Akiner 1998; FAO 2003). The majority of research takes place in China where, in the last decade, there has been an increasing focus on degradation, ecology, land management and human and livestock impact (Huang and Siegert 2006; Jun Li *et al.* 2007; Wang *et al.* 2008). A growing openness among Chinese researchers now enables discussion of environmental challenges resulting from potentially poor land use practices (farming, intensification, irrigation, fencing), settlement, increasing populations, government policy, socio-economic factors and concerns about climate change and ecosystem sustainability (Chen and Tang 2005; Normile 2007). Findings can potentially inform research and debate in Mongolia.

Largely missing is a discussion of mobile pastoralism; it is seldom practised in Inner Mongolia and is limited among minority groups (Uighur, Kazakh) in western areas of China. Government schemes, economic development, *de facto* land possession, agriculture, fencing and related issues limit the relevance of China in a transhumance context (Banks 2001; Shaoliang *et al.* 2007). Zhang *et al.* (2007) note the loss of ecologically sustainable nomadism in northern China and identify the conversion to cropland as destroying the grassland ecosystem. For pastoralism a Chinese perspective is most instructive in delineating the impact human action and state policy can have on the Gobi environment and herding practices.

Former Soviet states in Central Asia, traditional pastoral regions, are not often researched. A major factor for this is the 'collapse' of livestock numbers and the breakdown of transhumance since independence in Kazakhstan and a similar decline in Kyrgyzstan (Ellis and Lee 2003). Additional factors limiting study include a focus on mineral resource development and government restrictions on foreign participation. Thus an area that has a shared pastoral history, including collectivisation and similar climatic and physical conditions, is not well engaged in the scientific pastoral debate.

SUMMARY

As environmental conditions and herder motivations evolve, the context in which pastoralism is practised is transformed. Ecological constraints, economic pressures and limited resources challenge pastoralism and affect its role in Mongolia. Action and engagement that recognise physical limitations and inherent strengths are the key to ongoing herding viability. This takes leadership based on current realities and awareness of the multiple forces shaping pastoralism now and in the near future. Research, development and sustainability on the steppe will take a concerted effort across society.

Mongolia needs a broad outlook to better understand its position in the pastoral world, acknowledge its relative strengths and weaknesses and fairly evaluate environmental processes, livestock-raising and related development issues. Currently China is viewed negatively for political and historical reasons and as not relevant to the country. A more constructive assessment would acknowledge its relative advancement and examine northern China's development arc and resultant environmental challenges and pastoral impacts. In a similar landscape China's experience – mistakes and successes – can be instructive to Mongolia's nascent development. This would clarify the impact of current livestock-raising techniques including the effect of fencing, *de facto* privatisation, animal quality and numbers, over-extraction of groundwater, government support, improved infrastructure, economic organisation and the resulting pastoral environment.

Interdisciplinary research is key to assessment and understanding; much research in Mongolia has been dependent on international efforts and funding. Though relevant public and university departments exist, an organised research programme on pastoralism could be implemented to address drought and degradation on the steppe, improve understanding of *dzud* and clarify management and policy roles. Such efforts play to Mongolian strengths – a desire for education, improving capacity, a growing international perspective among younger members of society and a reasonably open and democratic government system, factors that encourage and recognise the practical benefits of research. Efforts can include national and provincial government staff, particularly in the Ministry of Nature and the Environment, the Institute of Geography and university departments of Geography and Remote Sensing that can provide the skills and training for significant research.

These issues point to how a developing country can engage with a larger world and benefit from knowledge and experience of other nations in similar circumstances. Research, particularly by Mongolians, that bridges distances and histories can be of great benefit to the country by encouraging approaches that have been successful elsewhere, maximising rural investment and avoiding failed programmes, with China as the obvious starting point despite cultural barriers. Recognising development challenges may encourage traditional Mongolian strengths and engender societal stability as herding remains a key part of the country's cultural identity.

Pastoralism faces an uncertain future around the world. To create viability over vulnerability will take simple solutions – greater expectations are unreasonable. Work that informs this paradigm, contributes to livelihood improvement and encourages sustainable environmental use will be most relevant to herders. As Fernandez-Gimenez (1999) states, 'Mongolia stands out as a nation in which pastoralism has thrived and where – if anywhere – it may survive.'

BIBLIOGRAPHY

Akata, N., Hasegawa, H., Kawabata, H., Chikuchi, Y., Sato, T., Ohtsuka, Y., Kondo, K., Hisamatsu, S. 2007. 'Deposition of 137Cs in Rokkasho, Japan and its relation to Asian dust', *Journal of Environmental Radioactivity* **95**: 1–9.

Akiner, S. 1998. *Sustainable Development in Central Asia.* New York: St Martin's Press.

Allen, T., Warren, A. (eds.) 1993. *Deserts: the Encroaching Wilderness* London: Mitchell-Beazley.

Banks, T. 2001. 'Property rights and the environment in pastoral China: evidence from the field', *Development and Change* **32**: 717–740.

Batima, P., Dagvadorj, O. 2000. 'Climate change and its impacts in Mongolia', National Agency for Meteorology, Hydrology and Environmental Monitoring. Ulaan Bataar.

Batima, P., Natsagdorj, L., Gombluudev, P. Erdenetsetseg, B. 2005. 'Observed climate change in Mongolia', *AIACC Working Paper No. 12.* www.aigccproject.org

Batjargal, Z. 1997. 'Desertification in Mongolia', *RALA Report No. 200*: 107–113.

Bayarjargal, Y., Karnieli, A., Bayasgalan, M., Khudulmur, S., Gandush, C., Tucker, C. 2006. 'A comparative study of NOAA–AVHRR derived drought indices using change vector analysis', *Remote Sensing of Environment* **105**: 9–22.

Bazargur, D. 2002. 'Territorial Organization of Mongolian Pastoral Livestock Husbandry in the Transition to a Market Economy', *Focus on Geography* **47**: 20–25.

Bedunah, D., Harris, R. 2002. 'Past, present & future rangelands in China', *Rangelands* **24**: 17–22.

Begzsuren, S., Ellis, J., Ojima, D., Coughenour, M., Chuluun, T. 2004. 'Livestock reponses to droughts and severe winter weather in the Gobi Three Beauties National Park, Mongolia', *Journal of Arid Environments* **59**: 785–96.

Bilskie, J., Arnold, H. 2002. 'An examination of the political and economic transition of Mongolia since the collapse of the Soviet Union', *Journal of Third World Studies* **19**: 205–218.

Bold, B. 2001. *Mongolian Nomadic Society*. New York: St. Martin's Press.

Chen, Y. and Tang, H. 2005. 'Desertification in north China: background, anthropogenic impacts and failures in combating it', *Land Degradation and Development* **16**: 367–76.

Chuluundorj, O. 2006. 'A Multi-Level Study of Vulnerability of Mongolian Pastoralists to Natural Hazards and Its Consequences on Individual and Household Well-Being', Ph.D. Thesis, University of Colorado, Denver.

Dearing, J. 2006. 'Climate–human–environment interactions: resolving our past', *Climate of the Past* **2**: 187–203.

Ellis, J., Lee, R. 2003. 'Collapse of the Kazakstan livestock sector', in C. Kerven (ed.) *Prospects for Pastoralism in Kazakstan and Turkmenistan: from State Farms to Private Flocks*. London: RoutledgeCurzon. pp. 52–76.

Evans J., Geerken R. 2004. 'Discrimination between climate and human-induced dryland degradation', *Journal of Arid Environments* **57**: 535–54.

FAO (Food and Agriculture Organization). 2003. Transhumanent grazing systems in Temperate Asia. '*Plant Production and Protection Series No. 31*' Fao.org/docrep/ 006/Y4856E/ Y4856E00.HTM

FAO (Food and Agriculture Organization). 2006. '*Country Pasture/Forage Resource Profiles – Mongolia*' Fao.org /ag/AGP/ AGPC/doc/Counprof/Mongol2.htm

Fernandez-Gimenez, M. 1999. 'Sustaining the Steppes: A Geographical History of Pastoral Land Use in Mongolia', *The Geographical Review* **89**: 315–42.

Fernandez-Gimenez, M. 2000. 'The role of Mongolian nomadic pastoralists' ecological knowledge in rangeland management', *Ecological Applications* **10**: 1318–26.

Fernandez-Gimenez, M. 2006. 'Land use and land tenure in Mongolia: a brief history and current issues', *USDA Forest Service Proceedings RMRS-P-39*. pp 30–36.

Fernandez-Gimenez, M., Swift, D. 2003. 'Strategies for sustainable grazing management in the developing world', in N. Allsopp, A. Palmer, S. Milton, K. Kirkman, G. Kerley, C. Hurt, and C. Brown (eds.) *Proceedings of the VIIth International Rangelands Congress*. 26 July–1 August 2003, Durban, South Africa. pp. 821–31.

Flores-Flores, J., Santha, S., Thomas, D., Safriel, U., Eswaran, H., Solh, M., Davies, J., Kowsar and Bissonnette, J. 2008. 'Experts address the question: "Are poverty and land degradation inevitable in desert-prone areas?"' *Natural Resources Forum* **32**: 77–80.

Geist, H. 2005. *The Causes and Progression of Desertification*. Burlington: Ashgate.

Geographical Atlas of Mongolia. 2004. Administration of Land Affairs, Geodesy and Cartography. Ulaan Baatar.

Goudie, A. 1990. 'Desert Degradation', in A. Goudie (ed.) *Techniques for Desert Reclamation*. Chichester: John Wiley & Sons.

Hayes, M., Svoboda, M., Wilhite, D. and Vanyarkho, O. 1999. 'Monitoring the 1996 drought using the Standardized Precipitation Index', *Bulletin of the American Meteorology Society* **80**: 429–38.

Hedin, S. 1925. *My Life as an Explorer*. New York: Kodansha International.

Hein, L. 2006. 'Impacts of grazing and rainfall variability on the dynamics of a Sahelian rangeland', *Journal of Arid Environments* **64**: 488–504.

Troy Sternberg

Herrmann S., Hutchinson C. 2005. 'The changing contexts of the desertification debate', *Journal of Arid Environments* **63**: 538–55.

Huang S. and Siegert F. 2006. 'Land cover classification optimized to detect areas at risk of desertification in North China based on SPOT VEGETATION imagery', *Journal of Arid Environments* **67**: 308–327.

Independent Commission on International Humanitarian Issues (ICIHI). 1986. *The Encroaching Desert: the consequences of human failure*. London: Zed Books.

Janzen, J. and Bazargur, D. 2003. 'The transformation process in mobile livestock keeping and changing patterns of mobility in Mongolia – with special attention to western Mongolia and Ulaanbaatar', in Y. Ishikawa and A. Montari (eds.) *The New Geography of Human Mobility – Inequality Trends?* Rome: Societa Geografica Italiana.

Johnson, D., Sheehy, D., Miller, D. and Damiran, D. 2006. 'Mongolian *Rangelands* in transition', *Secheresse* **17**: 133–41.

Jun Li, W., Ali, S. and Zhang, Q. 2007. 'Property rights and grassland degradation: A study of the Xilingol Pasture, Inner Mongolia, China', *Journal of Environmental Management* **85**: 461–70.

Kawamura, K., Akiyama, T., Yokota, H., Tsutsumi, M., Yasuda, T., Watanabe, O., Wang, G. and Wang, S. 2005. 'Monitoring of forage conditions with MODIS imagery in the Xilingol steppe, Inner Mongolia', *International Journal of Remote Sensing* **26**: 1423–36.

King, C., Bigas, H. and Adeel, Z. 2007. *Desertification and the International Policy Imperative*. Hamilton: UNU.

Krader, L. 1955. 'Ecology of Central Asian pastoralism', *Southwestern Journal of Anthropology* **11**: 301–25.

Lamprey, H. 1975. 'Report on the desert encroachment reconnaissance in northern Sudan' *UNESCO/UNEP.* p.16.

Landsberg, J., James, C., Morton, R. and Muller, W. 2003. 'Abundance and composition of plant species along grazing gradients in Australian Rangelands', *Journal of Applied Ecology* **40**, 6: 1008–24.

Lepers, E., Lambin, E., Janetos, A., Defries, R., Achard, F., Ramankutty, N. and Scholes, R. 2005. 'A Synthesis of Information on Rapid Land-cover Change for the Period 1981–2000', *BioScience* **55**: 115–24.

Li, X., Jia, X. and Dong, G. 2006. 'Influence of desertification on vegetation pattern variations in the cold semi-arid grasslands of Qinghai-Tibet plateau, north-west China', *Journal of Arid Environments* **64**: 505–22.

Lioubimtseva, E., Cole, R., Adams, J. and Kapustin, G. 2005. 'Impacts of climate and land-cover changes in arid lands of Central Asia', *Journal of Arid Environments* **62**: 285–308.

Lloyd-Hughes, B. and Saunders, M. 2002. 'A drought climatology for Europe', *International Journal of Climatology* **22**: 1571–92.

Mainguet, M. 1991. *Desertification: Natural Background and Human Mismanagement*. Berlin: Springer-Verlag.

Mandzy-Herring, L. 2008. *Vegetation dynamics and environmental change in Mongolia* D.Phil. Thesis, Oxford University, Oxford.

Middleton, N. (1992), *Last Disco in Outer Mongolia*. (Sinclair-Stevenson, London).

Middleton, N. and Thomas, D. 1997. *World Atlas of Desertification,* 2nd Edn. London: Arnold.

Miller, R. 1952. 'A selective survey of literature on Mongolia', *The American Political Science Review* **46**: 849–66.

Mongolian Statistical Yearbook. 2006. Ulaan Baatar.

Moses, L. and Halkovic, S. 1985. *Introduction to Mongolian History and Culture.* Bloomington: Research Institute for Inner Asian Studies.

Munkhtsetseg, E., Kimura, R., Wang, J. and Shinoda, M. 2007. 'Pasture yield response to precipitation and high temperature in Mongolia', *Journal of Arid Environments* **70**: 94–110.

Nandintsetseg, B., Greene, J. and Goulden, C. 2007. 'Trends in extreme daily precipitation and temperature near Lake Hovsgol, Mongolia', *International Journal of Climatology* **27**: 341–7.

Normile, D. 2007. 'Getting at the Roots of Killer Dust Storms', *Science* **317**: 314–16.

Okayasu, T., Muto, M., Jamsran, U. and Takeuchi, K. 2007. 'Spatially heterogeneous impacts on rangeland after social system change in Mongolia', *Land Degradation & Development* **18**: 555–66.

Perkins, J. and Thomas, D. 1993. 'Spreading deserts or spatially confined environmental impacts? Land degradation and cattle ranching in the Kalahari Desert of Botswana', *Land Degradation and Rehabilitation* **4**: 179–94.

Reynolds, J., Stafford Smith, D., Lambin, E., Turner II, B., Mortimore, M., Batterbury, S., Downing, T., Dowlatabadi, H., Fernandez, R., Herrick, J., Huber-Sannwald, E., Jiang, H., Leemans, R., Lynam, T. Maestre, F. Ayarza, M. and Walker, B. 2007. 'Global desertification: building a science for dryland development', *Science* **316**: 847–51.

Rossabi, M. 2005. *Modern Mongolia: from khans to commisars to capitalists.* Berkeley: University of California Press.

Rudaya, N., Tarasov, P., Dorofeyuk, N., Kalugin, I. and Andreev, A. 2008. 'Holocene vegetation and environments in the Mongolian Altai derived from the Hoton-Nur pollen and diatom records', *Geophysical Research Abstracts* **10**: 1–2.

Sallu, S. 2008. *Biodiversity dynamics, livelihoods, and knowledge in Kalahari dryland biomes.* D. Phil. Thesis, Oxford University, Oxford.

Sasaki, T., Okayasu, T., Jamsran, U. and Takeuchi, K. 2008. 'Threshold changes in vegetation along a grazing gradient in Mongolian rangelands', *Journal of Ecology* **96**: 145–54.

Shaoliang, Y., Ning, W., Peng, L., Qian, W., Fusun, S., Geng, S. and Jianzhong, M. 2007. 'Changes in Livestock Migration Patterns in a Tibetan-style Agropastoral System', *Mountain Research and Development* **27**: 138–45.

Shinoda, M., Ito, S., Nachinshonhor, G. and Erdenetsetseg, D. 2007. 'Phenology of Mongolian grasslands and moisture conditions', *Journal of the Meteorological Society of Japan* **85**: 359–67.

Sneath, D. 2003. 'Land use, the environment and development in post-socialist Mongolia', *Oxford Development Studies* **31**: 441-459.

Sonmez, K., Komuscu, A., Erkhan, A. and Turgu, E. 2005. 'An analysis of spatial and temporal dimension of drought vulnerability in Turkey using the Standard Precipitation Index', *Natural Hazards* **35**: 243–64.

Sorbo, G. 2003. 'Pastoral ecosystems and the issue of scale', *Ambio* **32**: 113–17.

Sporton, D. and Thomas, D.S.G. 2002. 'Sustainable livelihoods in Kalahari environments: a contribution to global debates', in D. Sporton and D.S.G. Thomas (eds.) *Sustainable Livelihoods in the Kalahari Environments*. Oxford: Oxford University Press.

Sternberg, T. 2008. 'Environmental challenges in Mongolia's dryland pastoral landscape', *Journal of Arid Environments* **72**: 1294–304.

Sternberg, T., Middleton, N. and Thomas, D. 2009. 'Pressurized pastoralism in South Gobi Province, Mongolia: What is the role of drought?' *Transactions of British Geographers – IBG* **34**: 364–77.

Sternberg, T., Thomas, D. and Middleton, N. 2011. 'Drought dynamics on the Mongolian Steppe 1970–2006', *International Journal of Climatology*. DOI : 10.1002/joc.2195.

Stringer, L. 2008. '*Reviewing the International Year of Deserts and Desertification 2006: what contribution towards combating global desertification and implementing the United Nations convention to combat desertification?' Journal of Arid Environments* **72**: 2065–74.

Sugita, M., Asanuma, J., Tsujimura, M., Mariko, S., Lu, M., Kimura, F., Azzaya, D. and Adyasuren, T. 2007. 'An overview of the Rangelands atmosphere–hydrosphere–biosphere interaction study experiment in northeastern Asia (RAISE)', *Journal of Hydrology* **333**: 3–20.

Suttie, J. 2005. 'Grazing management in Mongolia', in J. Suttie, S. Reynolds and C. Batello (eds.) *Grasslands of the world*. Rome: FAO Plant Production and Protection Series No. 34.

Tanaka, T., Abe, Y. and Tsujimira, M. 2005. 'Groundwater recharge process in the Kherlen River basin', *Journal of Groundwater Hydrology* **47**: 1–4.

Thomas, D. 1997. 'Science and the desertification debate', *Journal of Arid Environments* **37**: 599–608.

Thomas, D. and Middleton, N. 1994. *Desertification: Exploding the Myth*. Chichester: John Wiley & Sons.

Thomas, D., Sporton, D. and Perkins, J. 2000. 'The environmental impact of livestock ranches in the Kalahari, Botswana: Natural resource use, ecological change and human response in a dynamic dryland system', *Land Degradation & Development* **11**: 327–41.

UNCCD (United Nations Commission to Combat Desertification). 2002. *Second report on the implementation of the UN Convention to Combat Desertification*. www.unccd.int/cop/reports/asia/national/2002/mongolia-eng.pdf

UNEP (United Nations Environmental Programme). 2002. *Mongolia: State of the Environment 2002*. Ulaan Bataar: United Nations Environmental Program.

UNU (United Nations University). 2007. *Desertification: experts prescribe global policy overhaul to avoid looming mass migrations*. www.unu.edu/media /archives/2007/files/mre29-a-07.pdf

Veron, S., Paruelo J. and Oesterheld M. 2006. 'Assessing desertification', *Journal of Arid Environments* **66**: 751–63.

Wang, X., Chen, F., Hasi, E. and Li., J. 2008. 'Desertification in China: an assessment', *Earth-Science Reviews* **88**: 188–206.

Washington-Allen, R., Ramsey, R., West, N. and Norton, B. 2008. 'Quantification of the ecological resilience of drylands using digital remote sensing', *Ecology and Society* **13**:1–18.

Williams, M., Balling, R. 1996. *Interactions of Desertification and Climate*. London: Arnold.

World Bank. 2004. *Mongolia Environmental Monitor*. Ulaan Baatar.

Wu, H., Hayes, M., Weiss, A. and Hu, Q. 2001. 'An evaluation of the Standardized Precipitation Index, the China-Z Index, and the Statistical Z-Score', *International Journal of Climatology* **21**: 745–758.

Wu, H., Svoboda, M., Hayes, M., Wilhite, D. and Wen, F. 2007. 'Appropriate application of the Standardized Precipitation Index in arid locations and dry seasons', *International Journal of Climatology* **27**: 65–79.

Yang, X., Zhang, K, Jia, B. and Ci, L. 2005. 'Desertification assessment in China: An overview', *Journal of Arid Environments* **63**: 517–31.

Yang, X., Rost, K., Lehmkuhl, F., Zhenda, Z. and Dodson, J. 2004. 'The evolution of dry lands in northern China and in the Republic of Mongolia since the last Glacial Maximum', *Quaternary International* **118**: 69–85.

Ykhanbai, H., Bulgan, E., Beket, U., Vernooy, R. and Graham, J. 2004. 'Reversing grassland degradation and improving herder's livelihoods in the Altai Mountains of Mongolia', *Mountain Research and Development* **24**: 96–100.

Zhang, M., Borjigin, E. and Zhang, H. 2007. 'Mongolian nomadic culture and ecological culture: On the ecological reconstruction in the agro-pastoral mosaic zone in Northern China', *Ecological Economics* **62**: 19–26.

Zhao, H., Zhao, X., Zhou, R., Zhang, T. and Drake, S. 2005. 'Desertification processes due to heavy grazing in sandy rangeland, Inner Mongolia', *Journal of Arid Environments* **62**: 309–19.

~ 8 ~

THEORISING ECOLOGICAL MIGRATION[1]

Emily T. Yeh

University of Colorado – Boulder

INTRODUCTION: ECOLOGICAL MODERNISATION AND ITS DISCONTENTS

A consensus appears to be growing about China and its environment: the country is experiencing a devastating ecological crisis but the state has woken up and is working hard to rescue the environment as it teeters on the brink of collapse. China has become an environmental state, one in which concerns about the environment are being integrated into the fabric of governmental logics, as demonstrated by Chinese Communist Party General Secretary Hu Jintao's exposition of his 'new theory' of the 'scientific outlook on development' which has sustainable development as its basic requirement (Xinhua 2007a). The question that lies before us is whether the country can 'go green', undertaking a 'green leap forward' fast enough to avoid 'environmental meltdown' and ensure planetary survival. This is the story being told, in different ways, by Western public intellectuals (Economy 2004, 2006; Friedman 2006a,b 2008), environmental scientists (Cann *et al.* 2005; Zhang *et al.* 2000) and geographers (e.g. Shen 2004), among others. For example, despite the failure of the national Green GDP initiative in 2005 and 2006, Thomas Friedman notes optimistically that 'it is almost as if a light went on in the Chinese politburo ... finding a way to go green was becoming an imperative, not an option' (2008: 353).

This dominant story of 'going green' is essentially a narrative of ecological modernisation, a perspective that has been called 'a more specific interpretation of the key ideas prevailing in the more general notion of sustainable development' and which, like sustainable development before it, privileges entrepreneurship and market dynamics in creating environmental solutions (Mol 2006: 30; Spaargaren and Mol 1992). It suggests that there is no zero-sum trade off between environmental concerns and economic growth and that environmental problems can be solved through more, rather than less, modernisation, industrialisation and technological innovation (Buttel

---

1.   A longer version of this piece has been previously published as Yeh, Emily T. 2009. 'Greening western China: A critical view', *Geoforum* **40**: 884-894.

2000; Fisher and Freudenberg 2001; Mol 1995). Broadly, its usage connotes a stance that holds radical structural change to be unnecessary and even infeasible; instead, sustainability can and should be achieved through the internalisation of environmental impacts and the greening of business (York and Rosa 2003).

Although the concept of ecological modernisation was developed in studies of Europe, Western scholars have argued that China's environmental reforms can also be interpreted as ecological modernisation, although of 'a different mode' (Mol 2006: 53; Carter and Mol 2007; Ho 2006). Through dialogue between Chinese and Western scholars, ecological modernisation has also gained traction within China itself, as demonstrated by a recent major study by the Chinese Academy of Sciences, China Modernization Report 2007: Study on ecological modernisation. The report states that the basic requirements of ecological modernisation, which it calls 'an inexorable historical trend', are dematerialisation (high efficiency and low waste), greening (hazard free and healthy), ecologisation (waste recycling and innovation) and decoupling (decoupling economic growth from environmental degradation) (CAS 2007). It also states that ecological modernisation requires principles of prevention and innovation, pursuit of win-win results for both economy and environment, and a decoupling of economic growth and environmental degradation (*ibid*).

While these themes are familiar from the European literature on ecological modernisation, the discussion in the report is primarily limited to the technical dimensions of sustainable development, rather than 'the more political innovations in ecological modernization' such as equity, equality and citizen empowerment (Zhang *et al.* 2007: 664–5). In other words, China's emergent official version of ecological modernisation leaves out the elements of ecological modernisation that the framework's critics find most promising (cf. Buttel 2000). Ecological modernisation has been critiqued not only for being easily co-opted as a 'greenwash' for capitalist business-as-usual, but also for lacking coherence as a social theory (Buttel 2000; Hajer 1995; Harvey 1996). After reviewing the many ways in which environmental modernisation is used, Buttel (2000) argues that 'a full-blown theory of ecological modernization must ultimately be a theory of politics and the state,' such as found in literature on state–society synergy and civil society, rather than only a collection of optimistic associations about the potential for industrialisation and modernisation more generally to cure its own ills. Thus western observers of China's 'greening' have been focused on searching for signs of civil society in the growing environmental movement (Mol 2006; Yang 2005, Economy 2004; Friedman 2008). However, in China's own articulation of ecological modernisation, these concerns drop out and emphasis is placed instead on the environmentalisation of the state (Zhang *et al.* 2007). China's official account of its ecological modernisation thus aligns with arguments such as Cann *et al.*'s (2005: 11) that the future is optimistic, because 'for developing and implementing the new market economy in a sustainable manner, China has established a cadre of ambitious plans, policies and projects'.

In this paper I review recent scholarship about environmental protection programmes in China focusing particularly on programmes of ecological construction in

Emily T. Yeh

China's west, and placing ecological migration within this context. My approach is to demonstrate some of the limitations of green triumphalist accounts of these programmes and more generally of assumptions often found in ecological modernisation frameworks and to argue for alternative ways of analysing the greening of western China, including ecological migration. In addition to providing evidence from recent studies that these programmes of greening frequently fail on their own terms, I suggest that insights from political ecology are more suited to helping us understand why this is the case than is ecological modernisation. Political ecology calls for attention to the always and inevitably political dimensions of human–environment interactions, and particularly to the ways in which environmental management efforts may be based upon flawed assumptions and have the effect of expropriating access to and control over natural resources. The Marxian political economy orientation of political ecology calls attention to the social and environmental justice questions elided by ecological modernisation. Furthermore, it suggests that environmental projects are always linked to broader political-economic processes. While ecological modernisation looks to 'economic institutions [to] play a major role in articulating, communicating, strengthening, institutionalizing, and extending (in time and place) environmental reforms by means of their own (market and monetary) "language", logic and rationality' (Mol 2006: 53), a political ecology approach directs our attention to the distributive effects of those market logics. Further, rather than assuming (as claims of greening often appear to do) that environmental reforms *ipso facto* result in environmental goods, it takes the environmental effects as an empirical question. Finally, it suggests that environmental projects are always more than environmental projects – that they accomplish other things too, particularly with regard to governance (cf. Harvey 1996; Robbins 2004).

In addition to questions of access and distributive effects, I include in my framework of critical political ecology the analytic of governmentality. French post-structuralist philosopher Michel Foucault (1991) used the term to understand the emergence of new rationalities of rule that challenged and supplemented sovereignty's logic of the power over death; instead of death, governmentality was concerned with the regulation of life, with the 'right disposition of things' and the regulation of the social body. Thus, it required both the population and the other 'things' to be regulated to come into existence. As an analytic, governmentality draws attention to the ways in which particular forms of representation and ways of knowing of a phenomenon (such as 'the economy') allow the phenomenon to come into existence as a separate domain about which knowledge can be gained; once delineated, it becomes an object upon which actions can be performed (Miller and Rose 2008).

Extending Foucault's formulation of 'life and its mechanisms' to include the human–environment relationship means drawing attention to the ways in which grasslands come into existence as 'nature' and are thus enabled as objects of political and economic calculation. In other words, governmentality calls attention to how 'the apprehension of knowledge about how it is that ecosystems are central to human survival (eco-knowledge) becomes a political technology through which geo-power is exercised' (Baldwin 2003: 419; Luke 1999; Lövbrand *et al.* 2008; Luke 1999; Rutherford, 2007). Sustainability, in this analytical view, is not a politically neutral and universally achievable condition but rather a political project that creates the conditions of possibility for thinking about 'nature' as well as its intervention by experts. Ecology is a discursive regime, a set of ideas and practices that produces truth about nature, authorises certain ways of telling that truth and certain people to speak that truth, as well as enabling new identities with respect to nature (Darier 1996; Rutherford 2007). As Foucault's way of linking his concerns about technologies of the self with those of technologies of domination, governmentality directs our attention to the productive effects of power, including the ways in which environmental projects can produce environmental subjects, subjects for whom 'the environment' is a category in relation to which they think and act (Agrawal 2005; Darier 1996; Snodgrass *et al.* 2008).

The analytical framework I am suggesting as an alternative to ecological modernisation for understanding recent trends in China's environmental protection calls for the bringing together of several modes of examination. First is an analysis of ecological modernisation projects on their own terms, for whether they produce their desired environmental effects. Second, regardless of whether they produce their desired environmental effects, is an inquiry into what the distributive effects of these environmental projects are. Third, if the projects fail in some way, this framework calls for a consideration of the failure not just as a matter of technical flaws in implementation but rather for directing attention to what else is accomplished through the projects – what types of subjects are produced and what other 'regular effects' project flaws or failures may accomplish (cf. Ferguson 1990). This includes a consideration of what forms of power/knowledge enabled these particular environmental projects to be enacted in the first place. Fundamentally, the greening of China must be understood as more than an environmental project; it is also a project that creates new rationalities of rule, new forms of subjectivity and new economic and ecological practices. The creation of a technical 'environment' that can be acted upon by environmental projects has implications beyond the realm of the environment itself. These dynamics are important enough that they should not be simply ignored or bracketed, as they usually are in discussions of sustainable development or greening. While the analysis of environmental protection efforts through what I am calling a critical political ecology framework is not novel, its use for thinking through China's recent 'greening' projects is significant because of the dominance through which these are viewed in terms of ecological modernisation by officials, pundits, environmental scientists and scholars.

CHINA'S WEST

As a framework, ecological modernisation has most frequently been used to describe the ways in which societies respond to increasing awareness of ecological risks associated with industrial processes – that is, technological innovations and policy processes in 'brown' manufacturing and pollution issues such as those highlighted in the run-up to the Beijing Olympics (Fisher and Freudenburg 2001; Gouldson *et al.* 2008; Koppen 2003; Mol 2006). However, the Chinese Academy of Sciences report very clearly includes 'green' natural resource management issues in the purview of China's ecological modernisation. Indeed, according to the report, one of the ten challenges that China's ecological modernisation will face in the first half of the twenty-first century is 'to implement the National Plan for Ecological Environment Construction and quicken ecological modernization in the west region'. This leads to the following strategic measures recommended by the report to ensure ecological modernisation:

> The projects designed to protect natural forests, to facilitate forestation and to build planted forests should continue so as to increase forest coverage to about 35 percent in 2050 and about 40 percent in 2100. Construction of nature reserves should be sped up, the project to 'revert cultivated land back to forestation' should be improved and the natural grassland and pasture should be protected and improved. The goals and tasks specified in the 'National Plan for Ecological Environment Construction' should be implemented in a comprehensive way ... The construction of national nature reserves should be strengthened and the ratio of nature reserves should be raised. (CAS 2007)

This passage refers to a set of dramatic environmental projects begun in China in 1998, at the conjuncture of a series of 'natural disasters' and the launching of the Open Up the West (*xibu da kaifa*) campaign. In response to severe droughts that caused the lower reaches of the Yellow River to run dry for a record 267 days in 1997 and massive flooding on the Yangtze River in 1998, which caused more than 3000 deaths and an estimated 12 billion US dollars in property damage, the government initiated the Natural Forest Protection Plan (NFPP; referred to above as 'protect natural forests, to facilitate forestation and to build planted forests'); and the Sloping Land Conversion Project (SLCP, 'revert cultivated land back to forestation') (Katsigris *et al.* 2004; Shen 2004; Xu *et al.* 2001; Yin *et al.* 2005). The NFPP, often referred to as 'the logging ban', is a ten-year plan launched in full in 2000 to rehabilitate forests by banning commercial logging in the upper reaches of the Yangtze River and middle and upper reaches of the Yellow River, reducing timber output in other state-owned forest areas, providing alternative employment for workers in state-owned logging enterprises and accelerating reforestation and silvicultural treatments. SLCP, sometimes dubbed 'grain for green', is the largest land retirement programme in the world, calling for the conversion of 14.67 million hectares of cropland, especially cropland on steep slopes of greater than 25 degrees, to forest, as well as afforesting 17.33 million hectares of 'wasteland', by 2010 (Bennett 2008; Zhang *et al.* 2008). Made possible by national grain surpluses, it promised farmers grain and cash subsidies lasting five years for those planting 'economic forests' (e.g. orchards), eight years for 'ecological' forests, and two years for grasslands (Xu *et al.* 2007; Yin *et al.* 2005; Zhang *et al.* 2008).

The Sloping Land Conversion Project alone has a budget of over 40 billion US dollars, an indication of the massive scale of the environmental rehabilitation efforts currently underway. It is among the suite of 'ecological construction' projects targeted primarily at western China that have accompanied the national Open up the West campaign, launched in 1999 to reverse the 'trickle-west' economic strategy that characterised development in China since the late 1970s and help the Western region close the development gap with the eastern and coastal provinces (Goodman 2004). This was to be accomplished through investment in major infrastructure projects for communication, transportation and power generation, in order to establish the conditions necessary to attract private and foreign investment to link these places more tightly to the global economy and thus generate wealth. Simultaneously, the campaign called for large-scale ecological construction projects. Environmental protection and specifically ecological construction is a major component of Open up the West, which promised to create national level committees and commit billions of yuan to environmental improvement and to 'check the deteriorating ecological and environmental situation by putting increased investment in basic infrastructure and ecological construction' (People's Daily Online 2000, 2001, 2005).

Initially used in the 1950s, the term 'ecological construction' is now widely employed to refer to all programmes and efforts to improve the rural environment (Jiang 2006), though the largest and most visible of these projects are in China's west. In addition to SLCP and NFPP, these also include *tuimu huancao*, ecological migration and an accelerated programme of nature reserve declaration. These extraordinarily large scale projects have been hailed by both Chinese policy-makers and Western observers as a major sign of China's 'greening', its transformation into an environmental state and hence its ecological modernisation. For example, writing about SLCP, Zhang *et al.* (2008: 68) state that 'the program appears to be a perfect model of ecological modernization'. Indeed, the China Modernization Report 2007 concludes that the 1998 publication of the National Plan for Ecological Environment Construction marks the point at which China took off for ecological modernisation along 'pathway 2 – the canal strategy', one of three possible pathways toward ecological modernisation identified by the report. Surprisingly, it lists not just Beijing and Shanghai but also the Tibet Autonomous Region (TAR) and Qinghai, two of the poorest western provincial-level units, usually designated as 'backward' and lagging behind technologically as well as economically, as among the 'most ecologically modernized' of provincial-level units in China (Zhang *et al.* 2007). The vast land areas of Qinghai and TAR that have come under ecological construction projects, including China's largest and second-largest nature reserves, as well as NFPP, SLCP, ecological migration and *tuimu huancao*, are what give the two provincial level units their 'most ecologically modernized' status. This underscores the importance of ecological construction projects in western China in the national project of ecological modernisation and the conceptualisation of China's transformation into an environmental state.

Drawing on the perspective of critical political ecology discussed above, this article argues that the enthusiastic narrative of China's greening in relation to these ecological construction projects is limited and flawed. In part because most of China's ethnic minorities live in the PRC's geographical western half and because there has long been an assumption that studies that address minorities in China speak only to 'minority' issues rather than to knowledge about China as such (Vasantkumar 2006), western China is often treated in scholarly work as somehow marginal or peripheral to the 'real' China. However, the centrality of these ecological construction projects to China's ecological modernisation story suggests that a view from China's west can offer an important perspective on a broader analysis of the emerging environmental state. Here I borrow from the notion of 'anthropology in the margins of the state', in which the margins are important not as a set of exotic practices but rather as 'a necessary entailment of the state, much as the exception is a necessary component of the rule' (Das and Poole 2004: 4). Thus, while specific issues with green industrialisation, pollution control and recycling in eastern, urban areas are surely different from the management of the rangelands on the Tibetan plateau, a view from the latter is just as important as the former for understanding the nature of the Chinese environmental state.

Shen's (2004) assessment of ecological construction and degradation in western China provides a typical example of a positive account of the environmentalisation of the state *vis-à-vis* the ecological construction programmes that have accompanied the Open up the West campaign. As such it is worth examining in some length. His premises are that there is massive ecological degradation across western China and that this has been induced by population pressure and the conversion of forestry, pasture and sloping land to farmland (2004: 649). As a result of population growth and agricultural land conversion, 'China's western region has the most serious ecological crisis, which poses a major threat not only to the western region itself but also to the ecological security of the whole country' (637). A Malthusian trap leads to increased ecological degradation:

> With low agricultural productivity, more and more labour is employed to produce grain for increased population ... more and more hilly areas and pastures are converted to arable land which is susceptible to soil erosion and ecological degradation ... This necessitates the conversion of more land from hilly areas and pasture. Such a vicious circle is close to the familiar concept of the Malthusian trap (641).

This cycle needs to be reversed by converting cropland back to forests, but

> it is difficult for peasants to find alternative and adequate means of economic sustenance if they switch from farming to forestation ... the peasants' private interests are not consistent with the state's goal for ecological construction for the benefit of the public at large (657).

The solution is a suite of ecological construction projects. The environmentalisation of the state, that is, the internalisation of environmental logics into government programmes, is viewed as a positive step to achieving the win-win combination of economic growth and environmental improvement that is central to the ecological modernisation paradigm:

> Will agricultural and economic development help the fight against ecological degradation? The answer is yes ... government-led projects do show the potential to reverse the trend of ecological degradation in the poor western region. (661).

Theorising Ecological Migration

The problem, in this view, is that 'the top priority of peasants is to survive and their private interests are not consistent with the state's goal of ecological construction'; but by paying farmers to plant trees, the contradictions of the farmers' purported 'private interests' are internalised, and through the poverty relief that subsidies are supposed to provide, these programs can convert the situation to one of mutually reinforcing economic development and environmental improvement.

This rather common way of understanding the ecological construction of China's West is flawed in a number of ways that a critical political ecology approach helps reveal. First, embedded within the narrative are the implications that deforestation, cultivation of steep hillsides and conversion of pastures to farmland result simply from population growth, and that local resource users cannot and will not properly manage their forests without state intervention. This ignores a long history of local forest management in China (Menzies 1994; Sturgeon 2005), as well as the national political campaigns throughout the Maoist period to 'open up the wasteland' and 'learn from Dazhai' that called for grain agriculture in ecologically unsuitable areas, including both high altitude grasslands as well as steep hillsides. Moreover, much of this conversion was done by resettled youth from eastern China who set up large state farms in the west (Rohlf 2003; Shapiro 2001). In ignoring the broader forces that led to significant farmland conversion, the narrative implicitly blames local villagers. Further, by posing the 'private interests of the peasants' of the west in opposition to both the goals of the state and the good of the 'public at large', this narrative implies the western peasants' marginal status as those who are not part of the general 'public'; they are not citizens with whose goals and wellbeing the state is aligned. Instead, the Chinese 'public' appears to refer only to the citizens of China's wealthy eastern areas. Insofar as the NFPP and SLCP were enacted directly and explicitly as a consequence of flooding and drought downstream, they are designed to stabilise the western environment in order to protect the wealth generated through increasingly dense articulations with global capital in the east.

Since the early 1980s, and especially since the 7th Five Year Plan (1986–1990), China's west had been given the role of supplying energy, raw materials and other natural resources support to the centre and 'coastal front' engaged with the global economy. The Open up the West campaign was supposed to put an end to this, allowing the west to finally catch up with the east. Yet, the new suite of ecological construction programs suggests a reinscription, rather than an undoing of the long-standing territorialisation of western China as the provider of natural resources – and now ecological services – needed by the rest of China (Blaikie and Muldavin 2004; Jhaveri 2003; Yeh 2005). Indeed, a number of scholars who have examined aspects of Open up the West other than its environmental components have argued that it is most accurately conceptualised as a programme of state and nation-building, a renewed 'civilising mission' to closely incorporate minority ethnic groups and a reconsolidation of central state control after two decades of decentralisation and localism (Goodman 2004; Holbig 2004; Lai 2003; Oakes 2004, 2007; Shih 2004). These critical examinations of Open up the West as a new state and nation-building exercise have tended to gloss over the ecological construction aspects of the programme, generally stating only that a massive level of investment into environmental protection is part of the program. Yet a closer look at the processes of territorialisation at work in the ecological construction projects of Open up the West show that the environmental components fit well into the larger projects of state building.

As Vandergeest and Peluso (1995: 387; 412) argue, 'all modern states divide their territories into complex and overlapping political and economic zones, rearrange people and resources within these units, and create regulations delineating how and by whom these areas can be used'; these processes of territorialisation include functional territorialisation, 'controlling what people do according to detailed land-classification criteria.' The Chinese Academy of Sciences report on China's ecological modernisation provides a vision of a future that greatly intensifies processes of zoning according to ecological function and land use type:

> If all the above tasks [of ecological modernization] are fully accomplished, China's ecological modernization will reach the world's middle level in 2050 ... about one-third of the national territory will be covered by forests (about 35 percent), one-third of the territory will be used for agricultural purpose (about 36 percent) ... land for construction purpose will account for about 9 percent of the national territory and land for natural landscaping will account for 20 percent (CAS 2007).

Thus, while ecological construction projects are signs of an ecology-inspired transformation, as the ecological modernisation framework suggests, their functional zoning of the west as primarily forests and grasslands that provide ecosystem services to the downstream, capital-accumulating east, suggest that they are also part and parcel of power-laden processes which sort not only territories but also different segments of the population into different roles.

Reading Shen's (2004) account through a governmentality approach also suggests that the territorialisation of the west as a source of ecological services for the east is contingent upon something else taken for granted: a system of ecological knowledge in which it becomes possible to think of vast pieces of territory as 'degraded' and in which a clear connection is posited between the degradation of the landscape and the 'security' of downstream areas, which thus authorises interventions in the form of projects such as NFPP, SLCP, *tuimu huancao* and ecological migration. At the same time, however, using a governmentality approach to analyse rationalities of rule should not imply that rule is seamlessly accomplished (Rutherford 2007; cf. Li 1999, 2007). Instead, it is necessary to analyse both rationalities of rule and how the interventions predicated upon particular discursive regimes are engaged with and compromised in practice at their points of application. I do this below in discussions of the implementation of afforestation and grasslands protection projects, including discussions of environmental degradation and of how these projects produce new forms of subjectivity.

AFFORESTATION

As the Chinese Academy of Sciences report makes clear, dramatically increasing national forest coverage from the current estimate of some 18 per cent to 35 per cent and eventually 40 per cent, is a major component of the country's plans for ecological modernisation (Démurger *et al.* 2005). One part of the plan for reaching this goal is the Natural Forest Protection Program, the implementation of which has dramatically increased China's log imports from other countries, including those with unsustainable and sometimes illegal harvesting practices, such as Papua New Guinea and Myanmar (White *et al.* 2006), a result which points to the limitations of nation-state scale analyses of sustainability. The complete logging ban aspect of the program was designed only to apply to state-owned forests but when it was initially implemented, overzealous officials in Sichuan, Yunnan and Xinjiang extended the ban to collective forests, in some cases even going so far as to prohibit access to non-timber forest products and fuelwood without offering compensation, thus denying collective owners rights guaranteed to them by the Chinese Constitution (Zuo 2001). In places where this happened, communities reduced their active management of forests, resulting in increased illegal activities and forest fires and a shift from community patrol to policing of forests by government workers (Miao and West 2004).

Studies of the ecological effectiveness of the programme to date have thus far been very limited, with case studies suggesting large variations in implementation (Démurger *et al.* 2005). Shen *et al.* (2006) argue that 'if properly implemented', the programme will have both large-scale environmental and economic benefits, a win-win scenario for the environment and the economy. However, Zackey's (2007) study in northwest Yunnan, which showed that logging by local villagers continued despite the logging ban, provides some insight into the difficulties of 'proper implementation'. He found that the reason they logged was neither because of some innate lack of affinity for nature nor because of absolute poverty (indeed the poorest villagers logged the least) but rather because of their frustration at how national economic reforms had apparently left them behind, leaving them feeling further marginalised within the ever more prosperous country. Long-standing patterns of uneven development produce resentment among those who perceive both state corruption and their own marginalisation. Thus it is not economic considerations alone that can lead to environmental improvement, as the ecological modernisation story of greening suggests; instead, moral economy and issues of citizenship must inevitably also play a role in socio-environmental outcomes.

Like NFPP, the Sloping Land Conversion Project has also seen significant variation in local implementation patterns. The programme's rationale, as discussed above, is to pay farmers cash and grain subsidies for five to eight years to plant trees on sloping farmland to '[provide] an opportunity to break through the vicious cycle of poverty-ecological degradation-poverty, and to enter a path of sustainable development' (Zhang *et al.* 2008: 67). However, there are currently no provisions in place for farmers after their short-term subsidies run out; one survey of 316 participating households in Ningxia found that 79 per cent believed they would not have enough grain after the subsidised period, and thus only 8 per cent said they would not re-convert their land back to cropland after compensation ends (*ibid*). There is evidence in some areas that not all farmers have received their subsidies; even where full compensation has been received, it has in some cases fallen short of farmers' revenue before conversion. Moreover, compensation was not adequate for many farmers successfully to develop off-farm income generating opportunities. Multiple studies have also found that most farmers were not consulted in advance and felt they could not choose whether or not to participate in the programme, nor what kinds of trees to plant (Bennett 2008; Xu *et al.* 2004; Zhang *et al.* 2008).

Other problems include the fact that survival rates for planted trees are often quite low. Bennett (2008) argues that from an environmental perspective, provision of subsidies should be conditioned upon higher survival rates but that here the environmental protection and poverty relief aspects of the programme come into contradiction with each other (rather than being mutually reinforcing). Furthermore, Xu *et al.* (2007) argue that one of the unstated goals of the program has been to subsidise the State Grain Bureau, a factor that contributed to the relatively high grain (as opposed to cash) subsidy in the program. Farmers also complain that the grain is poor quality and that they would prefer more cash compensation. Rent seeking, where villages with connections to the local forest bureaus are able to obtain larger quotas, is yet another problem that has been identified (Bennett 2008).

Emerging out of a new rationality of rule, ecological construction projects also help forge distinct forms of subjectivity. Sturgeon (2009) describes the effects of both NFPP and SLCP in Mengsong village, a cluster of Akha hamlets in Yunnan, on the border with Burma. While SLCP was supposed to have been implemented, farmers had received no grain or money subsidies. More importantly, the implementation of NFPP severely restricted villagers' rights to use their collective and even household forests and also made shifting cultivation, long practiced in the area, impossible. Previous shifting cultivation fields in the process of regenerating into forests were also lost to farmers, leading to a 25 per cent drop in household incomes between 1997 and 2002. Furthermore, these Open up the West ecological construction projects were implemented simultaneously with a strengthened national emphasis on raising the 'quality' (*suzhi*) of China's population, believed necessary to transform the nation's citizens into the educated, scientific, rational and entrepreneurial subjects needed for China's entrance into the World Trade Organization (Sturgeon, 2009). The result was the sorting of citizens into those deemed 'high quality', deserving and advanced and those considered 'low quality', blamed both for China's continuing backwardness and increasingly its environmental problems. Marginalised minorities such as the Akha not only became positioned as 'low quality', a discourse which deflected blame for their loss of livelihood opportunities away from government policies and which also led them to blame themselves for environmental destruction – to come to see themselves as environmentally destructive (*ibid*).

This production of environmental subjects through ecological construction can also be seen in a case described by Jiang (2006) in the pastoral Uxin banner of Inner Mongolia. In part because of the way in which local government officials are evaluated, successful performance of ecological construction has come to be equated with increased vegetation cover and practices such as the planting of trees, shrubs and grasses, in order to make sandy land look green and productive. This has led in Uxin banner to a failure of tree planting policies, including SLCP, on their own terms: not only is the survival rate of tree seedlings very low but the overdrawing of groundwater for areas planted with trees has led to worsening degradation at the landscape level through lowering of the groundwater table and expansion of areas of mobile sand (Jiang 2004, 2006). However, while these projects, which also include grassland seeding and other improvement efforts, are thus arguably failures on their own terms, they have had productive effects in terms of producing environmental subjects. Ecological construction programmes have succeeded in influencing local perceptions, such that pastoralists have come to equate ecology with greening the landscape and to believe that intensified planting efforts can accomplish the desired greening. Jiang (2006: 1914) notes with respect to these environmental programmes that

> government policies first alter behaviours, which then help alter perceptions of what is 'right' or 'effective' ... suggest[ing] ... that individual behavioural changes (often significantly enforced by the state) can precede and lead to changing perceptions.

This is strikingly similar to Agrawal's (2005) governmentality approach to understanding community-based natural resource management in the Indian Himalayas. For Agrawal, participatory, decentralised management in forest councils sets conditions through the arrangement of repeated, embodied action for the production of self-governing environmental subjects; through bodily participation in monitoring and enforcement in village forest council rules, the rhetoric offered by villagers for why they wish to protect the forests comes to echo precisely the objectives pursued by the colonial Forest Department more than a century ago (*ibid*). In other words, environmental behaviour precedes environmental interests.

In addition to commenting indirectly on how ecological construction projects produce subjects, Jiang (2006) also makes another important observation about ecological construction: the 'green' that villagers come to associate with ecology is not just the colour of the (newly) desired landscape but also of money or financial benefit. Government funding, including household loans, has been linked to efforts to increase economic growth through grassland improvement, with households expressing interest in both financial growth and grassland improvement receiving loans for land use intensification in the form of seeds and irrigation equipment. Households were also offered other incentives, such as awards of 10,000–50,000 yuan and use rights for 50 years for those that managed to reclaim 5,000 mu of sandy land. As Jiang (2006: 1918) puts it, 'the local government has used ecology to represent material results (trees, shrubs, grasses, and crops) on the landscape, and followed a goal-oriented ecological construction that considers ecology as a means for growth.' While this is precisely what ecological modernisation suggests should be the goal, we have already seen that these programmes have failed ecologically on their own terms, when viewed at the landscape level.

Furthermore, the prevalent slogan in Uxin Ju that 'to have the economy soar, forestry must lead' (*ibid*: 1915) and the belief that ecology is a means for growth, resonate with greening processes elsewhere in China, where greening has become primarily a means to compete economically. The rush to designate nature reserves of all kinds from the 1990s onward can be attributed in part to deregulatory strategies which have allowed local governments to play an active role in their designation – often in the hopes of achieving the administrative status and the tourist income that typically accompany reserves (Jim and Xu 2004). Similarly, Boland and Zhu (forthcoming) show that China's growing urban 'green communities' programmes are fundamentally linked to broader processes of urban restructuring in China; the 'greener' a city can market itself as being, the brighter its economic prospects, in the competition between cities to attract investment capital. Eco-ideals alone cannot explain the emergence of the 'green community' model in China; instead 'the emergence of communities as socioecological objects of regulation is a spatial strategy adopted by cities in response to the increased importance placed on the environment in formulas for economic development', a strategy that relies on state and Communist Party efforts to strengthen the 'community' as a territorial base unit of urban administration (*ibid*). Just as urban green communities often focus on practices that are arguably not the most urgent ones for environmental protection, such as reminding residents to stay off of lawns, removing security bars and adding potted plants (*ibid*), nature reserves often have little significant biodiversity value or are too small to be ecologically viable (Harkness 1998; Harris 2008) and afforestation programmes can result in the growth of patches of trees but also the expansion of sandy areas (Jiang 2006). While often failing to have significant ecological benefits, tree-planting, green communities and the declaration of new nature reserves can work more effectively as spatial strategies for competitive advantage among local governments seeking to attract capital. Ecological modernisation suggests that economic and ecological success should be mutually reinforcing, but numerous examples from China suggest this not to be the case.

RANGELAND IMPROVEMENT AND ECOLOGICAL MIGRATION

Like forestry programmes, successive policies that have been launched to manage rangelands, which constitute about forty per cent of the PRC's land area, also appear to increasingly incorporate ecological considerations into institutional developments. Furthermore, these rangeland protection programmes have recently been incorporated into China's national climate adaptation plans, a move which suggests a further reflexive internalisation of ecological rationales into governance. In particular, both China's National Climate Change Program, prepared by the National Reform and Development

Commission and released in June 2007, and the State Council's White Paper on China's policies and actions on climate change, released in 2008, include specific references to current rangeland policies, including *tuimu huancao*, other measures to control grazing intensity and continued fencing as key measures to enhance climate change adaptation (NRDC 2007; State Council 2008). These policies were put in place before the formulation of climate adaptation strategies but are assumed to be 'win-win' for both rangeland health and climate change adaptation. However, as I will argue, evidence suggests that these policies are likely to fail on their own terms, neither significantly improving rangeland conditions nor enabling successful climate adaptation. They also have unjust distributive effects. At the same time, implementation of the interventions varies significantly from place to place, and is often compromised in practice.

One of the basic premises of the rangeland policies that are now also considered useful for climate adaptation is that there is large-scale, severe grassland degradation across China's pastoral areas, particularly the Tibetan plateau. Since 2002, the statistic that '90% of China's grasslands are degraded, and that the degradation is increasing at a rate of 200 km/year' has become pervasive in scientific papers as well as official publications. However, these figures have not been subject to much scrutiny. As Harris (2010) notes these statistics 'derive from undocumented surveys conducted by local-level staff of grassland and livestock bureaus', without a baseline, or training in field methods. More rigorous attempts to quantify the extent of rangeland degradation have had much more ambiguous and conflicting results (*ibid*). While there is little question that there is overgrazing and very severe degradation in some areas, the dire national-level statistics that provide justification for recent rangeland policies, particularly *tuimu huancao*, remain questionable (see Goldstein and Beall 2002; Holzner and Kreicshbaum 2000).

In addition to an assumption of pervasive, severe degradation, rangeland policies implemented since the extension of the household responsibility system from farmlands to rangelands beginning in the mid-1980s, have also been based on a tragedy of the commons assumption that overgrazing and poor management are the cause of the problems. First introduced in Inner Mongolia shortly after the decollectivisation of livestock, and then gradually to other pastoral areas in western China, the assumption of the household responsibility system is that only privatisation of rangeland use rights can give herders the needed incentive to control their livestock numbers, properly manage their grasslands and convert their 'unproductive' way of life into an efficient, market-oriented system. However, anthropologist Dee Mack Williams (1996, 2002) found in Inner Mongolia that only rich households could afford to buy barbed wire fences; they fenced more than they were allocated but saved their fenced land for emergencies, grazing instead on unfenced common land. This significantly increased grazing pressure on unfenced land, creating a tragedy of the commons (or rather, a tragedy of open access) where none existed before (see also Ho 2000; Jiang 2005, 2006).

In pastoral Xinjiang in far north-western China, despite the allocation of rights to individual households, little land has actually been fenced (Banks 2001, 2003). Instead, groups of households continue to graze in common and fuzzy boundaries persist. These apparently inefficient aspects of rangeland tenure may in practice actually have benefits such as economies of size in herding and boundary monitoring for the group as a whole, abatement of environmental risks and a better match for the spatially concentrated nature of resources such as water. These benefits, which derive in part from biophysical differences between pastoralism and farming, are often ignored but could present opportunity costs in further privatisation (*ibid*). These costs have been noted on the Tibetan plateau as well, where most winter (but not summer) pastures have been legally divided to households, except in the TAR, where implementation is still ongoing. Implementation varies widely even within provinces. As in the case of Xinjiang, in parts of pastoral Ganzi prefecture in Sichuan province, the actual division of the winter grasslands exists more on paper than in practice. In pastoral Aba prefecture of Sichuan province, by contrast, both boundary fencing and the household allocation of winter pasture have been more extensively implemented and in some areas, such as Ruoergai's Xiamai township, pastoralists no longer have distinct summer and winter pastures but rather one single pasture per family, as in a western ranching model (Yan and Wu 2005).

   Where winter rangelands have been divided, inequitable allocation has in some cases severely limited some households' access to both pasture and water resources. According to some researchers, rangeland privatisation on the Tibetan plateau has, by reducing flexibility in a non-equilibrium ecosystem, exacerbated rather than ameliorated degradation (e.g. Miller 2000). Rangeland division has also been associated, in various parts of the plateau, with reduced access to social and economic services, an increase in conflicts over access to rangeland, reduced mobility for wildlife and, in places where wells have been drilled to compensate for lack of access to water after fencing, vegetation change due to lowered groundwater levels (Goldstein 1996; Wu and Richard 1999; Yan and Wu 2005; Yan *et al.* 2005; Yeh 2003). In Ruoergai county of Sichuan province, the estimated number of pastoralists facing lack of water availability tripled after rangeland allocation, to 60–70 per cent of the population, with pastoralists reporting spending an average of two to three hours a day fetching drinking water (Yan *et al.* 2005). Much of the area, including Xiamai township, was once a productive wetland, which was drained in the early 1970s in order to create more pasture. This drainage, exacerbated now by the digging of wells by households whose pastures do not have access to water, has led to significant drying and deterioration of grassland condition in an area that was once a significant wetland.

   Research on grassland policies has been conducted for some time but its impact in the policy arena has been slow to be felt. Blaikie and Muldavin (2004: 542) argue that this is because of the exclusion from 'legitimate discourse [of] other types of knowledge about the environment and the practices of natural resource use by the resource users themselves'. There are signs of change, such as the recent formation of the People and Grasslands Network in Beijing, whose members hope to use insights from scholarly studies to prevent the 'mistakes of Inner Mongolia' from being replicated in other areas (Chang 2007).

At the same time, though, another challenge to herders' livelihoods has been launched recently through a new programme known as *tuimu huancao*, sometimes implemented in conjunction with ecological migration. *Tuimu huancao* began as a variant of SLCP but has grown into a programme that territorialises grasslands into various zones (the specific rules of which vary from place to place): zones declared either off limits to grazing for ten years or permanently; zones to be free from grazing for several to ten years; and zones where pastures will be managed through rotational grazing. In some cases, the areas to be fenced off for several to ten years are also to be seeded. Implementation, again, varies widely. In some parts of Sichuan's Ganzi prefecture, the programme has taken the form of new concrete-post fencing along the highway, some of which is not necessarily even fully enclosed away from the highway. However, local residents must guard the valuable fence from thieves, lest the fence goes missing when officials come to inspect; the programme thus becomes a form of corvee labour for villagers.

The program takes a very different character in the areas of Qinghai province that have been designated the Sanjiangyuan ('headwaters of the Three Rivers', referring to the Yellow, Yangtze and Mekong Rivers) Nature Reserve. Within the 150,000 square kilometre area of the declared reserve, *tuimu huancao* is being implemented in a more dramatic way, with restrictions on livestock numbers, as well as long-term off-limit zones combined with ecological migration. Throughout the area, those who stay on the land are now allowed to keep one sheep unit equivalent per 12 mu (Dell'Angelo 2007). Herders who take part in the programme are to sell all of their livestock and be relocated in settlements in towns, where the government provides a house as well as cash and grain subsidies over a 5–10 year period. Thus, unlike SLCP and other rangeland programs to date, this form of *tuimu huancao* does not seek to privatise resources to give herders better incentive to manage them but rather removes them from the land altogether. In one ecological migration resettlement area just outside of Jyeku town in Yushu prefecture, where 240 households were resettled in 2005, each household is supposed to receive 6,000 RMB per year, as well as 100 kilograms of flour, for five years as a feed grain subsidy. In addition, the households that previously had title to their houses on the grasslands were to receive an additional 70,000 RMB as compensation, though some herders claimed that 38,000 RMB was taken out for the house they were given in the relocation area, with the remaining amount distributed over ten years. Those who do not have a title were to receive 60,000 RMB, again with 38,000 RMB taken out. In return, these herders pledge not to return to their pastures to graze livestock for ten years. Other accounts suggest that herders receive compensation varying between 2,600 and 5,700 RMB per year and that 90 per cent of the cost of their houses at the relocation site are paid by the government (Dell'Angelo 2007; Perrement 2006). According to a Qinghai government plan in 2004, households who resettle voluntarily in groups and who permanently give up livestock herding would be given subsidies of 80,000 RMB as compensation, as well as 8000 RMB grain subsidies over five years; those who voluntarily resettle as individual households and who give up herding for at least ten years are given 40,000 RMB and 6,000 RMB as grain subsidies. Finally, herders who had moved for reasons of deteriorating environmental conditions ahead of programme implementation are to receive a 20,000 RMB compensation package and 3,000 RMB of grain subsidies per year.[2]

According to at least a few official news reports, between the beginning of programme implementation in 2003 and the end of 2007, 60,000 out of the 200,000 Tibetan herders living in the area had participated in the programme and been resettled, with another 40,000 to move, for a total of 100,000 by 2010 (Foggin 2008; Xinhua 2007b). Among these, all 43,000 nomads living in the eighteen designated core areas (20 per cent of the reserve area) are to be moved out (Wang and Jiao, 2008). Other reports suggest that, because of an unwillingness among herders to move, original targets have not been met and the number resettled is much lower.

In the Jyeku resettlement area, an early pilot of the programme, residents reported that they moved voluntarily, though some expressed regrets about having moved. As appears to be the case in other resettlement areas as well, government compensation is inadequate for supporting many families. While many agree that the houses are indeed better than the ones they lived in as pastoralists, they also find that life is too expensive in the town, where they must pay for electricity and water. In Jyeku, many residents appear not to have fully realised the extent to which everything in town must be purchased with cash. They also state that inflation is driving up the prices of goods up while subsidies have stayed the same; some claim that the subsidies are not even enough to buy the fuel they consume annually. Similarly, another study of 113 resettled households in the Sogrima area of Golok found that after two years, the annual income of those resettled in towns was 47 per cent lower than their earlier subsistence income, whereas their expenditures were 52 per cent higher. In this study area, many respondents also stated that their health conditions were getting worse after resettlement in town, because of changes in living conditions as well as diet (Sonamkyid 2009).

Contributing significantly to the problems is the fact that the Tibetan ex-pastoralists do not have Chinese language and other skills needed to earn an income in the towns, leading to unemployment and no income stream in the future. Many are currently living entirely off government subsidies, having already used up whatever money they earned selling off their livestock, leaving important questions about what they will do once their subsidies run out (*ibid*). Indeed, some social problems have already emerged, with resettlement areas quickly earning nicknames such as 'robber villages'. In Jyeku, people in town claimed that the area was dangerous and crime-ridden because the idle former pastoralists had all become thieves and taxi drivers routinely refused to drive to the settlement.

Current problems with pastoralist livelihoods are thus likely to be further exacerbated once subsidies run out. Despite the fact that several skills training workshops

---

2.   '7300 nomadic households in Qinghai voluntarily implement *tuimu huancao* and settle down in towns' (Qinghai 7300 hu mumin ziyuan *tuimu huancao* dingju chengzhen) http://www.agri.gov.cn/gndt/t20041220_287659.htm Last accessed 3 May 2009.

(carpet weaving and motor engine repair) were eventually provided in Jyeku, those who participated have still been unable to find jobs. While some herders have found work as unskilled construction labourers or from new income opportunities such as breeding and selling Tibetan mastiffs, most are subsisting only on temporary subsidies and income from digging caterpillar fungus. Those who do not have the labour power to dig caterpillar fungus are the worst off. Furthermore, though educational opportunities for children are said to be one of the major benefits of resettlement, the biggest complaint of the residents a year after they moved was that they wanted an elementary school for their children, because the one in the main town was too far to walk to. In other resettlement areas, children have been able to access compulsory education but government training schemes have been found to be ineffective and problems have been reported with receiving subsidies in time (Dell'Angelo 2007).

Dell'Angelo (2007) identifies a 'threshold of dissatisfaction' in which families that owned more than 30 yaks prior to resettlement were generally unhappy with moving, even though they had done so voluntarily, whereas those who had fewer livestock felt they were better off, though they also worried about future livelihood prospects. One local intellectual in Jyeku argued in 2006 that once the subsidies run out the social problems (which he claimed were fighting and alcoholism) that had arisen as a result of the resettlement, would be pointed out to show what a backward ethnic group the Tibetans are. Some have argued that Tibetan culture will not be lost because of resettlement, as 'nobody is stopping them from carrying out their culture … they can still sing and dance' (Fan 2008). However, an understanding of culture as both material and inextricably linked to embodied practices, suggests that a sudden shift to a more urbanised economy and concentrated settlements cannot but have cultural effects. In addition, the movement of large numbers of rural herders to settled life in urban areas is likely to have an effect on the prevalence of use of Tibetan language.

Furthermore, although this programme has been officially listed as an important climate adaptation measure and hailed as a sign of the state's commitment to future sustainable development, there is minimal evidence that removing herders will guarantee greatly improved grassland conditions. In fact, recent ecological evidence from warming and grazing experiments on the eastern Tibetan plateau suggests that the presence of moderate grazing modulates the expected effects of global warming on reduction of biodiversity and rangeland quality. While experimental warming leads to decreased species richness, including a specific decline in medicinal plants species, as well as decreased biomass, including palatable biomass, these effects are dampened in the presence of grazing (Klein *et al.* 2004, 2007). These results, particularly those having to do with biodiversity, suggest that ecological migration together with *tuimu huancao* cannot be considered to be necessarily adaptive for climate change. Another recent ecological study also suggests the need to explore the possibility that the implementation of ecological migration makes no significant difference in grassland species richness or composition (Wende 2008).

Thus, here too, the 'greening' of state governance with respect to grasslands may be more effective as a form of internal territorialisation than as a form of either development or environmental improvement. Indeed, just as 'political forests' refer to the declaration by states around the world of certain lands as 'forests', thus constituting them as proper targets of intervention (Peluso and Vandergeest 2001; Siviramakrishnan 1999), *tuimu huancao* in conjunction with ecological migration can be thought of as creating 'political grasslands' or perhaps 'political deserts'; it declares as desertified or degraded territories that are to be conceived of as grassland (*cao*) rather than pasture (*mu*), thus targeting them for particular state logics of expropriation and care. More generally, ecological migration is a component of a broader reterritorialisation of China into different types of zones, from Special Economic Zones to zones deemed too 'degraded' for certain kinds of citizens and livelihoods. The protection of China's 'water tower', as the Sanjiangyuan region has been dubbed, is also said to be vital to the country's ecological security, suggesting the way in which this particular discursive regime of environmental protection is tied to the reproduction of the nation. The logic in which the purported improvement of both the environmental conditions of Tibetan plateau grasslands (which in turn is to protect the wealthy cities downstream from further flooding and thus the ecological security of the country) and the nomads (who are to become more 'developed' by becoming urban residents) will be accomplished is part of a power/knowledge regime that authorises interventions upon a recalcitrant population.

However, it is important not to read governmental rule as a completed project uniformly and passively received by its objects (Li 2007; Rutherford 2007). Understanding the state as a 'self-conflictual institutional ensemble' (Lin and Ho 2005: 436) highlights the incentive structures that lead local officials to fence primarily along highways and to require villagers to patrol fencing material rather than the grasslands. Similarly, fencing programmes are favoured by local officials in some areas despite problems, because they are seen as an effective way of capturing state subsidies (Bauer 2005). At the same time, in many parts of the Sanjiangyuan area, including Maduo, it is primarily those families with few or no livestock who have migrated (Du 2009). In some areas, their pastures are still being grazed by other families, in part because of the lack of monitoring and the non-contiguous nature of the pastures under the programme, thus undermining the ecological rationales of the programme.

Furthermore, environmental interventions also produce new subjectivities and desires, in sometimes unexpected ways. In parts of pastoral Xinjiang and Tibet, herders find some aspects of environmental programmes objectionable while simultaneously desiring other elements, such as settled housing and fencing, as indices of modernity and of the development that they deserve (Zukosky 2007; cf. Li 2005, Sturgeon 2007). Some herders, particularly those who are better off, choose to participate in ecological migration specifically as a way of leaving behind their herding lifestyles (Du 2009); the presence of the ecological migration project may further encourage this shift toward a desire for a new identity and the association of town life with modernity for herders. Thus, projects of ecological construction, which render particular state interventions as technical projects of environmental improvement, lead their subjects to identify and position themselves in new ways, which in turn sets the terrain for further socio-natural transformations and interventions.

CONCLUSION

Ecological construction projects in the west, including *tuimu huancao* and ecological migration, play a prominent role in China's plans for national ecological modernisation. While China has made major improvements in environmental protection, it is important also to take note of the fact that many environmental protection programs that have been celebrated have also sometimes had the effect of further marginalising already marginalised citizens, while producing only questionable environmental benefits. Multiple cases of the implementation of forestry and rangeland protection programs show that a key assumption of ecological modernisation, that economic growth and ecological protection will feed each other in a virtuous, mutually sustaining circle, often does not hold. Though China's ecological construction projects do reflect an integration of certain environmental logics and rationales into state governance, the environmental rationales are in some cases not backed by scientific evidence and the results often disproportionately take away access to resources of some groups over others. These kinds of problems, however, are not addressed by an ecological modernisation framework, which focuses instead on questions of the extent to which technical innovation and economic institutions help extend environmental reforms and to which ecological phenomena are inserted into modernisation processes more generally.

Thus I have argued that a critical political ecology approach is a more productive way of analysing the greening of western China in general, and ecological migration in particular, than the more common ecological modernisation approach. In this perspective, it is important to understand what forms of knowledge and representation allow 'the environment' to come into being as an object of regulation and intervention and what the implications of these authorised interventions are, not only for ecological outcomes and the livelihoods of specific groups of affected people but also for the relationship between the state and different groups of citizens and for the production of new subjectivities. It becomes clear that ecological construction projects in western China can be seen as having acted as a form of reterritorialisation, categorising citizens into those who are considered aligned with the interests of the state at large and others, seen as marginal to the broader Chinese public, who become the targets of intervention of ecological construction projects. At the same time, we cannot assume that green governmentality is a completed project of rule. Instead, there is much more grounded research to be done on how ecological migration and other programmes intended to improve both the environment and promote development, are being implemented and experienced in differentiated, place-specific ways, and with what effects.

Emily T. Yeh

BIBLIOGRAPHY

Agrawal, A. 2005. *Environmentality: Technologies of Government and the Making of Subjects.* Durham, N.C: Duke University Press.

Baldwin, A. 2003. 'The nature of the boreal forest: governmentality and forest-nature', *Space & Culture* 6, 4: 415–428.

Banks, T. 2001. 'Property rights and the environment in pastoral China: evidence from the field', *Development and Change* 32: 717–740.

Banks, T. 2003. 'Property rights reform in rangeland China: Dilemmas on the road to the household ranch', *World Development* 31,12: 2129–2142.

Bauer, K. 2005. 'Development and the enclosure movement in pastoral Tibet since the 1980s', *Nomadic Peoples* 9, 1–2: 53–81.

Bennett, M. 2008. 'China's sloping land conversion program: Institutional innovation or business as usual?' *Ecological Economics* 65, 4: 699–711.

Blaikie, P. and Muldavin, J. 2004. 'Upstream, downstream, China, India: The politics of environment in the Himalayan region', *Annals of the Association of American Geographers* 94, 3: 520–548.

Boland, A. and Zhu J. Forthcoming. 'Public participation in China's green communities: Mobilizing memories and structure incentives', *Geoforum* http://faculty.geog.utoronto.ca/boland/ab_home.htm.

Buttel, F.H. 2000. 'Ecological modernization as social theory', *Geoforum* 31: 57–65.

Cann, C., Cann, M. and Gao, S. 2005. 'China's road to sustainable development: An overview' in K. Day, K. (ed.) *China's Environment and the Challenge of Sustainable Development.* Armonk, NY: M.E. Sharpe. pp. 3–34.

Carter, N.T. and Mol, A.P.J. (eds.) 2007. *Environmental Governance in China.* London: Routledge.

CAS (Chinese Academy of Sciences). 2007. Ecological Modernization Report 2007 (overview) http://www.chinagate.cn/english/reports/50007.htm (last accessed 15 Feb 2009).

Chang, T. 2007. 'Scholars question division of pastoral lands', *China Development Brief.* 3 July. Available at http://www.chinadevelopmentbrief.com/node/1166. Last accessed 28 February 2008.

Darier, E. 1996. 'Environmental governmentality: The case of Canada's green plan', *Environmental Politics* 5, 4: 585–606.

Das, V. and Poole, D. (eds.) 2004. *Anthropology in the Margins of the State.* Santa Fe: School of American Research Press.

Dell'Angelo, J. 2007. 'The Sanjiangyuan Environmental Policy and the Tibetan Nomads' Last Stand: A Critical Political Ecology Analysis', Unpublished MS Thesis, London School of Economics and Political Science.

Démurger, S., Fournier, M. and Shen, G. 2005. 'Forest Conservation Policies and Rural Livelihood in North Sichuan Tibetan Areas', http://ssrn.com/abstract=876870

Du, Fachun. 2009. 'From eco-refugees to Eco-migrants: A research in Maduo county in the source area of the Yellow River'. Draft version.

Theorising Ecological Migration

Economy, E. 2004. *The River Runs Black: The Environmental Challenge to China's Future*. Ithaca: Cornell University Press.

Economy, E. 2006. 'Environmental governance: the emerging economic dimension', *Environmental Politics* 15, 2: 171–189.

Fan, M. 2008. 'For China's nomads, relocation proves a mixed blessing', *Washington Post*, 20 Sept. http://www.washingtonpost.com/wpdyn/content/article/2008/09/19/AR2008091904053. html Last accessed 4 May 2009.

Ferguson, J. 1990. *The Anti-politics Machine: Development, Depoliticization and Bureaucratic Power in Lesotho*. Minneapolis: University of Minnesota Press.

Fisher, D. and Freudenberg, W. 2001. 'Ecological modernization and its critics: Assessing the past and looking toward the future', *Society and Natural Resources* 14: 701–9.

Foggin, J.M. 2008. 'Depopulating the Tibetan grasslands: National policies and perspectives for the future of Tibetan herders in Qinghai province, China', *Mountain Research and Development* 28, 1: 26–31.

Foucault, M. 1991. 'Governmentality', in G. Burchell, C. Gordon and P. Miller (eds.) *The Foucault Effect: Studies in Governmentality*. London: Harvester Wheatsheaf. pp. 87–104.

Friedman, T. 18 November 2006. 'China's Green Leap Forward', *New York Times*.

Friedman, T. 19 Nov. 2006. 'China faces environmental crisis', *The Charlotte Observer.* 27A.

Friedman, T. 2008. *How, Flat and Crowded.*(New York: Farrar, Straus and Giroux.

Goldstein, M. 1996. 'Nomads of Golok: A Report', Available at http://www.case.edu/affil/tibet/ tibetanNomads/books.htm

Goldstein, M.C. and Beall, C.M. 2002. 'Changing patterns of Tibetan nomadic pastoralism', in W.R. Leondard and M.H. Crawford (eds.) *Human Biology of Pastoral Populations*. Cambridge: Cambridge University Press. pp. 131–150.

Goodman, D.S.G 2004. 'The Campaign to "Open up the West": National, provincial-level and local perspectives', in D. Goodman (ed.) *The Campaign to 'Open up the West'*. China Quarterly Series Special No. 5. Cambridge: Cambridge University Press, pp. 3–20.

Gouldson, A., Hills, P. and Welford, R. 2008. 'Ecological modernization and policy learning in Hong Kong', Geoforum 39: 319–330.

Hajer, M. 1995. *The Politics of Environmental Discourse: Ecological Modernization and the Policy Process*. Oxford: Clarendon Press.

Harkness, J. 1998. 'Recent trends in forestry and conservation of biodiversity in China', *The China Quarterly* 156: 911-934.

Harris, R.B. 2008. *Wildlife Conservation in China: Preserving the Habitat of China's Wild West*. Armonk, N.Y.:M.E. Sharpe.

Harris, R.B. 2010. 'Rangeland degradation on the Qinghai-Tibetan plateau: A review of the evidence of its magnitude and causes', *Journal of Arid Environments* 74, 1: 1–12.

Harvey, D. 1996. *Justice, Nature and the Geography of Difference*. New York: Blackwell.)

Ho, P. 2000. 'China's Rangelands under Stress: A Comparative Study of Pasture Commons in the Ningxia Hui Autonomous Region', *Development and Change* 31: 385–412.

Ho, P. 2006. 'Trajectories for greening in China: Theory and practice', *Development and Change* 37, 1: 3–28.

Emily T. Yeh

Holbig, H. 2004. 'The emergence of the campaign to Open up the west: ideological formation, central decision-making and the role of the provinces', *The China Quarterly* **178**: 335–357.

Holzner, W. and Kreichbaum, M. 2000. 'Pastures in south and central Tibet (China): Methods for a rapid assessment of pasture conditions', *Die Bodenkultur* **51**: 259–266.

Jhaveri, N. 2003. 'Ecological construction, China's "Go West" campaign and globalization'. Paper presented at the Annual Meeting of the Association of American Geographers.

Jiang, H. 2004. 'Cooperation, land use and the environment in Uxin Ju: A changing landscape of a Mongolian-Chinese borderland in China', *Annals of the Association of American Geographers* **94**,1: 117–139.

Jiang, H. 2005. 'Grassland management and views of nature in China since 1949: Regional policies and local changes in Uxin Ju, Inner Mongolia', *Geoforum* **36**: 641–653.

Jiang, H. 2006. 2006. 'Decentralization, ecological construction, and the environment in post-reform China: Case study from Uxin Banner, Inner Mongolia', *World Development* **34**, 11: 1907–1921.

Jim, C.Y. and Xu, S.W. 2004. 'Recent protected-area designation in China: An evaluation of administrative and statutory procedures. *Geographical Journal* **170**, *1: 39–50.*

Katsigris, E., Xu, J. and Schmitt, U. (eds.) 2004. *Implementing the Natural Forest Protection Program and the Sloping Land Conversion Program: Case Studies.* Beijing: China Forestry Publishing House.

Klein, J., Harte, J. and Zhao, X. 2004. 'Experimental warming cause large and rapid species loss, dampened by simulated grazing, on the Tibetan Plateau', *Ecology Letters* 7, 12: 1170–79.

Klein, J., Harte, J. and Zhao, X. 2007. 'Experimental warming, not grazing, decreases rangeland quality on the Tibetan Plateau', *Ecological Applications* **17**, 2: 541–557.

Koppen, C. 2003. 'Ecological modernisation and nature conservation', *International Journal of Environment and Sustainable Development* **2**, 3: 305–323.

Lai, H. 2003. 'National security and unity, and China's Western development program', *Provincial China* **8**, 2: 118–143.

Li, T. 1999. 'Compromising power: development, culture and rule in Indonesia', *Cultural Anthropology* **14**, 3: 295–322.

Li, T. 2005. 'Beyond "the State" and Failed Schemes', *American Anthropologist* **107**, 3: 383–394.

Li, T. 2007. *The Will to Improve: Governmentality, Development, and the Practice of Politics.* Durham, N.C.: Duke University Press.

Lin, G.C.S. and Ho, S.P.S. 2005. 'The state, land system and land development processes in Contemporary China', *Annals of the Association of American Geographers* **95**, 2: 411–436.

Lövbrand, E., Stipple, J., and Wiman, B. 2008. 'Earth system governmentality: Reflections on science in the Anthropocene', *Global Environmental Change* **19**: 7–13.

Luke, T. 1999. 'Environmentality as green governmentality', in E. Darier (ed.) *Discourses of the Environment.* Oxford: Blackwell. pp. 121–151.

Menzies, N. 1994. *Forest and Land management in Imperial China.* New York: Palgrave Macmillan.

Miao, G. and West. R. 2004. 'Chinese collective forestlands: contributions and Constraints', *International Forestry Review* **6**, 3–4: 282–298.

Miller, D. 2000. 'Tough times for nomads in western China: Snowstorms, settling down, fences and the demise of traditional nomadic pastoralism', *Nomadic Peoples* 4, 1: 83–109.

Miller, P. and Rose, N. 2008. *Governing the Present*. Cambridge: Polity Press.

Mol, A. 1995. *The Refinement of Production: Ecological Modernization Theory and the Chemical Industry*. Utrecht, Netherlands: Van Arkel.

Mol, A. 2006. 'Environment and modernity in transitional China: Frontiers of ecological modernization', *Development and Change* 37, 1: 29–56.

NDRC, National Development and Reform Commission. 2007. China's National Climate Change Programme. www.ccchina.gov.cn/WebSite/CCChina/UpFile/File188.pdf Last accessed 3 May 2009.

Oakes, T. 2004. 'Building a southern dynamo: Guizhou and state power', in D.S.G. Goodman (ed.) *China's Campaign to 'Open up the West': National, Provincial and Local Perspectives. The China Quarterly* special issues No. 5. Cambridge: Cambridge University Press. pp. 153–173.

Oakes, T. 2007. 'Welcome to paradise! A Sino-US Joint Venture Project', in L. Jensen and T. Weston (eds.) *China's Transformations: The Stories Beyond the Headlines*. Boulder: Rowman and Littlefield. pp. 240–264.

Peluso N. and Vandergeest, P. 2001. 'Genealogies of the political forest and customary rights in Indonesia, Malaysia and Thailand', *Journal of Asian Studies* 60, 3: 761–812.

People's Daily Online. 2000. Feb. 16. 'Take good care of forests and green drive launched in China'. http://english.peopledaily.com.cn/english/200002/16/eng20000216N101.html Last accessed 12 January 2007.

People's Daily Online. 2001. Sept. 14. 'China injected 20bn into ecological construction in West Regions'. http://english.peopledaily.com.cn/english/200109/14/eng20010914_80228.html Last accessed 12 January 2007.

People's Daily Online. 2005. March 31. 'China sets forth objectives for ecological construction in the west'. http://english.peopledaily.com.cn/200503/31/eng20050331_178933.html Last accessed 12 Jan 2007.

Perrement M. 2006. 'Resettled Tibetans "can't live on charity forever"'. China Development Brief, 1 May. http://www.chinadevelopmentbrief.com/node/573 Last accessed 4 May 2009.

Robbins, P. 2004. *Political Ecology: A critical introduction*. New York: Blackwell.

Rohlf, G. 2003. 'Dreams of oil and fertile fields: The rush to Qinghai in the 1950s', *Modern China* 29, 4: 455–489.

Rutherford, S. 2007. 'Green governmentality: insights and opportunities in the study of nature's rule', *Progress in Human Geography* 31: 291–307.

Shapiro, J. 2001. *Mao's War against Nature: Politics and the Environment in Revolutionary China*. Cambridge: Cambridge University Press.

Shen, J. 2004. 'Population growth, ecological degradation and construction in the western region of China', *Journal of Contemporary China* 13, 41: 637–661.

Shen, Y, Liao, X. and Yin, R. 2006. 'Measuring the socioeconomic impacts of China's Natural Forest Protection Program', *Environment and Development Economics* 11: 769–788.

Shih, V. 2004. 'Development, the second time around: the political logic of developing Western China', *Journal of East Asian Studies* 4, 3: 427–451.

Emily T. Yeh

Sivaramakrishnan, K. 1999. *Modern Forests: Statemaking and Environmental Change in Colonial Eastern India.* Stanford: Stanford University Press.

Snodgrass, J., Lacy, M., Sharma, S., Jhala, Y., Advanai, M., Bhargava, N.K. and Upadhyay, C. 2008. 'Witch hunts, herbal healing and discourses of indigenous ecodevelopment in North India: Theory and method in the anthropology of environmentality', *American Anthropologist* 110, 3: 299–312.

Spaargaren, G. and Mol, A. 1992. 'Sociology, environment and modernity: ecological modernization as a theory of social change', *Society and Natural Resources* 5, 4: 323–344.

State Council of the PRC. 2008. White paper on China's policies and actions on climate change. http://www.china.org.cn/government/news/200810/29/content_16681689.htm Last accessed 3 May 2009.

Sturgeon, J. 2005. *Border Landscapes: The Politics of Akha Land Use in China and Thailand.* Seattle: University of Washington Press.

Sturgeon, J. 2007. 'Globalizing rubber: "Outsourcing" rubber to Laos from Xishuangbanna', Paper presented at the annual meeting of the Association of American Geographers.

Sturgeon, J. 2009. 'Quality Control: Resource access and local village elections in rural China', *Modern Asian Studies* 43, 2: 481–509.

Vandergeest, P and Peluso, N. 1995. 'Territorialization and state power in Thailand', *Theory and Society* 35: 385–426.

Vasantkumar, C. 2006. *Ethnicity's Entanglements: Intersections of Minzu and Development in China's 'Little Tibet'.* Ph.D. Dissertation, University of California, Berkeley.

Wang, K. and Jiao, W.N 2008. 'Sanjiangyuan ecological migrants face new problems. (sanjiangyuan shengtai yimin mianlin xin nanti)', *Economic Times*, Nov 10 2008. www.amdotibet.com/cn/environment/jsgc/2008/11/amdotibet_9441053_2.htm Last accessed 4 May 2009.

Wende Drolma. 2008. *The ecological migration project: The case of Ca Chogs, Mtsho Sngon Province, China.* Unpublished thesis. Environmental Studies, Miriam College.

Williams, D.M. 1996. 'Grassland enclosures: Catalyst of land degradation in Inner Mongolia', *Human Organization* 55, 3: 307–312.

Williams, D.M. 2002. *Beyond Great Walls: Environment, Identity and Development on the Chinese Grasslands of Inner Mongolia.* Stanford: Stanford University Press.

Wu, N. and Richard, C. 1999. 'The privatization process of rangeland and its impacts on pastoral dynamics in the Hindu-Kush Himalaya: The case of Western Sichuan, China', in D. Eldridge and D. Freudenberger (eds.) *People and Rangelands: Building the Future.* Proceedings of the VI International Rangeland Congress, pp. 14–21.

Xinhua. 2007a, Oct. 15. 'Hu Jintao proposes Scientific Outlook on development for tackling China's immediate woes, challenges', http://news.xinhuanet.com/english/2007-10/15/content_6883135.htm Last accessed 1 March 2008.

Xinhua. 2007b. Oct. 6. 'China's largest ecological resettlement program making smooth progress'. (zhongguo zui da de shengtai yimin gongcheng jinzhan shunli) at http://www.chinapec.com.cn/qysq/ShowArticle.asp?ArticleID=597 Last accessed 4 May 2009.

Xu J., Katsigris, E. and White, T. (eds.) 2001. *Implementing the Natural Forest Protection Program and the Sloping Land Conversion Program: Lessons and Policy Recommendations.* Beijing: China Forestry Publishing House.

Xu, Z., Bennett, M.T., Tao, R. and Xu, J. 2004. 'China's Sloping Land Conversion Program Four Years on: Current Situation and Pending Issues', *International Forestry Review* 6, 3–4: 317–326.

Xu, J., Tao, R., Xu, Z. and Bennett, M. 2007. 'China's sloping land conversion program: does expansion equal success?' CCAP working paper, at www.efdinitiative.org/research/publications/publications-repository/chinas-sloping-land-conversion-program-does-expansion-equal-success.

White, A., Sun, X., Canby, K., Xu, J., Barr, C., Katsigris, E., Bull, G., Cossalter, C. and Nilsson, S. 2006. *China and the global market for forest products: Transforming trade to benefit forests and livelihoods.* Washington DC: Forest Trends.

Yan, Z. and Wu, N. 2005. 'Rangeland privatization and its impacts on the Zoige wetland on the Eastern Tibetan Plateau', *Journal of Mountain Science* 2, 2: 105–15.

Yan, Z., Wu, N., Yeshi Dorji and Jia, R. 2005. 'A review of rangeland privatization and its implications on the Tibetan plateau, China', *Nomadic Peoples* 9, 1: 31–52.

Yang, G. 2005. 'Environmental NGOs and institutional dynamics in China', *The China Quarterly* 181: 46–66.

Yeh, E.T. 2003. 'Tibetan range wars: Spatial politics and authority on the grasslands of Amdo', *Development and Change* 34, 3: 499–523.

Yeh, E.T. 2005. 'Green governmentality and pastoralism in western China: Converting pastures to grasslands', *Nomadic Peoples* 9, 1–2: 9–30.

Yin, R., Xu, J., Li, Z. and Liu, C. 2005. 'China's ecological rehabilitation: the unprecedented efforts   and dramatic impacts of reforestation and slope protection in western China', *China Environment Series* 7: 17–32.

York, R. and Rosa, E. 2003. 'Key challenges to ecological modernization theory', *Organization & Environment* 16, 3: 273–288.

Zackey, J. 2007. 'Peasant perspectives on deforestation in southwest China: Social discontent and environmental mismanagement', *Mountain Research and Development* 27, 2: 153–161.

Zhang, P., Shao, G., Zhao, G., Le Master, D., Parker, G., Dunning Jr., J. and Li, Q. 2000. 'China's Forest Policy for the 21st Century', *Science* 288: 2135–36.

Zhang, L., Mol, A.P.J. and Sonnenfeld, D. 2007. 'The interpretation of ecological modernization in China', *Environmental Politics* 16, 4: 659–668.

Zhang, L., Tu, Q. and Mol, A. 2008. 'Payment for environmental services: The sloping land conversion program in Ningxia Autonomous Region of China', *China & World Economy* 16, 2: 66–81.

Zukosky, M. 2007. 'Making pastoralist settlement visible in China', *Nomadic Peoples* 11, 2: 107–133.

Zuo, T. 2001. 'Implementation of the NFPP', in J. Xu, E. Katsigris and T.A. White (eds.) *Implementing the Natural Forest Protection Program and the Sloping Land Conversion Program: Lessons and Policy Recommendations.* Beijing: China: Forestry Publishing House.

CAN *ECOLOGICAL MIGRATION* POLICY IN THE TIBETAN PLATEAU REGION ACHIEVE BOTH CONSERVATION GOALS AND HUMAN DEVELOPMENT GOALS? A REVIEW OF THE CANADIAN EXPERIENCE OF RELOCATION AND SETTLEMENT

J. Marc Foggin[1]

Plateau Perspectives (Canada); School of Geography and Life Sciences, Qinghai Normal University (China); Durrell Institute for Conservation and Ecology (DICE), School of Anthropology and Conservation, University of Kent (United Kingdom)

Gongbu Zhaxi

Department of Environment and Natural Resources, Agriculture and Animal Husbandry College of Tibet University (China)

The stated goals of 'ecological migration' in the Tibetan plateau region of China are to protect the fragile ecology of grassland ecosystems and to improve the wellbeing (quality of life) of Tibetan herders. According to an official government document entitled *Settlement Project for Tibetan Nomads in Qinghai Province*, all Tibetan herders in Qinghai province who have not yet 'settled down' – that is, over 530,000 people – now will be settled/urbanised within the next five years (*People's Daily*, 11 March 2009).

However, the underlying assumption that the planned relocations and settlement will improve environmental conditions and enhance socio-economic development has not been adequately tried or tested. Few demonstration sites in the Tibetan plateau region have been established and studied over appropriate time periods. First, there are preliminary findings from other grassland areas that indicate detrimental ecological effects from the full removal of domestic livestock. Second, there are many social problems that may emerge following rapid, top-down relocation programmes.

---

1. Corresponding author.

Focusing on the latter challenges, the Canadian experience is particularly relevant and informative with its long history (from the early 1800s to the 1960s) of state-sponsored resettlements. The health consequences have in fact been devastating and local people's overall wellbeing and sense of identity have also been affected negatively; a social situation that often has lasted for multiple generations.

With high levels of unemployment, low levels of schooling (despite all the investment in infrastructure), relatively low income, very high levels of suicide and a significantly poorer health status than other social groups in Canada – a situation that was engendered by well-intentioned but faulty development approaches including large-scale resettlements, sedentarisation, and inappropriate education policies – the present state of most Inuit and other aboriginal/minority communities in Canada in fact does *not* support the premise or assumption that (re-)settlement will necessarily bring about the socio-economic improvements that China seeks to introduce in its vast pastoral regions.

Learning from the Canadian experience, it appears that the development of aboriginal (minority) communities, even in remote settings, would have been more successful if greater attention had been given to increasing the involvement of affected populations in decision-making; if more culturally-appropriate forms of education were promoted; if social services such as health care were adapted to serve sparsely populated regions, instead of requiring urbanisation; and if appropriate forms of adult education (such as vocational training) were more accessible to assist people integrate into new jobs and livelihoods, as desired. Taken as a whole, this suite of development and sociological factors may be recognised as contributing to an enhanced sense of 'cultural continuity' within the population under consideration.

In the context of current 'ecological migration' policy, social stability would likely be enhanced if some of the above features were integrated into development plans (even if applied to the new settlements). Furthermore, even greater stability would be achieved if the option existed for Tibetan herders to remain on the grassland, if they so chose, to practise a modified (more sustainable) form of their traditional livelihood.

ENVIRONMENTAL AND SOCIO-CULTURAL BACKGROUND

The Tibetan plateau covers about one-quarter of China's land area, or 2.5 million km^2 – that is, approximately the size of Sudan or six times the size of California, USA. Not only is this region important for endangered wildlife species such as snow leopard, wild yak and black-necked crane and for Tibetan herders who live in this fragile alpine environment – but also for 40 per cent of the world's population that lives downstream, depending on or influenced by the major rivers that have their source and headwaters on the plateau – the Yellow (*Huanghe*), Yangtze (*Changjiang*), Mekong (*Lancangjiang*), Salween (*Nujiang*) and Brahmaputra (*Yalong*) rivers. The Tibetan plateau also has significant regional and global impact through the carbon sequestered in its grasslands, which risks being released into the atmosphere due to land degradation, which is both anthropogenic and natural in cause (though more targeted research is necessary to determine the relative contributions of the different putative causes of land degradation, including especially better measurements and impact assessments of climate change and livestock grazing).

It is also noteworthy that the first significant human migration into the central parts of the Tibetan plateau may have occurred around 20 to 25,000 years before the present, and animal husbandry in this high altitude region probably began about 5,000 years before the present. Since then, pastoralism has developed in such a way that environmental and nutritional benefits of the grassland ecosystem could be 'harvested' by herders over long periods of time (that is, across generations) and the natural resource management practices of local herders have proven to be generally sustainable (Figure 1). Local ecological knowledge (or traditional ecological knowledge, TEK) has thus accumulated over many centuries and it would be most beneficial now to integrate such 'traditional' experience with current 'scientific' knowledge systems (Figure 2) – instead of rejecting the past outright, which would be to our loss. Indeed, local herders have long been good environmental stewards, or conservationists, in these high altitude grasslands; and they may indeed be our best allies in future conservation endeavours.

Figure 1. Tibetan pastoralists have sustained their livelihood in grassland environments for centuries. Livestock have long been the main 'tool' to convert natural resources into productive materials, transport and food.

Figure 2. Over the past decade, traditional and modern approaches have merged (for example, with the *Sipeitao* Programme focused on building winter homes for nomads).

GLOBAL CONTEXT OF CONSERVATION INITIATIVES

Most of the conservation agenda through the twentieth century and into the twenty-first century has been based on a North American 'national parks' model. This approach has also been termed 'fortress conservation' or 'exclusionary conservation', with local people (often Aboriginal and/or ethnic minority people) regularly being forced to move off the land. Given this history, Mark Dowie has appropriately coined the term, not of 'ecological refugees' (a situation in which people move off the land due to environmental stress) but rather of '*conservation* refugees' (Dowie 2009) – a situation when people who have traditionally used a geographic area or habitat as the basis of their livelihood are either encouraged or forced to move away for the sake of implementing a conservation plan, often the establishment of a protected area (PA) but sometimes 'environmental policy' too.

Worldwide, the proportion of land now included under 'protected area' status is around 12 per cent. In China that figure is even higher, around 15 per cent. And within China, broken down regionally, we note that about one third of the land area in the Tibetan plateau region is included within protected areas in the form of provincial- and national-level nature reserves. In parallel with this, there are several national policies, generally promoted as environmental or conservation-oriented policies, that also serve similar purposes – namely, policies or programmes that seek to protect the region's natural environment (e.g., to restore grassland and forest vegetation, in order to limit soil erosion and thus protect downstream populations from potential flooding). However all of these policies, programmes or projects tend to be – in Dowie's (2009) terminology – exclusionary in approach, i.e. promoting conservation through the removal or exclusion of local people and communities from designated regions. And these regions are huge, and the populations large – in Qinghai province, for example, the target population for such new exclusions (or relocation) is now set at *100 per cent of Tibetan herders over the next five years*, from 2009 through 2013, *in total over half a million people* whose livelihoods and lives are now being changed, irreversibly. Not only will there be socio-economic and cultural challenges for all the people relocated, but also – just as importantly – such relocations have inherent within them major loss for conservation, both lost knowledge (cf. TEK) and loss of genuine, able allies for wildlife conservation, on the one hand, and for sustainable use of resources, on the other.

On the global scene, the first experiment with PAs was the creation in 1871 of Yellowstone National Park, in Wyoming, USA. Other famous early PAs include Yosemite and Banff national parks, the latter situated in the Canadian Rocky Mountains. In these localities, as elsewhere throughout Africa and Asia over the next 100 years and more, national parks and other exclusionary models have been the primary means by which wildlife and wilderness preservation has been attempted – initially with a focus on focal species or 'charismatic mega-vertebrates', and later shifting toward habitat protection or in some instances 'umbrella species'. However, around the world, approximately half the land included in such reserves created over the past century was either previously occupied, or regularly used, by indigenous people – indigenous being defined here as people that have 'occupied the land where they reside, or in the case of pastoral nomads, if they grazed their livestock through a region before the particular area in question was [incorporated into] the nation-state … within which it now exists' (Dowie 2009). In the Americas, over 80 per cent of the PAs were previously occupied or regularly used by Aboriginal people, before they were removed in the creation of PAs, purportedly in order to 'preserve wilderness'. In total, the estimated number of Aboriginal (ethnic minority) people who have been evacuated or relocated for the creation of reserves is between 5 million and over 10 million people. Most of these people now are among the poorest of the poor, very often marginalised within the broader society and with little hope for the future.

While there are indeed recent attempts to consider local development needs and listen to the aspirations and hopes of local communities situated in or near to PAs – for example, there is a recent trend to design and implement 'community co-management projects' – already, after only a few years, an increasing number of local communities are beginning to express feelings that such approaches are, at least in the case of certain non-government organisations, just a façade or public relations spin. In few instances are local people really kept centre stage.

ECOLOGICAL MIGRATION POLICY ON THE TIBETAN PLATEAU

Ecological Migration (Chinese, *shengtai yimin*) is a national policy in China that refers to relocation programmes (Figure 3), mostly in grassland regions, undertaken primarily for the purpose of restoring the environment in places where it is recognised or assumed to be degraded or otherwise deemed unsuitable for continued human habitation (Foggin 2008). In most of these situations, the term 'ecological refugee' has been used in the media as it refers to the movement (or relocation) of people away from lands that, it is reported, no longer can support them. It is, however, the latter position that should in fact be at the heart of the debate – namely, *whether or not it is even necessary* to move people (i.e., to relocate and settle people) in order to achieve sustainability. As this question has yet to be resolved, with many of the longer-term social and environmental costs still to be assessed, a more accurate terminology would therefore be 'conservation refugees'.

The two main rationales given for implementation of ecological migration (EM) in the Tibetan plateau region of China are, firstly, environmental conservation and, secondly, socio-economic development. With regard to the environment, it must also

Figure 3. A view of one of the numerous 'ecological migration villages' recently built on the Tibetan plateau, requiring major socio-cultural changes. Photo: Du Fachun.

be noted that humans are themselves a part of the broader environment, and always have been. Specifically in the Tibetan grasslands, local people have used and indeed have helped to shape and create the grassland environment through livestock grazing and related livelihood practices over the past several thousand years. In the process, they will also have gained an intricate knowledge of the natural environment, of grassland ecology and of wildlife, livestock, climate and innumerable other aspects of their surroundings. As such, they have an inordinate amount of knowledge and experience to contribute to our current conservation efforts, gained not through modern, scientific or reductionist approaches but through a more holistic and empirical understanding of the natural environment – this is the approach understood in the word 'traditional' within the phrase 'traditional ecological knowledge' (as opposed to a meaning of old, non-scientific, backward, etc.). Working with local people and communities, in this case nomadic pastoralists, they can and should therefore be recognised as excellent allies for biodiversity conservation. Failing to do so not only is an opportunity lost, it can also all too easily lead to the creation of new opponents and increased conflict between local people and, for example, a new nature reserve.

The second main rationale for EM policy is socio-economic development. In the case of grassland regions, however, there are few alternative livelihoods available to local people (Figures 4 and 5). Traditional nomadic pastoralism has developed over long periods of time – with strong evolutionary or selective pressures (i.e., a necessity to survive) – such that it is generally well suited to the local environment. Even with a changing climate, this livelihood still remains the best way yet found for humankind to successfully gain material benefit from the grassland environment. In addition, local livelihoods are intertwined with history and language and other aspects of culture to form the matrix in which development is, and always will be, enmeshed. It would be most prudent, therefore, to move somewhat more slowly with regard to EM policy, so as not to work counter to cultural interests or predispositions, lest speed and direction of change lead to unexpected (at least by decision-makers) frustration, discontent or even instability. As will be seen below, the relocation, settlement and/or urbanisation of people does not always lead to improved health, income, etc. In fact, if the Canadian experience has any predictive value, the opposite situation may be the most likely outcome of rapid, sustained resettlement programmes such as carried out under EM policy.

In Qinghai province, implementation of the EM policy on a larger scale started around 2005. Already by 2007, at least 35 new settlements had been built (i.e., small towns or suburbs created to house former herders who had moved off the land.) It is officially maintained that all decisions to relocate are voluntary – yet local government also has annual quotas to meet, for which purpose it organises community meetings to discuss options and to encourage relocation according to plan. A further 51 settlements were also under construction in the same year, with a planned total of around 62,000 people (over 13,000 families) to be relocated and settled in the Sanjiangyuan region. By 2010, plans were for more than 100,000 people to settle in new towns, with a total investment around 646 million Chinese Yuan, or nearly 100 million US dollars.

Ecological Migration Policy in the Tibetan Plateau

Figure 4. In many new settlements (built under EM policy), new 'urban herders' seek to maintain traditional/pastoral livelihoods; yet have no pastures. Alternatives are few.

Figure 5. With little land available in the new settlements, high population densities and few livelihood options, unemployment is high. Social problems are predicted.

J. Marc Foggin and Gongbu Zhaxi

The most recent official goal is even more drastic, indeed devastating:

Starting this year, Qinghai will complete a settlement programme for nomadic people within five years. By then, more than 112,000 households, over 530,000 nomadic people in the Tibetan-inhabited areas of Qinghai Province [i.e., 100 per cent of Tibetan herders], will leave their nomadic lives. (*People's Daily*, 11 March 2009)

According to the above article, the programme entitled *Settlement Project Planning for Tibetan Nomads in Qinghai Province* has already been issued and approved by the government.

Given the potential loss of culture and of cultural knowledge (including traditional ecological knowledge, TEK), how does such policy fit within the context of the Convention on Biological Diversity (CBD) to which China is a signatory? For example, CBD ensconces the value and need to conserve TEK; in Article 8, it specifically states that each nation 'subject to its national legislation [will] respect, preserve and maintain knowledge, innovation and practices of indigenous and local communities embodying traditional lifestyles relevant to the conservation and sustainable use of biological diversity'. The onus is therefore now increasingly on China to determine how much it values local culture and TEK, on the one hand, and the development of a broader spectrum of effective conservation allies (in the form of Tibetan herders, living sustainably on the grassland), on the other.

The EM policy does have a set of environmental as well as development rationales, yet the social costs are potentially very high and still insufficiently addressed – and this could, if such costs are deemed too high by the affected populations, ultimately lead to the undoing, or counter-acting, of any hoped-for benefits.

What costs may be expected? For historic comparative purposes, we turn our attention now to consider government-sanctioned relocations of Aboriginal people in Canada, many undertaken in the name of preserving wilderness (which in modern language would be termed biodiversity conservation), with an overview of some of the major socio-economic consequences in the affected (relocated, settled) communities that have lasted for multiple generations.

WHAT CAN BE LEARNED FROM THE CANADIAN EXPERIENCE OF RELOCATION/SETTLEMENT?

The establishment of many protected areas in Canada, starting with the creation of Banff National Park in 1885, included the removal/relocation of native people – with given reasons being that this was done in the interest of game conservation, tourism, and Indian assimilation.

Who are Canada's Indian or aboriginal people? Aboriginal populations in Canada have been classified into 12 major ethno-linguistic families (though sadly one has gone extinct, Beothuk) with more than 50 unique languages. Aboriginal people also have over 2,200 reserves, ranging in size from only several hectares up to 900 km². The main categories generally used when referring to Canada's aboriginal peoples are the

First Nations, Métis and Inuit. In 2006, nearly four per cent of Canada's population was recognised as aboriginal: 698,025 First Nations people; 389,785 Métis people; 50,485 Inuit people; and 34,500 people with multiple or other aboriginal descent.

Around 50 years after the first national park was created in Canada, and its original inhabitants forcibly removed, the *National Parks Act* was passed. The Act was written to ensure that parks could only be established, or changed, by an Act of Parliament and to ensure that mineral exploration and development was prohibited and only limited use of timber essential for park management was allowed. While this may have made some conservation sense, from the European perspective, it still impacted on the excluded aboriginal communities to a very large extent, people who previously had used, mostly in sustainable ways, local natural resources for many generations.

Relocation of Inuit Communities

Historically a nomadic hunting and fishing people, the Inuit people now are settled in 46 northern communities (where they are the majority) and eight towns (where they form a significant minority); no more than 10 per cent of Canada's Inuit live outside of these 54 communities and towns. Early government policy *vis-à-vis* the Inuit aimed to enable Inuit to be 'self-sufficient'. Later policies, however, included the first official Eskimo [Inuit] relocation project, which occurred from 1934–1947. In the 1950s, three options were officially presented to the Inuit: (1) to maintain their basic way of life, where natural resources would allow; (2) relocate to areas of White settlement, and adapt to new ways; or (3) in areas that could not support native people, relocation. The official rationale for relocation was the government's concern about the ability of the Inuit to sustain themselves on the land and also a desire to extend and centralise government services to the Inuit people. However, following relocations, many problems rapidly emerged: livelihoods were lost and people became dependent on social welfare. These problems have become endemic, enduring even for decades (Marcus 1995; INAC 2004).

Relocation of Cree Communities

Another nation, the James Bay Cree, has also been subjected to a relocation policy. In this instance, the main rationale has been the development of a massive hydro-power station, the James Bay Hydroelectric Project. Here too, relocation and consolidation 'into settlement patterns designed according to southern urban models has often resulted in cultural confusion and an increase in interpersonal tension, alcohol abuse, and violence' (Feit 2004).

The Residential School System

With many other aboriginal communities across Canada, the policy that most changed their culture and way of life was the residential school system, a devastating policy that continued well into the twentieth century. The predominant view behind this strategy was that only a European approach or worldview was valid, as opposed to traditional/ holistic worldviews, or native languages, or experience-based forms of education, etc. Young children were therefore forcibly taken from their parents and community, in the name of compulsory education, and sent to boarding schools where English was the only medium of education and all native languages were forbidden. Because of this, or at least through this difficult process, many of the young generation began to reject their parents and elders, which translated over time into alienation within families and loss of cultural identity (Anderson 2008).

LONG-LASTING (NEGATIVE) SOCIO-CULTURAL IMPACTS AMONGST FIRST NATIONS IN CANADA

Nearly all aboriginal communities in Canada have been affected, to a greater or lesser extent, by such significant disruptions, upheavals, relocations, transitions, alienations. What has been the result, in terms of development and society, of such histories? The social and development outcomes of such policies have been, to put it mildly, long-lasting and extremely detrimental to both the aboriginal communities themselves and the nation as a whole. Beyond the qualitative aspects of loss of cultural identity and loss of hope within many communities, there are also many quantifiable measures, almost all negative:

– High unemployment rates: 2.6 times higher in aboriginal communities

– Lower life expectancy at birth: 7 years less for men, 5 years less for women

– Infectious diseases prevalent: e.g., TB over 7 times higher than national rates

– Endemic urban poverty: around 50% of aboriginal people living in cities live below poverty line (national average, 4.8%)

– High rates of suicide: around 6 times national average (also high levels of self-injury, especially among young people)

All these figures – and these are but a few examples, many more can be produced – are indicative or symptomatic of deep-rooted sociological and psychological 'disconnects' and cultural confusion. That is, most Aboriginal people are now living simultaneously in two very different realities, with resultant crises of identity and the burden generally remains heavy across the generations (Frideres and Krosenbrink-Gelissen 1998).

In summary, past government policies in Canada vis-à-vis Aboriginal people have had some serious negative impacts, including especially the following:

– Serious disparities in health, income/poverty, education, etc.

– Some loss of heritage, sense of belonging, sense of broader community

– Legacy of alienation with distrust of government, also (in some instances) breakdown of family and community

- Large financial burden, even up to the national level due to long-term costs (and lost opportunities) related to unemployment, poor health, alcoholism, crime, etc.

HOW DOES THIS CANADIAN EXPERIENCE RELATE TO CHINA'S PRESENT SITUATION?

There are many historic similarities between Canada's development and some current policy in China, particularly in relation to the relocation and settlement of Aboriginal or ethnic minority populations for the purpose of environmental conservation and/or the provision of social services. In China as in Canada, not only has uneven development (disparities) between regions or communities been given as a rationale for relocations, but such relocations and settlement projects have in fact also in turn led to, or further exacerbated, disparities in health and other aspects of socio-economic development.

In the case of Tibetan pastoralists in China, such disparities will further increase due to radical livelihood changes that are required by some related government policies (e.g., ban on livestock grazing in some areas) and the lack of alternative employment or vocational training opportunities for (former) herders who have moved to town.

The financial burden of long-lasting unemployment, loss of hope, poor health, limited education … the real financial cost of such transformation of the social land-scape, when such costs are properly internalised, may be enormous. In addition to the financial cost, the significant matter of social stability and security should also be factored within the broad development equation.

What Should be Done Now?

Based on some of the important lessons we have already learned in Canada and China, as discussed above, we now make the following key development recommendations.

Specifically, because EM policy (1) is still experimental in nature (that is, it is a policy that has not previously been attempted on such a large scale, with over half a million people to be settled in five years in Qinghai province alone); (2) carries serious social risk (see the Canadian experience of aboriginal relocations and settlements, with break-up of communities and other long-lasting/generational harmful impacts, lasting to the present); and (3) is likely to be irreversible (with low likelihood of people being able to return to pastoral livelihoods in the future) – it is advisable that the process of moving/transitioning people from a rural pastoral economy toward semi-urban, market-based livelihoods with an uncertain future for former herders (cf. EM policy) *be slowed down, even suspended at least temporarily.*

In particular, we propose the following development options be considered immediately:

- Slow down implementation of EM policy in the Tibetan plateau region, at least until more is known about the root causes of environmental degradation and the potential social impacts of socio-cultural transitions required by EM policy

- Study more about possible root causes of (perceived) environmental degradation

- Study more about (potential) social and environmental impacts, both good and bad, of the proposed/current EM policy

- Involve more stakeholders, especially stakeholders from the affected region, in both the local/regional and global dialogues on conservation and sustainability

Furthermore, also based on the Canadian experience, it is suggested that the following issues are equally important for environmental protection and sustainable development in the Tibetan plateau region – development which, if/when done properly, will benefit the whole nation. That is, there should also be concerted effort and focus in the Tibetan plateau region on increasing, *inter alia,*

- the level of genuine community engagement and participation in development

- research and development of alternative (new) livelihood options for herders

- opportunities and access to adult education and vocational training programmes

- accessibility to social services (e.g., health, education) in rural and urban settings

- opportunities for teaching/studying in maternal as well as national languages

- the integration of traditional knowledge with 'scientific' knowledge systems

If further thought and deliberation as well as academic research are properly focused on such critical topics, conservation and sustainable development in the plateau region will be much better served (with benefits accruing to local Tibetan communities), and China as a whole will benefit.

BIBLIOGRAPHY

Anderson, C. 2008. 'Assimilation through Education: Applying Lessons from Canada's Residential Schools Experiment to the Education of China's Ethnic Minorities', in P. Potter and F. Du (eds.) *Proceedings of the Canada–China Forum, Western Development and Socio-Economic Change.* Beijing, China: Institute of Ethnology and Anthropology, Chinese Academy of Social Sciences and University of British Columbia.

Dowie, M. 2009. *Conservation Refugees: The Hundred-year Conflict between Global Conservation and Native Peoples.* Cambridge, Massachusetts: The MIT Press.

Feit, H.A. 2004. 'Hunting and the Quest for Power: The James Bay Cree and Whiteman Development', in R.B. Morrison and C.R. Wilson (eds.) *Native Peoples: The Canadian Experience.* Toronto: Oxford University Press.

Foggin, J.M. 2008. 'Depopulating the Tibetan Grasslands: A Review of Current National Policies Affecting Tibetan Herders in the Sanjiangyuan Region of Qinghai Province, People's Republic of China', *Mountain Research and Development* **28**, 1: 26–31.

Frideres, J. and Krosenbrink-Gelissen, L. 1998. *Aboriginal Peoples in Canada: Contemporary Conflicts.* Toronto: Prentice-Hall Allyn/Bacon.

INAC (Indian and Northern Affairs, Canada). 2004. 'Encouraging Self-sufficiency: Dispersing the Baffin Island Inuit: Looking Forward, Looking Back: False Assumptions and a Failed Relationship', http://www.ainc-inac.gc.ca/ch/rcap/rpt/lk_e.html

Marcus, A.R. 1995. *Relocating Eden: The Image and Politics of Inuit Exile in the Canadian Arctic.* Hanover, New Hampshire: University Press of New England.

Morrison, R.B. and Wilson, C.R. (eds.) *Native Peoples: The Canadian Experience.* Toronto: Oxford University Press.

People's Daily. 2009, 11 March. 'Nomadic People in Qinghai to Settle within Five Years', http://english.peopledaily.com.cn/90001/90776/90882/6611715.html

Potter, P. and Du, F. (eds.) 2008. *Proceedings of the Canada–China Forum, Western Development and Socio-Economic Change.* Beijing, China: Institute of Ethnology and Anthropology, Chinese Academy of Social Sciences and University of British Columbia.

FURTHER READINGS

Anderson, J. 2003. 'Aboriginal Children in Poverty in Urban Communities: Social Exclusion and the Growing Racialization of Poverty in Canada'. Ottawa: Canadian Council on Social Development. http://www.ccsd.ca/pr/2003/aboriginal.htm

Cao, H. (ed.) 2009. *Ethnic Minorities and Regional Development in Asia: Reality and Challenges.* Amsterdam, Holland: Amsterdam University Press.

Chandler, M.J. and Lalonde, C.E. 1998. 'Cultural Continuity as a Hedge against Suicide in Canada's First Nations', *Transcultural Psychiatry* **35**, 2: 193–211.

Du, F. 2006. 'Grain for Green and Poverty Alleviation: The Policy and Practice of Ecological Migration in China', *Horizons* **9**, 2: 45–8.

Foggin, J.M. 2005. 'Highland Encounters: Building New Partnerships for Conservation and Sustainable Development in the Yangtze River Headwaters, Heart of the Tibetan Plateau', in Velasquez, Yashiro, Yoshimura and Ono (eds.) *Innovative Communities: People-centered Approaches to Environmental Management in the Asia–Pacific Region.* Tokyo: United Nations University Press.

Foggin, J.M. 2011. 'Rethinking 'Ecological Migration' and the Value of Cultural Continuity – A Response to Wang, Song and Hu', *AMBIO: A Journal of the Human Environment* **40**, 1: 100–1.

Foggin, J.M. 2012. 'Pastoralists and Wildlife Conservation in Western China: Collaborative Management within Protected Areas on the Tibetan Plateau', *Pastoralism: Research, Policy and Practice* **2**, 17.

Foggin, J.M. and Torrance-Foggin, M.E. 2011. 'How can social and environmental services be provided for mobile Tibetan herders? Collaborative examples from Qinghai Province, China', *Pastoralism: Research, Policy and Practice* 1, 21. doi:10.1186/2041-7136-1-21.

Foggin, P.M. and Foggin, J.M. 2008. 'The Practice and Experience of Settlement and Relocation among Canada's Aboriginal Peoples', in P. Potter and F. Du (eds.) *Proceedings of the Canada–China Forum, Western Development and Socio-Economic Change.* Beijing, China: Institute of Ethnology and Anthropology, Chinese Academy of Social Sciences and University of British Columbia.

Foggin, P.M., Torrance, M.E. and Foggin, J.M. 2009. 'Accessibility of Healthcare for Pastoralists in the Tibetan Plateau Region: A Case Study from Southern Qinghai Province, China', in H. Cao (ed.) *Ethnic Minorities and Regional Development in Asia: Reality and Challenges.* Amsterdam, Holland: Amsterdam University Press.

Gruschke, A. Forthcoming. 'Yushu Nomads on the Move: How Can the Use of Pastoralist Resources be Sustainable?' paper given at the International Symposium on Human Dimensions of Ecological Conservation on the Tibetan Plateau. Xining: Qinghai Academy of Social Sciences.

Henderson, D. Forthcoming. 'Public Participation, Leadership and Sustainable Development: Canadian Context and Issues for China', keynote speech given at the International Symposium on Human Dimensions of Ecological Conservation on the Tibetan Plateau. Xining: Qinghai Academy of Social Sciences.

Lee, M. (ed.) 2005. *Inuit in Urban Space.* Fairbanks: University of Alaska Press.

Lobo, S. 2005. 'Theoretical Perspectives on Inuit Urbanization', in M. Lee (ed.) *Inuit in Urban Space.* Fairbanks: University of Alaska Press.

MacMillan, H.L., MacMillan, A.B., Offord, D.R. and Dingle, J.L. 1996. 'Aboriginal Health', *Canadian Medical Association Journal* 155, 11: 1569–78.

Mendelson, M. 2004. *Aboriginal People in Canada's Labour Market: Work and Unemployment – Today and Tomorrow.* Ottawa: Caledon Institute of Social Policy.

Murray, D. Forthcoming. 'Parks Canada: Working with Aboriginal Peoples, Establishing New National Parks', paper given at the International Symposium on Human Dimensions of Ecological Conservation on the Tibetan Plateau. Xining: Qinghai Academy of Social Sciences.

NAHO (National Aboriginal Health Organization). 2006. *Suicide Prevention: Inuit Traditional Practices that Encouraged Resilience and Coping.* Ottawa: Ajunnginiq Centre. http://www.naho.ca/inuit/english/documents/Eldersproject-FinalVersion.pdf

Peters, E.J. 2001. 'The Geographies of Aboriginal Populations and Rights in Canada', *The Canadian Geographer* 45: 138–44.

Peters, E.J. and Starchenko, O. 2006. 'Changes in Aboriginal Settlement Patterns in Two Canadian Cities: A Comparison to Immigrant Settlement Models', *Canadian Journal of Urban Research* 14: 315–37.

Ptackova, J. 2011. 'Sedentarisation of Tibetan Nomads in China: Implementation of the Nomadic Settlement Project in the Tibetan Amdo area; Qinghai and Sichuan Provinces', *Pastoralism: Research, Policy and Practice* 1, 4.

Satterthwaite, D. 2007. 'The Transition to a Predominantly Urban World and its Underpinnings', Human Settlements Discussion Paper Series. London: International Institute for Environment and Development.

StatCan. 2008. *Aboriginal Population Profile, 2006 Census*. Ottawa: Stats Canada.

Tashi, G. and Foggin. J.M. 2009. 'Evaluation of Migration Village: Namsaling Dekhi Village', *Journal of Agriculture and Animal Husbandry College of Tibet* 2009, 3: 31–8.

Tester, F.K. and Kulchyski, P.K. 1994. *Tammarniit (Mistakes): Inuit Relocation in the Eastern Arctic, 1939–63*. Vancouver: UBC Press.

Torrance, M. 2008. 'Health Consequences of Rapid Urbanization', paper presented at the XVI Congress of the International Union of Anthropological & Ethnological Sciences (IUAES) International Workshop on Ecological Resettlement: Local Participation and Policy Improvement, held on 30 July 2009, Kunming, China.

Velasquez, J., Yashiro, M., Yoshimura, S. and Ono, I. (eds.) 2005. *Innovative Communities: People-centered Approaches to Environmental Management in the Asia–Pacific Region*. Tokyo: United Nations University Press.

Waldram, J.B. 2005. 'Relocation, Consolidation, and Settlement Pattern in the Canadian Subarctic', *Human Ecology* **15**: 117–32.

Waldram, J.B., Herring, D.A. and Young, T.K. 2006. *Aboriginal Health in Canada: Historical, Cultural and Epidemiological Perspectives*. Toronto: University of Toronto Press.

Wang, Z., Song, K. and Hu, L. 2011. 'Response to "Rethinking Ecological Migration and the Value of Cultural Continuity"', *AMBIO: A Journal of the Human Environment* **40**, 1: 102–3.

Zinsstag, J., Taleb, M.O. and Craig, P.S. 2006. 'Health of Nomadic Pastoralists: New Approaches towards Equity Effectiveness', *Tropical Medicine and International Health* **11**, 5: 565–8.

INDEX

Index

Index

Index

Lightning Source UK Ltd.
Milton Keynes UK
UKHW011044070819
347551UK00003B/661/P